A History of the 1957 Federation of Malaya Constitution

Fernando examines important aspects of the drafting of 1957 Federation of Malaya constitution related to the system of governance, division of legislative and executive powers, the conceptualisation of citizenship and the roles of the judiciary and election commission.

The book sheds new light on the balances that the Reid Commission sought to embed in the constitution and the historical constitutional debates and discussions which greatly shaped the framing of the new federal constitution between 1956 and 1957. Drawing on historical evidence mainly from declassified primary constitutional documents, it analyses the submissions, debates and discussions among the framers and various interest groups during the drafting of the constitution between 1956 and 1957 to discern more clearly the intentions of the framers on many aspects of governance and distribution of powers embedded in the constitutional provisions. This book reveals more deeply the nature and complexity of the constitutional issues faced by the framers and how they attempted to reach compromises between the various interest groups in Malaya.

It is a valuable resource for scholars and academics of Malaysian, Asian and Commonwealth constitutional history as well as those interested in history, law, political science and important aspects of governance and distribution of powers in the system of parliamentary democracy.

Joseph M. Fernando was formerly an associate professor at the Department of History at the Faculty of Arts and Social Sciences in the University of Malaya (2000–2018) and taught undergraduate and postgraduate courses on Malaysian political and constitutional history and the history of modern Southeast Asia. He was a visiting Fulbright Scholar at the Department of History, Harvard University, in 2004/2005, and Chapman Fellow at the Institute of Commonwealth Studies, University of London, in 2004, and is presently an independent researcher. He has authored several books on Malaysian constitutional and political history and published widely in international academic journals.

Routledge Studies in the Modern History of Asia

191. Cultures of Modernity and the U.S.-Japan Cold War Alliance
Masami Kimura

192. Sino-Muslims, Networks, and Identity in Late Imperial China
Longstanding Natives and Dispersed Minorities
Shaodan Zhang

193. Traditional Malay Monarchy
Asbol bin Haji Mail

194. Comfort Women of the Japanese Empire
Colonial Rule and the Battle over Memory
Park Yu-Ha

195. The Rice Trade in Asia
A. J. H. Latham

196. The Crafting of the Postwar Peace Treaty with Japan, 1945–1951
Seung Mo Kang

197. Winning Vietnam's Hearts and Minds during the Vietnam War (1954–1975)
Chosen Glories
Hai-Chung Pham

198. A History of the 1957 Federation of Malaya Constitution
Joseph M. Fernando

For a full list of available titles, please visit: www.routledge.com/Routledge-Studies-in-the-Modern-History-of-Asia/book-series/MODHISTASIA

A History of the 1957 Federation of Malaya Constitution

Joseph M. Fernando

Routledge
Taylor & Francis Group
LONDON AND NEW YORK

First published 2025
by Routledge
4 Park Square, Milton Park, Abingdon, Oxon OX14 4RN

and by Routledge
605 Third Avenue, New York, NY 10158

Routledge is an imprint of the Taylor & Francis Group, an informa business

British Library Cataloguing-in-Publication Data
A catalogue record for this book is available from the British Library

Library of Congress Cataloging-in-Publication Data
Names: Fernando, Joseph M., author.
Title: A history of the 1957 federation of Malaya Constitution / Joseph M. Fernando.
Description: Abingdon, Oxon [UK] ; New York, NY : Routledge, 2025. | Series: Routledge studies in the modern history of Asia | Includes bibliographical references and index. | Contents: Introduction—The System of Government—Division of Legislative and Executive Powers—Federal-State Financial Relations—Citizenship—The Other Voices—The Judiciary—The Election Commission.
Identifiers: LCCN 2024034505 (print) | LCCN 2024034506 (ebook) | ISBN 9781032893891 (hardback) | ISBN 9781032893914 (paperback) | ISBN 9781003542537 (ebook)
Subjects: LCSH: Constitutional history—Malaysia—Malaya. | Malaya. Constitution. | Constitutions—Malaysia—Malaya.
Classification: LCC KPG6672 .F469 2025 (print) | LCC KPG6672 (ebook) | DDC 342.595/1029—dc23/eng/20240731
LC record available at https://lccn.loc.gov/2024034505
LC ebook record available at https://lccn.loc.gov/2024034506

ISBN: 978-1-032-89389-1 (hbk)
ISBN: 978-1-032-89391-4 (pbk)
ISBN: 978-1-003-54253-7 (ebk)

DOI: 10.4324/9781003542537

Typeset in Times New Roman
by Apex CoVantage, LLC

Contents

Acknowledgements

I would like to thank several archives, institutions and libraries for allowing me access to primary and secondary sources related to the research conducted for this book. Most importantly, I would like to express my deep gratitude to the National Archives of Britain in Kew for allowing me access to the primary constitutional documents related to the framing of the 1957 Malayan federal constitution. I would also like to thank Arkib Negara Malaysia in Kuala Lumpur and the Institute for Southeast Asian Studies in Singapore for permitting me to refer to related primary and secondary material deposited in these institutions. I am grateful to the University of Malaya Library and the Institute of Commonwealth Studies in London for enabling me to refer to sources related to this research. A special note of thanks needs to be accorded to the University of Malaya and the Department of History at the Faculty of Arts and Social Sciences in the University of Malaya for their continuous support during my tenure as lecturer at the varsity. I would also like to thank the editors at Routledge for their editorial support in preparing this manuscript for publication. Finally, I would like to express my gratitude to my family who have always been supportive of my academic research. I hope this book, which is largely based on an examination of the primary constitutional documents, will enable us to understand better the complex and challenging historical processes in the drafting of the Federation of Malaya constitution between 1956 and 1957 and the intentions of its framers.

Joseph M. Fernando
Kuala Lumpur
July 2024

1 Introduction

Constitutions are the highest form of laws in a modern nation-state. Ivor Jennings defined the constitution as the document in which are set out the rules governing the composition, powers, and methods of operation of the main institutions of government and the general principles applicable to their relation to the citizens.[1] In the evolution and development of the modern nation-state, constitutions have become the central document that serves as a source of reference for the administration of the state by its elected executives and for the citizens to discern their inherent fundamental rights. In this sense, the 1957 Federation of Malaya (now Malaysia) constitution was a landmark document which shaped enormously the form and character of the independent post-colonial state. The new constitution determined and defined the system of governance, the powers of the organs of government and ancillary bodies, the division of powers between the federal government and the states and the fundamental rights of the citizens as the federation became a sovereign nation on 31 August 1957. Malaya inherited a federal parliamentary form of government with a constitutional monarchy based on the Westminster model and which borrowed considerably from the constitutions of India (1949) and Pakistan (1956). The history of the framing of the Malayan constitution provides a fascinating and revealing insight into the constitutional ideas, issues and debates that arose during the formulation of the document and how the framers resolved these challenges. The federal constitution was drafted between June 1956 and February 1957 by the Reid Commission after extensive consultations with all sectors of Malayan society and much deliberation within the constitutional commission. The Reid draft constitution was reviewed by a Working Party comprising the multicommunal Alliance Party leaders led by Chief Minister Tunku Abdul Rahman, representatives of the nine Malay rulers and the British High Commissioner Sir Donald MacGillivray between February and May 1957. The revised draft constitution was further examined at the London constitutional conference from 13 to 21 May 1957, then debated in the Malayan Federal Legislative Council and the British parliament in July and assented to by the nine Malay rulers before coming into force on 31 August 1957 as Malaya became independent.

Understanding the historical process of the formulation of the federal constitution and, particularly, the internal constitutional debates is thus crucial for an

DOI: 10.4324/9781003542537-1

appreciation of the provisions of the 1957 Malayan constitution. This book is therefore an effort to examine closely the primary constitutional documents and the ensuing debates between 1956 and 1957 to obtain a deeper understanding of the formulation of Malayan federal constitution and to discern the intentions and concerns of the framers. My previous book, *The Making of the Malayan Constitution* (2002),[2] had covered considerable ground in tracing the framing of the 1957 federal constitution but was not able to examine more deeply important aspects of the constitution because of the limitation of the scope of that study which was intended to provide a broader examination of the main elements of the constitution-making process and the deliberations. This book augments my earlier study by focusing more specifically on important constitutional aspects relating to the system of governance, the role and powers of the main institutions of government, the division of legislative and financial powers between the federal government and the states and aspects of the 1957 constitution that pertain to citizenship, the judiciary, the election commission and the views of the smaller voices in the process through an examination of the primary constitutional documents. This book hence fills a gap by providing a deeper understanding of many important aspects of the constitution that could not be adequately examined in my earlier study. Other existing literature on the 1957 Malayan federal constitution tends to take a legalistic approach using mainly secondary sources such as published text of the constitution, case studies of court judgements (post-1957) and the report of the Reid Commission. This approach does not enable us to understand adequately the historical processes entailed in the framing of the Malayan constitution and more specifically the various constitutional elements examined in my book. These include R. H. Hickling, *An Introduction to the Constitution of Malaysia* (Singapore: Malayan Law Journal, 1960); L. A. Sheridan, *The Federation of Malaya Constitution* (Singapore; University of Malaya Law Review, 1961); Mohamed Suffian Hashim, *An Introduction to the Constitution of Malaysia* (Kuala Lumpur: Government Printer, 1972); F. A. Trindade, and H. P. Lee (eds), *The Constitution of Malaysia: Further Perspectives and Development* (Singapore: Oxford University Press, 1986); Abdul Aziz Bari, *Malaysian Constitution: A Critical Introduction* (Kuala Lumpur; The Other Press, 2003); Andrew Harding, *Law, Government and the Constitution in Malaysia* (Kuala Lumpur: Malayan Law Journal, 1996); and Andrew Harding, *The Constitution of Malaysia: A Contextual Analysis* (London: Bloomsbury Publishing, 2012). This book examines the primary constitutional documents such as the records of the internal discussions of the Reid Commission, the Working Party which reviewed the draft constitution, the London constitutional conference (such as the CO 889, CO 941) and other related Colonial Office records (CO 1022 and CO 1030), party documents, memoranda by various organisations and individuals to discern more clearly the historical constitutional drafting process and the intentions of the framers.

After providing some background to the history of early Malaya and the movement for constitutional reform in the post-war period and the origins of the constitutional commission in 1956 in this introductory chapter, the book examines the primary constitutional debates on important aspects of the federal constitution.

These include the system of government, division of legislative and executive powers, distribution of federal-state financial powers, citizenship, the views of the smaller players in the constitution-making process, the judiciary and the election commission.[3] This approach, we believe, would provide a more holistic and deeper appreciation of the constitutional deliberations and the nature of the post-colonial state envisioned by the framers. Before examining the demands from the nationalist movement in the post-war period for constitutional reforms which led to the eventual appointment of an independent constitutional commission in 1956 to draft a new constitution, it will be useful to outline briefly the historical background to the emergence of the Federation of Malaya.

The modern nation-state of Malaya was largely a construct of the late nineteenth century and first half of the twentieth century by the British colonial power from a collection of princely states and crown colonies to strengthen its rein on what was viewed as economically valuable territories that were rich with natural resources.[4] Prior to Britain gaining territorial control over the Malay sultanates from the nineteenth century, the Portuguese and the Dutch colonial powers had significant territorial control of parts of the peninsula during the sixteenth and seventeenth centuries in an effort to gain control of the spice trade.[5] Before the European conquest, parts of the peninsula, mainly along the coastal areas, had come under the control of Malay sultanates from the outer islands while large areas in the interior remained inhabited by several aboriginal tribes who were the earliest inhabitants of Malaya. Winstedt provides a useful description of the early aboriginal tribes in Malaya – the details of which are beyond the scope of this book.[6] Two prominent kingdoms in the peninsula prior to the arrival of the European powers were the kingdoms of Kedah in the north and Malacca in the south.

Historians Barbara Watson Andaya and Leonard Y. Andaya observed that until the beginning of the fifteenth century CE, the history of Malaya would be difficult to reconstruct with certainty.[7] The leading Malay sultanate in the peninsula, known as the Malacca Sultanate, which was believed to have been founded in early 1400s, was a strong state and a centre of the spice trade in Southeast Asia which exercised control and influence over the smaller states in the peninsula in the fifteenth century until its defeat by the Portuguese in 1511.[8] The Dutch, who had begun trading in Southeast Asia in the sixteenth century, were keen to control the spice trade which the Portuguese dominated, and a strong rivalry ensued. In 1641, the Dutch defeated the Portuguese and gained control of Malacca.[9] Events in Europe, the French conquest of Holland, undermined Dutch interests at times, and in 1824 the Dutch signed a treaty with the British, the Anglo-Dutch Treaty, in which Malacca was exchanged for Bencoolen in Indonesia. Both the Portuguese and Dutch colonial powers did not have wide territorial control of the peninsula compared to the British, who gradually gained control over the whole of the territory by the mid-twentieth century.

British intervention in the mainland Malay states in Malaya can be said to have begun in the later part of the nineteenth century with the signing of the Pangkor Treaty on 20 January 1874 with the ruler of the state of Perak.[10] The Pangkor Treaty provided for the appointment of a British official, called the Resident, to administer the state and to offer some form of protection to the state from external threats. Prior to this, a British trading firm, the East India Company, had acquired three coastal territories in Malaya – Penang (1786), Singapore (1819) and Malacca (1824) – which became known as the Straits Settlements collectively. In 1867, the Straits Settlements were transferred to the control of the British government and became Crown Colonies under the direct jurisdiction of the British Crown. Until 1874, the British Straits Settlements government had adhered to a non-intervention policy vis-à-vis the mainland states while actively promoting trade. The disruption to the Settlements' trade with the Malay states caused by internal conflicts in 1860s and 1870s saw a shift in British policy and intervention in Perak and the signing of the Pangkor Treaty with the ruler of Perak.[11] Following this, further treaties were signed by the British government with the rulers of Selangor, Negeri Sembilan and Pahang. In all these states, the rulers were to accept the advice of the British Residents on all matters other than the Muslim religion and Malay customs.

British notions of law and governance thus were gradually adopted and implemented in the Malay states as a result of these treaties, which also offered protection to the rulers from external threats. In 1896, the four states (Perak, Selangor, Negeri Sembilan and Pahang) were brought together under a broader administration called the Federated Malay States (FMS) with a central legislature largely to strengthen the administrative and financial aspects of the British-controlled territories.[12] A proto federal system of governance can be said to have been introduced during this period. In the FMS, the Malay rulers continued to enjoy sovereignty, albeit a shared sovereignty with the colonial power, but the British Resident was in reality the *de facto* chief executive in each state. Over time, the British government also gained much influence in the Unfederated Malay States (UMS) comprising Kedah, Kelantan, Perlis, Terengganu and Johore, through the placement of British Advisers in these states. The British Advisers had lesser powers than the British Residents. From the late nineteenth century and the early part of the twentieth century, the British administration encouraged mass immigration of labour from India and China to Malaya to meet the needs of the developing modern colonial economy, which was based largely on the tin and rubber industries, and to build the rail and road infrastructure and to staff the lower administrative positions in the civil service.[13] In the process, a plural society was created in Malaya comprising mainly of the Malay, Chinese and Indian communities.

The outbreak of the Second World War in Europe soon led to the Japanese attack on Malaya on 8 December 1941 to gain control of its rich minerals and natural resources and resulted in territorial occupation from mid-February 1942 until August 1945. A Japanese military administration ruled Malaya during the Second World War.[14] The disruption to the British form of constitutional government, however, was a temporary hiatus. The British government in London was confident of regaining Malaya, and much discussion was conducted by a Malayan Planning Unit in the Colonial Office during the war period on the future governance of Malaya after the Japanese were defeated. The wartime planning led to a radical overhaul in the system of administration in Malaya and the introduction of the controversial Malayan Union scheme in 1946 providing for a unitary system of government incorporating the nine Malay states and the Crown Colonies of Penang and Malacca.[15] Singapore was left out of the Malayan Union scheme. Under the scheme, the sovereignty of the Malay rulers was transferred to the British Crown. The Malayan Union scheme met with strong protests from the Malay community because of the rulers' loss of sovereignty and the introduction of a common citizenship, which enabled the Chinese and Indians to embrace Malayan citizenship. In the later part of 1946, negotiations had begun between the British colonial government under Governor Sir Edward Gent, the Malay rulers and representatives of the United Malays National Organisation (UMNO), a newly established political party which had been formed in May 1946 to protest the Malayan Union scheme. Following negotiations, a new agreement was reached to replace the Malayan Union government with a federal form of government.[16] The sovereignty of the rulers was restored, and citizenship requirements proposed under the Malayan Union were made stricter. Some consultations were made with leaders and organisations representing the non-Malays on the new constitution by the H. R. Cheeseman committee, but essentially the agreements reached with the Malay rulers and UMNO prevailed.

The Malayan Union protests provided fertile ground for the growth of nascent nationalist movements. Most significantly, the Malayan Union led to the formation of the United Malays National Organisation (UMNO) to represent the interests of the Malays.[17] Other political organisations which emerged in the immediate post-war period were the *Parti Kebangsaan Melayu Malaya* (PKMM) or Malay Nationalist Party (MNP) and the Malayan Democratic Union in 1945.[18] The Malayan Communist Party (MCP)(formed in 1930) which cooperated with the British colonial government on the eve of the war to resist the Japanese military in Malaya also gained much prominence following their role in the anti-Japanese movement in Malaya during the war. The Malayan Indian Congress (MIC) was formed in August 1946, partly as a response to the Malayan Union debacle, to represent Indian interests.[19] The Malayan Chinese Association (MCA) was formed in February 1949 to represent Chinese interests and to offer a moderate alternative to the MCP.[20]

The 1948 Federation of Malaya Agreement was essentially a construct of British colonialism which enabled Britain to regain full control over the Malayan territories after the Malayan Union controversy, with the support of the Malay rulers and elites. The federation agreement was in essence a proto constitution as Malaya was still under the political and economic control of Britain with the British high commissioner being the chief executive of the federation. The federation agreement introduced a federal system of government for the whole of Malaya, incorporating the nine Malay states and the two former Crown Colonies, the settlements of Penang and Malacca. The British colonial administration introduced a wholly nominated Federal Legislative Council in 1948 headed by a British high commissioner to administer Malaya. A significant proportion of the 70 seats in the legislative council was filled by local political and business representatives. Gradually, local elections were introduced by the British colonial government under the leadership of High Commissioner Sir Henry Gurney from December 1951. State elections were introduced in several states in 1954. This was an effort by the British government to devolve greater powers to local political elites and to neutralise the growing influence of the MCP by indicating to the people that the local elites were involved in the political decision-making process.[21] Following the introduction of local elections and the growth of political parties, the local political elites began to push for a greater degree of participation in government with the ultimate aim to secure self-government for Malaya. The emergence of a coalition between UMNO and the MCA in the Kuala Lumpur municipal elections in February 1952 impacted considerably the growth of a nationalist movement. The banning of the MCP in June 1948 following a declaration of the Emergency after the killing of three British plantation managers in the state of Perak contributed significantly to the growth and advancement of moderate political movements.

The overwhelming victory of the UMNO-MCA ad hoc coalition in the Kuala Lumpur municipal elections in February 1952, which won nine of the 12 seats, altered considerably the pattern of development of Malayan politics.[22] The British colonial administration had hoped that the Independence of Malaya Party (IMP) formed in September 1951 by Dato' Onn Jaafar, the preeminent Malayan politician of the time, would lead to the emergence of a non-communal approach to politics and the growth of a centrist party. The victory of the UMNO-MCA coalition, known as the "Alliance," over the IMP in the Kuala Lumpur election altered the course of Malayan politics and contributed to the entrenchment of communally based political parties. The idea of communally based political parties cooperating in an inter-communal electoral coalition, while preserving their ethnic organisational make-up, began to take root in the Malayan political landscape. In 1952 and 1953, the UMNO-MCA alliance won most of the seats in the local elections held in several major towns throughout the country. Following the electoral success and inspired by the gains made by independence movements in India and Ghana, the leaders of the Alliance became more ambitious and began to push for self-government by demanding the introduction of federal elections from 1953.[23] Several conventions were organised by the Alliance in 1953 and 1954 at which resolutions urging the introduction of federal elections were passed.[24]

The Alliance also sent a three-man delegation led by Alliance leader Tunku Abdul Rahman to London in May 1954 to meet the secretary of state for Colonies in order to persuade him to introduce federal elections in 1954 with a 60% elected majority. The secretary of state declined the Alliance's request to hold federal elections in 1954 with a 60% elected majority. He told the Alliance delegation that elections would be held as planned in 1955 in line with the recommendations of the High Commissioner Sir Gerald Templer (who had recommended 52 elected seats from the 98 seats in the Federal Legislative Council instead of the minority of 44 elected from 92[25] seats suggested by the specially assembled Federal Elections Committee), and if there were shortcomings in the working of the new system, he would consider making the necessary changes. The Alliance was dissatisfied with the secretary of state's response and decided on their return to Kuala Lumpur that some form of direct-action protest was necessary to exert some pressure on the colonial administration. The Alliance decided to boycott the local councils and legislatures and asked their representatives to withdraw from them. The coalition also held a number of street protests in June and July 1954 to push for electoral and constitutional reforms, in addition to sending petitions to the Malay rulers on their demands. The political atmosphere became tense with the protests, and the British colonial administration became very concerned that the security situation could worsen particularly with an ongoing Emergency. The new High Commissioner Sir Donald MacGillivray, who had previously advised the Colonial Office to maintain a tough stance against the Alliance's demands, sought a compromise with the Alliance.[26] MacGillivray, who was beginning a tour of the east coast states, met the Alliance leader Tunku Abdul Rahman on board a Royal Navy frigate, the *H.M.S. Alert*, off the coast of Johore Bahru on 1 July 1954, and after talks agreed to the Alliance's suggestion that five of the seven reserved seats in the Federal Legislative Council, traditionally filled by the high commissioner's nominees, should be filled by the nominees of the majority party.[27] This would strengthen the majority party and bring the "elected" majority to nearly 60% of the total seats in the council that the Alliance sought. This compromise brought to an end the tense stand-off between the Alliance and the colonial administration. The Alliance representatives resumed their membership of the local councils, and a serious crisis was averted.[28]

Most significantly, apart from calling for the introduction of federal elections, the Alliance demanded the appointment of a constitutional commission to draft a new constitution to replace the 1948 Federation Agreement. Following a landslide win by the Alliance in the first federal elections in July 1955, winning 51 of the 52 elected seats, the coalition demanded to meet the British government to discuss the issue of Malayan independence and the appointment of an independent constitutional commission from the Commonwealth, which had been among the major campaign issues in the federal elections.[29] The Tunku informed the visiting Secretary of State Alan Lennox-Boyd in August 1955 that voters had supported fully the Alliance's position on independence in the federal election and it would be appropriate to discuss the issue immediately. The secretary of state was initially hesitant to discuss the issue but eventually agreed to hold a meeting in London to discuss the question of self-governance and several other issues such as finance and security together with representatives of the rulers.[30] The London conference was held in January 1956. There was some concern among the Malay rulers over the Alliance's push for independence. They felt that Malaya was not quite ready for independence yet. The Alliance nonetheless decided to push aggressively for speedier movement towards independence. An important turning point in the campaign for independence was the agreement reached between the Alliance and the representatives of the rulers before the delegations reached London, particularly in regard to safeguarding the position of the rulers as constitutional monarchs. Hence, in London the Malayan delegation was able to speak in one voice, and this strengthened considerably the delegation's bargaining power. The London conference agreed to the Alliance's demand for the appointment of an independent panel of constitutional experts from the Commonwealth to draft a new constitution for independent Malaya.[31] The date for Malayan independence, 31 August 1956, suggested by the Alliance, was also agreed to by the British government at the London conference.

The constitutional commission and its terms of reference

Thus, in the early months of 1956, a panel of constitutional experts was assembled from five Commonwealth countries – Britain, Australia, Canada, India and Pakistan – to frame a new constitution for Malaya. The constitutional commission was headed by Lord Reid, a Lord of Appeal in the Ordinary in the House of Lords; Sir Ivor Jennings, a constitutional expert from Cambridge University; Justice Abdul Hamid from West Pakistan; Justice B. Malik from the Allahabad high court in India and Sir William McKell, a former governor general from Australia.[32] The Canadian candidate withdrew for health reasons. The constitutional commission began its work in Malaya in June 1956.

The Terms of Reference given to the Reid constitutional commission were broad and a general statement of the potential lines of inquiry. The constitutional commission was asked to examine the existing constitutional arrangements in Malaya taking into account the positions and dignities of Her Majesty the Queen and their Highnesses the Malay rulers and to make recommendations for "a federal form of constitution for the whole country as a single, self-governing unit within the Commonwealth based on Parliamentary democracy with a bicameral legislature," which would include provision for:

(i) the establishment of a strong central government with the States and Settlements enjoying a measure of autonomy (the question of residual legislative power to be examined by, and to be the subject of recommendations by the Commission) and with machinery for consultation between the central Government and the States and Settlements on certain financial matters to be specified in the Constitution;
(ii) the safeguarding of the position and prestige of Their Highnesses as constitutional rulers in their respective States;
(iii) a constitutional *Yang di-Pertuan Besar* (Head of State) for the Federation to be chosen among Their Highnesses the rulers;
(iv) a common nationality for the whole Federation; and
(v) the safeguarding of the special position of the Malays and the legitimate interests of other communities.[33]

In essence, the constitutional commission was asked to frame a federal constitution which provided for a parliamentary system of governance with a bicameral legislature while safeguarding the constitutional position of the Malay rulers. The British Westminster-based parliamentary system of governance had already been adopted in several states which had gained independence from Britain, such as India, Pakistan, Ceylon and Burma and were useful points of reference. The older Commonwealth countries such as Australia and Canada also provided a good source of reference for the Westminster-based model of governance. Hence, the constitutional commission did not have to depart radically from the existing systems of parliamentary governance, and the challenge was in working out the details that would have to be explicitly stated in the constitution on the form of government. The constitutional commission was also asked to provide for a strong central government while ensuring that the state governments enjoyed a measure of autonomy. Here, too, there were numerous examples such as India, Pakistan and Australia and Canada which would serve as sources of reference for a federal form of governance.

The commission was asked to provide for a new constitutional head of state for the federation to be chosen from among the nine hereditary rulers. The terms of reference do not give details of the expected head of state, and hence the commission would have to frame this position in consultation with the rulers and the leading political organisations. The terms of the commission also required them to provide for a common nationality and to safeguard the special position of the Malays and the legitimate interests of the other communities. The constitutional commission in a sense was given wide room to frame the constitution to provide what they deemed as essential in a federal constitution without any explicit limits on the content of the constitution.

In this context, it was not surprising that the constitutional commission consulted closely the constitutions of India and Pakistan to the frame the new constitution and to a lesser extent the constitutions of Australia, Canada, Eire, Ceylon, United States and South Africa which were all Common Law based constitutions. The framing of the new Malayan federal constitution was a major challenge to the multinational constitutional commission from the Commonwealth, but there were plenty of sound sources of constitutional reference and they would not have to reinvent the wheel. Nevertheless, the challenge the commission faced was to ensure that the constitutional provisions were compatible and practicable in the complex Malayan political and socio-economic setting. Before we explore how the constitutional commission set about to frame the new Malayan constitution in accordance with the terms of reference and how they debated and discussed the various aspects of the constitutional provisions, it would be useful to briefly consider the background of the Reid Commission members and their roles and the constitutional processes involved in the framing of the Malayan federal constitution.

The members of the Reid Commission

The Reid Commission was made up of five members from the Commonwealth nations – two from Britain and one each from India, Pakistan and Australia. A sixth member from Canada had been selected but withdrew at the last minute for health reasons and was not replaced. The British government nominated Lord Reid as chairman. Sir Ivor Jennings, the second member from Britain, was actually appointed at the suggestion of the Malayan Chief Minister Tunku Abdul Rahman. The governments of India, Pakistan and Australia nominated their own candidates. The names of the candidates were then considered and approved by the Malay rulers and the Federation of Malaya government before they were formally appointed. This process took several months, and the full commission was able to assemble only in June 1956. The work of the constitutional commission took about nine months. In the first phase between July and August 1956, the commission took evidence in Malaya from federal and state departments, political and socio-economic organisations and individuals.[34] A total of 131 memoranda were received from organisations and individuals. These organisations and individuals were invited to express their views at private and public hearings held throughout the country by the constitutional commission. A total of 33 hearings were held in the nine states and two settlements of Penang and Malacca.[35] In the second phase from September, the commission began discussing working papers prepared by the panel members and formulating early drafts of articles to be inserted in the constitution. By the end of October after lengthy and detailed discussions, an early draft was prepared. The commission held 65 meetings in Kuala Lumpur, sometimes meeting twice a day, to discuss the drafts. In early November, the members of the commission left for Rome for the third stage of the work of the commission and to prepare the final draft of the new constitution. Jennings and Abdul Hamid flew to London in early November to look up further references at Cambridge University and to prepare advanced drafts. Lord Reid and E. O. Laird, the commission's secretary, left on the ship *m.v. Asia*, which reached Rome on 8 December 1956, having to make a detour round the Cape of Good Hope because of the Suez crisis. Malik and McKell travelled with Reid until Bombay, where they disembarked and flew out directly to Rome, arriving on 22 November 1956. The constitutional commission was only able to begin its work in Rome on 12 December 1956, and the draft constitution was signed by all members on 11 February 1957 and copies submitted simultaneously to the British government, the Malay rulers and the Federation of Malaya government.

The chairman of the constitutional commission, Lord Reid, 66, was a Lord of Appeal in the House of Lords. He was an experienced politician and had been a Member of Parliament for several years and had served as solicitor general for Scotland before serving as a judge. Lord Reid was born on 30 July 1890 in a village called Drem in East Lothian in Scotland.[36] From 1931 to 1935, Lord Reid was Unionist party member for Stirling and Falkirk Burghs in the House of Commons while practising law. According to *The Times*, he made his mark as a "skilled debater and wise administrator" in the House of Commons.[37] Reid was solicitor general for Scotland from 1936 to 1941 and Lord Advocate between 1941 and 1945.[38] In 1945, he was elected Dean of the Faculty of Advocates, the highest position in the Scottish Bar for practising lawyers. Three years later, he was made a Lord of Appeal in the Ordinary and given a life peerage under the title of Baron Reid of Drem.[39]

Sir William McKell, 65, a former governor general of Australia, was also an experienced politician having served as an Australian cabinet minister, including as justice minister. He had much experience in political administration and a sound understanding of the Australian federal system. Justice B. Malik, 61, was a former chief justice of the Allahabad high court in India and had wide experience in the interpretation of Indian constitutional law. Justice Abdul Hamid, 54, was an experienced high court judge and had served as secretary to the Ministry of Law in West Pakistan. He had worked with Sir Ivor Jennings in the drafting of the 1956 Pakistan constitution. Sir Ivor Jennings, 53, was a former King's Counsel, had served as a vice chancellor of Cambridge University and at the time of appointment was Master of Trinity Hall in Cambridge University. Jennings was the constitutionalist *par excellence* in the commission, having published several important works on the British and Commonwealth constitutions. His publications included *The Law and the Constitution* (London: University of London Press, 1933), *The Constitutional Laws of the British Empire* (London: Oxford University Press, 1938) and *The Constitution of Ceylon* (London: Oxford University Press, 1938).[40]

The constitutional commission's members had considerable knowledge of Commonwealth constitutions, particularly of their respective countries, and were trained in the English Common Law tradition. Jennings and Justice Abdul Hamid had constitution drafting experience, having been involved in drafting the constitution of Pakistan. They also had considerable understanding of the workings of the political systems in their countries. It can be said that the constitutional commission assembled to frame the Malayan constitution had much legal and political experience and a sound understanding of Commonwealth constitutions and parliamentary forms of government, and the Federation of Malaya benefited enormously from their expertise.

The constitution-making process

The Reid Commission began their work on 19 June 1956 when all the members had arrived in Malaya with the exception of the Indian member, Justice B. Malik, who arrived at the end of June.[41] Reid was an able organiser and identified and outlined clearly the work of the commission even before it held its first meeting.[42] The initial meetings of the commission were mainly focused on the procedures to be adopted by the commission and the schedule for taking evidence throughout the country and the manner in which the evidence was to be heard. That is, whether the hearings should be private or public hearings and whether the evidence could be published by either parties. Jennings and Hamid were tasked with preparing most of the working papers on various subjects that served as the basis for the formulation of the articles in the draft constitution. Reid himself prepared a few papers, including on the citizenship of the United Kingdom and the Colonies while McKell (Forestry, Agriculture, Australian Loan Council) and Malik (Education and Subjects of the Rulers) contributed several papers.[43] Even in the early stages of the work of the commission, Reid was faced with a number of challenges, apart from the six-week delay in the start of the commission's work. The commission was to have begun its work in early May 1956 but only held the first meeting on 19 June.[44] The first related to the publication of the commission's report. Reid was careful to ensure the independence of the commission and insisted it publish the report on its own. The Colonial Office had suggested that the report should be sent in the first instance to the secretary of state for Colonial Affairs. Reid was firm on the issue of the publication of the report, and the Colonial Office relented. Second, Reid faced some administrative problems. The secretary to the commission, H. P. Hall, resigned in late July, barely a month after the commission began its work, after complaining to the Colonial Office that he was "unable to work" with Lord Reid.[45] Reid was not happy with Hall's performance and asked the secretary of state for a replacement. High Commissioner Sir Donald MacGillivray's sensitive handling of the issue prevented a more serious crisis erupting. K. J. Henderson was initially appointed acting secretary, and E. O. Laird from the Malayan Civil Service was then appointed as the new secretary.[46] This crisis delayed the early work of the commission.

After the commission submitted its draft constitution on 11 February 1957 simultaneously to the Queen, the Malay rulers, the Malayan federal government and the Colonial Office, the draft constitution was further examined by a Working Party. The Working Party, comprising the British high commissioner, representatives of the Malay rulers and the Alliance government, met between 22 February and 22 May 1957 in Kuala Lumpur to review the Reid draft constitution. Following the meeting of the Working Party, the revised draft constitution was further examined by the London constitutional conference between 13 and 21 May 1957, which involved the Colonial Office, the representatives of the Malay rulers and the Alliance government. This was followed by the tabling of the draft constitution in the Federal Legislative Council in Malaya and the British parliament simultaneously in July 1957. The Malay rulers then assented to the new constitution which came into force on 31 August 1957 as Malaya became independent.

The draft constitution produced by the Reid Commission was the collective effort of the five experienced jurists. Each member of the commission brought with them a vast knowledge of constitutional law and public administration from the Commonwealth countries, and their contributions are reflected in the internal debates and the final document. The Reid draft constitution drew from the best of constitutional traditions in the Commonwealth and had the added benefit of hindsight of seeing the working of these constitutions in practice as is discernible from various case laws cited in the constitutional documents. The Working Party in Malaya and later the London constitutional conference in May 1957, which reviewed the Reid draft constitution, made significant changes to the draft constitution. Nevertheless, most of the Reid draft constitution remained intact and was adopted following parliamentary debates in Kuala Lumpur and London in July 1957. In the following pages, we examine the internal discussions on important aspects of the 1957 Malayan federal constitution during the drafting stages to obtain a deeper understanding of the historical process of the framing of the new constitution and intentions of the framers.

Notes

1 Ivor Jennings, *The law and the constitution* (London: University of London Press, 1961), p. 33.

2 Joseph M. Fernando, *The making of the Malayan constitution* (Kuala Lumpur: Malaysian Branch of Royal Asiatic Society, 2002).

3 For a discussion of fundamental liberties in the 1957 Malayan federal constitution, please refer to Joseph M. Fernando and Shanthiah Rajagopal, "Fundamental liberties in the Malayan constitution and the search for a balance, 1956–1957," *International Journal of Asia-Pacific Studies*, Vol. 13, No. 1, 2017, pp. 1–18.

4 Barbara Watson Andaya and Leonard Y. Andaya, *A history of Malaysia* (London: Palgrave, 2001), pp. 157–203.

5 Ibid., pp. 58–71.
6 R.O. Winstedt, *A history of Malaya* (Kuala Lumpur: Malayan Branch of Royal Asiatic Society, 1935), pp. 1–5. See also Leonard Y. Andaya, "Orang Asli and the Melayu in the history of the Malay Peninsula," *Journal of the Malaysian Branch of the Royal Asiatic Society*, Vol. 75, No. 1, 2002, pp. 23–48.
7 Andaya and Andaya, *A history of Malaysia*, p. 7.
8 Ibid., pp. 46–53.
9 Ibid., pp. 70–78.
10 Eunice Thio, *British policy in the Malay Peninsula, 1880–1910* (Kuala Lumpur: University of Malaya Press, 1969), pp. xi–xxxvii. See also C.N. Parkinson, *British intervention in Malaya, 1876–77* (Kuala Lumpur: University of Malaya Press, 1964).
11 Thio, *British policy in the Malay Peninsula*, pp. 3–27.
12 Yeo Kim Wah, *The politics of decentralization* (Kuala Lumpur: Oxford University Press, 1982), pp. 11–18.
13 Rajeswary Ampalavanar, *The Indian minority and political change in Malaya, 1945–1957* (Kuala Lumpur: Oxford University Press, 1981), pp. 1–8. See further, S. Arasaratnam, *Indians in Malaysia and Singapore* (London: Institute of Race Relations, 1967). See also Yen Ching-hwang, "Historical background," in Lee Kam Hing and Tan Chee-Beng (eds), *The Chinese in Malaysia* (Shah Alam: Oxford University Press, 2000), pp. 1–6. See further Victor Purcell, *The Chinese in Malaya* (London: Oxford University Press, 1967).
14 Paul H. Kratoska, *The Japanese occupation of Malaya, 1941–1945* (London: Allen and Unwin, 1998), pp. 26–85.
15 A.J. Stockwell, *British policy and Malay politics during the Malayan Union experiment, 1942–1948* (Kuala Lumpur: Malaysian Branch of the Royal Asiatic Society, 1979), pp. 17–72. See further, Albert Lau, *The Malayan Union controversy, 1942–1948* (Singapore: Oxford University Press, 1991).
16 Stockwell, *British policy and Malay politics*, pp. 73–107.
17 Ibid., pp. 108–128.
18 G.P. Means, *Malaysian politics* (London: Hodder and Stoughton, 1976), pp. 68–93.
19 Ampalavanar, *The Indian minority and political change in Malaya, 1945–1957,* pp. 83–85.
20 Fernando, *The making of the Malayan constitution*, pp. 13–14.
21 Ibid., pp. 10–29.
22 Ibid., pp. 20–29.
23 Ibid., pp. 38–58.
24 *Straits Times*, 3 August 1953, p. 7. See also *Straits Times*, 24 August 1953, p. 1. See further Fernando, *The making of the Malayan constitution*, pp. 37–45.
25 *Straits Times*, 1 February 1954, p. 6, and 2 February 1954, p. 1. See further Fernando, *The making of the Malayan constitution*, pp. 45–50.
26 *Straits Times*, 7 July 1954, p. 1.
27 *Straits Times*, 8 July 1954, p. 1, and 2 August 1954, p. 6. See also Fernando, *The making of the Malayan constitution*, pp. 50–57.
28 *Straits Times*, 8 July 1954, p. 1, and 30 July 1954, p. 4.
29 Ibid., pp. 58–63.
30 See Fernando, *The making of the Malayan constitution*, pp. 50–58.
31 Ibid., pp. 100–104.
32 For details on the composition of the constitutional commission, see CO 1030/129, The National Archives, Kew, London. See also Malayan Constitutional Commission, CO 1030/136 (7) and Fernando, *The making of the Malayan constitution*, pp. 103–115.
33 Report of the Federation of Malaya Constitutional Commission 1957, London: Her Majesty's Stationery Office, No. 330, p. 6.
34 See Federation of Malaya Constitutional Commission, CO 889/1.
35 Ibid.
36 *The Times*, 31 March 1975.

37 Ibid.
38 Ibid.
39 Ibid.
40 See CO 1030/136 (7) for details on the Commission's members. See also Fernando, *The making of the Malayan constitution*, pp. 109–110.
41 Summary record of First meeting of Constitutional Commission, 19 June 1956, CO 889/1, p. 14. Malik attended the sixth meeting of the commission on 30 June 1956. See also Summary record of Sixth meeting of Constitutional Commission, 30 June 1956, CO 889/1, p. 28.
42 See Summary record of First meeting of Constitutional Commission, 19 June 1956, CO 889/1, pp. 12–19.
43 See memoranda by members of the Commission, CO 889/2, 1956, pp. 112–179.
44 See Summary record of First meeting of Constitutional Commission, 19 June 1956, CO 889/1, pp. 14.
45 See Secretary of State to Reid, 2 August 1956, CO 1030/136 (2).
46 See Malaya: Constitutional Commission, FCO 141/7473, for details on the new appointment. See also Summary record of 12th meeting of Constitutional Commission, 30 July 1956, CO 889/1. K. J. Henderson, who was Assistant Secretary from the 7th meeting on 9 July 1956, took over from Hall at 12th meeting as Acting Secretary on 30 July 1956. E. O. Laird appears as the Secretary to the Commission for the first time at the 20th meeting of the Commission on 22 August 1956.

2 The system of government

The political testament, which we set out below, reflects the firm desire of the majority of the peoples of this country for a form of government which will ensure freedom, equality and unity of the new nation. We, therefore, desire that the future constitution of this country must provide for the establishment of a sovereign and fully independent State in which the people shall enjoy freedom and equality. This constitution shall also provide for a stable democratic government and ensure peace and harmony amongst all its peoples.

(Alliance memorandum, 27 September 1956)

The 1957 Federation of Malaya constitution defined the system of government that independent Malaya adopted after considerable constitutional deliberations between 1956 and 1957. The constitutional document, which took more than a year to produce if the work of the review committees and legislative debates are included, provided very detailed provisions on the structure and functions of the institutions of government, the distribution of powers between the institutions and the division of powers between the federal government and the states, in addition to stating the fundamental rights of the citizens.[1] The constitution also contained provisions outlining the powers of the ancillary bodies that were created or formalised to enable the full working of the system of parliamentary democracy such as the Public Services Commission, the Election Commission and the Police Service Commission.[2] The function and powers of parliament, the executive and the judiciary were all clearly defined in the new constitution. The Reid Commission, which prepared the draft constitution, drew from the existing constitutional provisions, practices and precedents in the Commonwealth, including Britain, to formulate the relevant articles in the Malayan constitution. The commission also formulated its own provisions in the new constitution to accommodate certain local peculiarities (as, for example, Article 89 which provided for the creation of a Consolidated Fund under the jurisdiction of the federal government, and the provisions relating to the newly created institution of the *Yang di-Pertuan Agong*, the supreme head of state), and at other times adapted the borrowed provisions to suit Malayan conditions. There is an interesting similarity in many of the provisions relating to the structure of government in the Malayan constitution and the constitutions of Commonwealth

DOI: 10.4324/9781003542537-2

countries such as India, Pakistan and Ceylon, all of which are parliamentary democracies and drew considerably from English Common Law principles.[3]

The final constitutional document was as close a compromise as possible that the framers, including the Working Party which reviewed the Reid draft constitution, could reach while adhering to the main tenets of parliamentary democracy and constitutional principles and, most importantly, the terms of reference. Interestingly, the provisions on the system of government were among the least contentious areas in the drafting of the new constitution although substantive debates took place during the constitutional deliberations on the specific provisions and wording in the constitution of various elements of governance. There were two main reasons for this. First, the Reid constitutional commission's terms of reference stated explicitly that the commission should provide for a federal parliamentary system of governance with a bicameral legislature. The commission's terms of reference required them: "To make recommendations for a federal form of constitution for the whole country as a single, self-governing unit within the Commonwealth based on Parliamentary democracy with a bicameral legislature."[4] It also required the constitution to safeguard the position of Their Highnesses as constitutional rulers of their respective states while providing for a paramount ruler at the federal level to be elected from among the nine monarchs. This meant that the nature of the system of government, a parliamentary democracy with a bicameral legislature and a constitutional monarchy, had largely been predetermined by the terms of reference of the commission which had been agreed at the London conference in January 1956. Second, the drafters of the constitution could draw on existing parliamentary practices in Britain and the Commonwealth countries in addition to existing institutional practices in Malaya. There was no need to reinvent the wheel. A proto parliamentary style of governance based on the House of Commons procedures had been in use in Malaya since 1896, and with the availability of details on the parliamentary practices and procedures used in Britain, India and Pakistan, a useful template for reference was readily available. The constitutional commission also learnt from existing weaknesses in these countries in the light of experience. Thus, the formulation of the provisions on the main functions and powers of the different organs of government was less contentious. Nevertheless, the commission had to scrutinise the "borrowings" to ensure that they were suitable and relevant to the Malayan conditions while adhering to the cardinal principles of parliamentary democracy.

The federal system of governance based on the 1948 Federation of Malaya Agreement, although not a full democratic entity as only 53% (52 out of the total of 98 seats) of the members of the Federal Legislative Council were directly elected since 1955, had worked reasonably well, and it remained for the commission to formulate a new constitution which could draw on this experience while providing for the changed political conditions in the post-independence period and potential contingencies that could arise. The provisions on the powers of the head of state to declare an emergency in the new constitution (Article 138 of Reid draft constitution), for example, were inserted in anticipation of possible future scenarios of threats to national security while drawing from the lessons of the ongoing communist insurgency in Malaya.[5] The federation agreement, however, was in essence a colonial constitution in which the chief executive was the British high commissioner who had to balance the various demands on the federal state, whereas the new system would provide for a fully elected legislature headed by a prime minister who would be more fully subjected to the pressures and vagaries of a party system. Thus, a distinctly different system had to be formulated for the new polity. Malaya needed a system of government that provided for the full working of a parliamentary democratic system and yet would be able to incorporate some traditional institutions in the country such as the institution of constitutional monarchs.

There was almost universal consensus among the Malayan political parties, the nine Malay rulers, socio-economic and political organisations and individuals who made submissions to the constitutional commission that a parliamentary system based on the Westminster model but with a federal structure would be the most suitable for the independent country. The ruling Alliance Party's desire is reflected in their memorandum to the Reid Commission:

> The Legislature of Malaysia should be bicameral consisting of an Upper House, to be known as the *Dewan Negara*, and a Lower House to be known as *Dewan Raayat*. . . . The constitution of Malaysia should provide for parliamentary democracy, and it is therefore imperative that the *Dewan Raayat* should be fully elected. The election of members of the *Dewan Raayat* should be under the system of direct elections from single-member constituencies held once at least in every five years.[6]

The Alliance had consistently maintained, right from the federal elections campaign in July 1955, that they preferred a parliamentary system of government with a bicameral legislature. They had considerable tutelage in the parliamentary system over the years and felt that it was the most suited to the country. In the 1955 election manifesto, for example, the Alliance stated:

> The Alliance believes that the democratic form of Government based on parliamentary institutions is the form of Government best suited to Malaya. We have learnt in the course of the past many years to accept this form of Government as the best and we have been educated in the parliamentary system of debating and discussion and have accepted the procedures.[7]

Nevertheless, the proposals of the Alliance on the form of government contained in their memorandum were thin on paper with very little details and were quite vague. The Alliance documents do not indicate that there were any serious debates among its leaders on the system of government or the division of powers among the main organs of government.[8] It was obvious that the Alliance had not thought out the matter deeply to be more forthcoming with details and left most of the detailed work on the system of government to the commission, having accepted in principle the Westminster parliamentary system of government. Hence, during the hearing before the constitutional commission on 27 September 1956, the Alliance leaders were probed and prodded by the commission to extract greater details on the ruling coalition's ideas of governance and preferences.[9] The Malay rulers also proposed the adoption of the system of parliamentary democracy with a bicameral legislature. They recommended the lower house should comprise single-member constituencies.[10] They felt that the upper house should act as a check on the "hasty" legislative proposals from the lower house and to ensure a representation of the states and settlements and other special interests that were not represented in the lower house.[11] The constitutional documents indicate that there was an engaging debate within the constitutional commission and with the main actors on the various elements of the system of government.

The other major political parties, while preferring the parliamentary system of government, had some significant differences with the Alliance Party on the make-up of the chambers. They, however, did not have a major impact on the recommendations of the commission which adopted the Alliance's recommendations. The People's Progressive Party (PPP) proposed a parliamentary system with bicameral legislature but stressed that the second house should be made up of members representing a cross section of the population not unduly influenced by the ruling party.[12] The PPP felt that if the second chamber was elected, in all probability the members would comprise representatives of the party which was successfully elected to the lower house. Further, if the nominations to the second chamber were made by the party in power, it would also result in the chamber being filled with members or supporters of the party in power.[13] This would fail to fulfil the purpose of a second chamber. Thus, the PPP suggested the second chamber should comprise the *Mentris Besar* of each state, a number of major or territorial chiefs from each state, a number of representatives from the Settlements (Penang and Malacca), not more than five members to be elected by the first chamber and five members to be nominated by the *Yang di-Pertuan Agong* to represent special interests.[14] The party argued that such a chamber would be more likely to carry out its duty effectively as the members would not be dependent on the goodwill of the party in power. The party suggested that the second chamber should not have power to introduce finance bills and its powers of delaying should be limited to a year.[15] The *Persatuan Islam sa-Malaya* (also known as the Pan-Malayan Islamic Party)[16] preferred a federal parliamentary system of government with a bicameral legislature but had no details in its memorandum.[17] The Labour Party of Malaya recommended that Malaya should be a unitary state rather than a federal state.[18] While supportive of parliamentary democracy, the party preferred a republican system of governance.[19] The party argued that the general tendency in Southeast Asia was towards republicanism. The Party Negara which submitted a memorandum through its Perlis branch suggested a single legislature with fully elected members without providing any details.[20] Hence, there was a basic consensus among all the political parties that Malaya should adopt a parliamentary system of governance, but there were differences in the need for a second chamber and its composition. We now examine the constitutional discussions related to nature and powers of the lower and upper house that the constitutional commission recommended after listening to the submissions of the various organisations.

Lower house of parliament

The Alliance proposed that the lower house of Parliament, which they wanted to be termed as *Dewan Raayat*, should be fully elected.[21] They felt that minority groups and other special interests could be represented in the nominated upper house. The coalition did not want to have any nominated members in the lower house although it was pointed out to them by the commission that there were precedents in some countries such as India where a small portion of the members were nominated by the president to represent minority and special interests.[22] A Speaker would be elected from among the members of the lower house with the exception of the first life of the lower house where the *Yang di-Pertuan Agong*,[23] the Paramount Ruler, would appoint the Speaker. This was because it was anticipated, and eventually agreed, that the sitting parliament would continue after independence until the first elections were held in 1959.[24] It was also intended to enable the constituency delineation commission to complete its work in relation to the creation of parliamentary and states seats for the whole federation. The Alliance unequivocally wanted the members of the lower house to be elected by direct elections to single-member constituencies.[25] The maximum life of the *Dewan Raayat* was to be five years as was the practice in many independent Commonwealth nations. The *Yang di-Pertuan Agong*, however, could exercise his prerogative "to prorogue, dissolve and in the event of national crisis to extend the life of the *Dewan Raayat*."[26] Members of the lower house must be nationals and at least 21 years of age.[27] The Alliance noted in their submissions that minorities and other interests would be represented in the upper house.[28] The Alliance did not state in their memorandum the total number of members they expected in the first post-independence lower house. The commission after discussion provided (Article 40 of Reid draft constitution) that the total number of members in the lower house to be elected after Merdeka Day should be 104, twice the existing total parliamentary constituencies.[29]

In their conception of the system of government, the Alliance was clear that the lower house of parliament would be the centre of power while the upper house would play a more secondary role. This is evident from the range of powers that was accorded to the respective houses. The *Dewan Raayat* and *Dewan Negara* would have "equal powers in initiating Bills, except Money Bills which should only be initiated by the *Dewan Raayat*."[30] Bills passed by the lower house should be passed by the upper house before they become law. The upper house could send bills passed by the lower house back for reconsideration. But if the bills, after being reconsidered by the lower house and sent back to the upper house, were not passed by the upper house within a period of 12 months from the date they were approved by the lower house, they would automatically become law after 21 days.[31] In other words, the Senate's powers would be mainly those of revising and delaying powers. The Senate could not reject a bill which had been reconsidered by the lower house. The Alliance's memorandum, however, was silent on whether the upper house could send the bill back to the lower house more than once. The commission's attempt to persuade the Alliance to consider the possibility of a small proportion of nominated members in the lower house was strongly resisted.

Justice B. Malik pointed out that in India a small proportion of the members of the lower house were appointed by the president to represent special interests and to raise particular interests: "Under Articles 331 and 332 of the Indian Constitution, there are special provisions relating to other classes. The idea is that in the Lower House, if there are some representatives, they can speak on behalf of their particular interest."[32] He noted that in Malaya there was a case, for example, for nominated representation for the aboriginal peoples who could not elect their own representatives. Abdul Razak responded that their interests would be represented in the upper house: "We want the Lower House to be fully elected; otherwise there will, I think, be objection."[33] When Malik probed further along the same lines, the Alliance leader, Tunku Abdul Rahman, remarked: "The object of having a second house is that we want the interests of minorities to be represented and to have a say in the legislature. We have reserved the Lower House for the representatives to be fully elected."[34] The Alliance leaders, as evident from the record of the discussions with the commission, had clearly not thought out deeply the composition of the two legislatures in the light of other practices in the Commonwealth and were really making up their arguments as the hearing proceeded, sometimes even contradicting each other's statements in their responses to queries from the commission.

On the extension of the life of the lower house, wherein the Alliance proposed that the *Yang di-Pertuan Agong* should be empowered to extend the life of the house, Justice Abdul Hamid asked if this was not "a dangerous provision."[35] To which, Razak replied that the provision was only intended to be used in the event of a "national crisis." Hamid raised the possibility of a ruling party, having lost the confidence of the people, advising the head of state to extend the life of parliament for another two years.[36] But the Alliance stood its ground. In order to avoid this, Hamid said, the phrase "national crisis," would have to be clearly defined in the constitution. In a departure from the practice in most Commonwealth countries, the Alliance proposed that members of the Cabinet could come from both houses and should have the right of audience in both houses. Reid thought this was unusual although it was practised in India. Hamid felt that such a provision would be advantageous as the minister could validate bills which originated in the lower house and which would need to be validated in the upper house.[37] The Tunku supported the idea, noting:

> I think it would be a good thing. Either House may like to hear the views of Government and the Minister who formulates the policy should be able to go and explain it to the Upper House. It would not be a bad idea.[38]

The Alliance, nevertheless, did not want any minister to be appointed from outside the House.[39]

The rulers' proposals on the system of government were in general similar to the Alliance's conception of the parliamentary system. The rulers' proposition on the make-up of the lower house was surprisingly brief, amounting to only a single paragraph in the 50-page memorandum. They proposed that the lower house should comprise members elected through direct popular elections in single-member constituencies, for a term of not less than three years.[40] They did not approve of dual membership, meaning that an elected member of the lower house should not be a member of the state legislature at the same time.[41]

The constitutional commission, in the main, followed closely the proposals of the Alliance on the composition and powers of the lower house of parliament. The commission provided for a lower house of 104 members to be elected on the basis of single-elected constituency members for a term of five years beginning with the first post-independence federal elections in 1959.[42] The functions and powers of the lower house were largely based on the Westminster model, and there was considerable borrowing from the relevant sections of the constitutions of India and Pakistan in particular to frame the articles in this section. Article 38 of the Reid draft constitution provided for a parliament that would consist of the *Yang di-Pertuan Agong* and two house of parliament, the House of Representatives and the Senate, in keeping with the Alliance proposals for a bicameral legislature based on the Westminster model.[43] The qualifications for membership of the lower house, members' privileges, the rules of procedures in the house and the powers of the lower house (Articles 38–63 of Reid draft constitution) were mainly drawn from the constitutions of India and Pakistan and House of Commons procedures. The commission barred double membership (Article 43 of Reid draft constitution), that is, membership of the lower and upper house at the same time,[44] but allowed simultaneous membership of the state legislature and either the lower house or the upper house of parliament. The commission felt such simultaneous membership was necessary as it would otherwise be difficult to find sufficient members who had suitable experience for the state legislatures.[45] This was also in recognition of the Alliance's request to allow such double membership of the legislatures.

The draft constitution provided that a person should be a citizen and at least 21 years of age to qualify to be a member of the lower house (Article 41 of Reid draft constitution). Individuals who were undischarged insolvent, hold any office of profit or were convicted for any offence for a term of not less than two years would be disqualified from being a member of the house (Article 42 of Reid draft constitution). These were quite similar to the provisions in the constitutions of India and Pakistan. The procedures relating to voting on bills in the house, the passage of the bills, money bills, assent of bills and remuneration of the members were also framed along the lines of similar provisions in the constitutions of India and Pakistan. The provisions relating to legislative procedures in the draft constitution followed the basic pattern found in most Commonwealth constitutions and were not controversial as most of the Commonwealth nations followed the procedures of the House of Commons, with some variations to accommodate local conditions.

The upper house of parliament

A second chamber in the national legislature is a fairly common feature in Commonwealth states, many of whom drew from the Westminster style of government where besides the lower house of parliament, called the House of Commons, there was an upper house called the House of Lords. Many newly independent former

British colonies in the post-second World War period followed this practice because it allowed for a measure of check and balance in the system of governance wherein the upper house, usually comprising elder statesmen and politicians and representatives of special interest groups, could play an advisory role to the lower house consisting mainly of younger politicians. It was believed that this bicameral legislative system could also moderate a little the considerable powers of the lower house. In some countries, such as the United States and Australia, the upper house was directly elected while in others they were nominated. There are, of course, some states which have a single chamber. In the context of Malaya, the constitutional records indicate that most of the political parties preferred a bicameral legislature with an upper house. The terms of reference of the commission agreed at the London conference in January 1956 further required the commission to provide for a bicameral legislature. The ruling Alliance Party also wanted the constitution to provide for an upper house to represent the states and special interests. They wanted the fully nominated upper house to be termed *Dewan Negara* with a total of 45 members.[46] According to the Alliance formula, each of the 11 states in the federation would provide two members and the balance would comprise prominent members who would be appointed by the *Yang di-Pertuan Agong* on the recommendation of the ruling government.[47] In the Alliance's view, the *Dewan Negara* or Senate should "reflect the national pattern of life in the country, including racial minorities."[48] The Senate would be headed by a "president" who would be appointed by the *Yang di-Pertuan Agong*. Hence, the Alliance wanted the upper house to represent the states and a cross section of Malayan society, including commerce and trade.

The rulers in their memorandum to the commission proposed an upper house to check upon what they called "hasty legislative proposals" by the lower house.[49] They wanted the upper house to represent the interests of the states and settlements and other interests that would otherwise not be represented in the lower house.[50] The rulers proposed that the upper house should comprise three state representatives – the *Mentris Besar* from the states and their equivalent officers in the settlements (i.e. chief ministers) and two others who would be appointed by the rulers or head of state (for the settlements) with the advice of the state executive.[51] The latter two representatives, they suggested, should consist of an elected member of the local legislature and another with experience in public affairs. In addition, the rulers submitted that the upper house should have nominees not exceeding 15 members appointed by the *Yang di-Pertuan Agong* to represent sections of the community not sufficiently represented in the lower house.[52] They proposed that the members of the upper house should serve for six years, one-third retiring every two years and being ineligible for re-nomination.[53] They wanted the members of the upper house to have full legislative powers with the exception of initiating money bills.[54] In essence, the propositions of the rulers were quite similar to the suggestions of the Alliance Party.

An interesting debate took place when the Alliance appeared before the commission in September 1956 for a hearing of their submissions contained in their memorandum. The commission, after some discussion among its members, appeared to favour a partially elected upper house by the voters and for a minority of nominated members. Lord Reid told the Alliance delegation that some quarters wanted a minority of nominated members in the upper house, either directly or indirectly elected, and wondered what the Alliance thought of the idea.[55] Lord Reid noted:

> I do not know whether you attach particular importance to half the House being Government nominees because, that is, of course, what they would be, or rather they would be selected on certain principles. I do not know whether the Alliance regarded such a large proportion of nominated members as really important.[56]

Abdul Razak, the Alliance deputy leader, explained that the elected element came from the states through nominations by state councils while the other nominated members came from "all walks of life." It was the Alliance's intention, he said, "not to give the States too strong a say in Federal matters."[57] He explained that the terms of office in the upper house would be for five years, and nominees might have to be changed when a new government came into office. Reid pointed out that this would mean that if a general election resulted in a new government, then half the upper house would be changed as they would comprise the nominees of the new government. The Alliance leader Tunku Abdul Rahman agreed that the party had anticipated this would happen. On the composition of the nominated representation of the various interest groups, the Alliance felt that apart from racial or ethnic minorities, the members would represent important sectors such as commerce, rubber, tin, and trade unions, among others, which reflected a national pattern of life.[58] The Alliance did not seem keen on the mention of trade unions in the document, to which Justice Abdul Hamid remarked: "The nomination will be in your hands, you should not be afraid of that. You will be able to silence the people."[59] And this was followed by laughter.

The Alliance told the commission they thought that the composition of the nominees to the upper house should be flexible to enable the government to vary the choices according to the times and were not keen on any rigid list. The Alliance was unanimous that only nationals should be nominated, even in the early stages of the introduction of the upper house.[60] Sir William McKell, the Australian member of the commission, was against the idea that the elected members could serve as members of both the state and federal legislatures. The Alliance had suggested that members could be elected to the state and federal legislatures at the same time simply because they felt that the country at that stage did not have sufficient people of calibre and hence double membership of the legislatures should be allowed. Tunku told the commission: "I feel very strongly that under the present circumstances we cannot avoid it because of a shortage of men."[61] Lord Reid interjected to state that in the United Kingdom a member of the Ulster parliament could also be at the same time a member of the Westminster parliament.[62] The commission eventually did not bar simultaneous membership of the lower and upper houses because it felt that such disqualification "might deprive the Legislative Assemblies of useful contacts with the Federal Parliament" and it would also pose some problems in finding suitably experienced candidates for the state assemblies.[63]

There was a further engaging debate during the hearing about the potential loyalty of the representatives in the upper house and the question of an equal voice for the states. McKell posed a question to the delegation as to whether the Alliance had considered the possibility that the elected members from the states, numbering 22, could with just the support of one additional nominated member dominate the upper house as those elected would primarily be responsible to their electors in the states. In this way, he felt, a small majority could delay government legislation. A member of the Alliance delegation, Ng Ek Teong from the Malayan Chinese Association (MCA), pointed out that the state representatives would to an extent come from the majority party in the legislature, and this scenario was less likely to arise.[64] When McKell pushed the point further to ask to whom the members of the upper house owed their first loyalty, Tunku pointed out that the Alliance at present controlled all the state and settlements' governments and the loyalty of the members of the state councils were first to the party. Tunku said:

> Every directive issued from our headquarters is respected most obediently. At the moment, personal loyalty is to the party itself, but later on, perhaps with a party less strong than ourselves, opinion might change, but in working on any plan, we have to see the picture as it exists today.[65]

He stressed that the Alliance wanted to ensure that there was a strong central government.

McKell was keen to have a fully elected upper house as was the case in Australia and to enable the states to have an equal voice at the centre. He disapproved of special interests being represented in the upper house.[66] Malik, however, felt nominated members were important to represent minorities as was the case in India.[67] McKell said:

> In Australia, the Upper House is elected on the same franchise by the people as members of the Lower House. You have an election for members of the Lower House and you have an election for members of the Upper House at the same time, but the Upper House represents the States because each State has an equal representation in the Senate, that is, the Upper House. It does not matter how small the State is – it has equal representation with the large States; but they are all elected – elected under exactly the same franchise.[68]

Justice Hamid supported McKell on the importance of having a directly elected upper house, noting that it was the same in India where they were directly elected:

> There is strong Central government but it does not mean that the Central government do not have the right to have nominated members. There are a

> few nominations but the rest of the members are elected by the people just like members of the Lower House.[69]

Razak suggested that the Alliance wanted to combine the two types together. The Alliance, however, agreed to the suggestion of the commission that state representatives to the upper house could be selected from outside the state councils to widen the choice as compared to their written proposition that the state representatives should merely come from the state councils.[70]

In keeping with the convention in parliamentary democracies, the commission gave more powers to the lower house whose members were elected directly compared to the Senate but with sufficient powers to the latter to delay legislation and to act as a check and balance. The commission noted in its report:

> Our recommendations will give to the Senate much less direct control over legislation and administration than to the House of Representatives. We are directed to base our recommendations on Parliamentary democracy, and in our view the principles of Parliamentary democracy require that ultimate responsibility should rest with that House of Parliament which has been elected by direct elections.[71]

Nevertheless, the commission, which envisioned that in time the Senate would be directly elected, did not think that the Senate would only be of secondary importance. It believed the Senate had an important role to play with revising and delaying powers.[72] The commission's report noted:

> Our recommendations are made with the intention of enabling the Senate to become an influential forum of debate and discussion, and a body which will contribute valuable revision to legislation and which will be able to impose a measure of delay in exceptional cases.[73]

The Senate could delay legislation, other than money bills, for up to 12 months. "Such delay will enable public opinion to express itself, and the Senate's power to impose delay should be a safeguard against hasty or ill-considered legislation," stated the commission's report.[74] In the first life of the Senate, the commission recommended (Article 39 of Reid draft constitution) that each state should elect two members and a further 11 should be nominated to represent minority and special interests.[75] They recommended that each member should be elected for a period of six years. McKell and Hamid issued a note of dissent on this issue, arguing that the Senate should be fully elected in keeping with the system of parliamentary democracy:

> It will be seen that none of the members of the Senate are to be elected by the people. We consider that a Senate so constituted does not conform to a system of parliamentary democracy, and is not in keeping with the aspirations of a people whose desire it is to enjoy self-government in the real sense and democracy in its purest form.[76]

McKell and Hamid recommended that the Senate should comprise equal number of members from each state to be elected on the same terms as the members of the House of Representatives.[77] The Working Party, which reviewed the Reid draft, adopted the recommendations of the majority in the Reid Commission but increased the nominated members in the Senate from 11 to 16 to enable a wider representation of interests.[78] The term of a senator was reduced to three years, and a senator would be eligible for a second term.

The head of state

The provisions on the position of head of state for the independent Federation of Malaya did not pose too much of a problem for the Alliance or the rulers. There was no question then of Malaya choosing a republican style of government and the possibility of electing a civilian head of state as was the case in India and many Commonwealth states. The constitutional documents do not indicate any discussion of any other alternatives among Malayan organisations. Only the Labour Party of Malaya had suggested that the country adopt a republican form of government, but this idea had not gained favour among the other parties and was not given any serious discussion during the constitutional deliberations.[79] The constitutional documents reveal that there was much consensus among most of the leading political organisations that one of the rulers should be appointed as the supreme head of state for a certain period of time and that the nine rulers should take turns to serve as the head of state of the federation. The idea of such an elective kingship can be said to have been inspired by practices observed in the states of Negri Sembilan and Perak where traditionally one of the main territorial chiefs (called *undangs* in Negri Sembilan) took turns to serve as the supreme head of that state. There were, however, considerable discussions during the framing of the constitution on the powers of the Paramount Ruler vis-à-vis the Executive. The Alliance Party proposed that the head of state should be called the *Yang di-Pertuan Besar* and would be chosen from among the Malay rulers to serve a term of three years. The Alliance memorandum stated:

> In keeping with the dignity and prestige of a sovereign and fully independent State, Malaysia should have a Head of State entitled the *Yang di-Pertuan Besar*, chosen by Their Highnesses the Rulers from amongst themselves and shall hold office for a term of not less than three years. The *Yang di-Pertuan Besar* should be the constitutional head of Malaysia.[80]

The term *Yang di-Pertuan Besar* was changed to *Yang di-Pertuan Agong* later when it was realised that this title was already held by the ruler of the state of Negri Sembilan. The rulers in their memorandum noted this and suggested that the paramount ruler should be called *Yang di-Pertuan Agong* or *Maha Besar*.[81] The counsel for the rulers, Neil Lawson, pointed out this anomaly during the hearing given by the commission.[82] It is interesting that the Alliance recommended in their memorandum that the *Yang di-Pertuan Besar* should be the constitutional head of "Malaysia." At the same time, it was noted in their memorandum that United

Malays National Organisation (UMNO) preferred the independent federation to be named "Malaysia" while the MCA said it preferred the continuation of the name "Malaya."[83] The Reid Commission, however, refused to be drawn into deciding the name for the federation, stating that it was beyond their terms of reference and asked the Alliance to set up a nomenclature committee to decide and standardize the terms to be used.

The Alliance submitted that Paramount Ruler should be chosen by Their Highnesses the Rulers from among themselves. The Alliance also proposed that a successor to the *Yang di-Pertuan Besar*, to be called the *Yang di-Pertuan Muda*, should be appointed to succeed as head of state "on the demise of the *Yang di-Pertuan Besar*."[84] The Alliance wanted provisions to be made in the constitution for the appointment of a successor within 24 hours in the event of the demise of both *Yang di-Pertuan Besar* and the *Yang di-Pertuan Muda*.[85] If this was not done, the Alliance wanted provisions to be made in the constitution to enable the Cabinet to appoint a "Council of Regency" from among the rulers.[86] The Alliance memorandum is quite clear on the status of the Paramount Ruler as a constitutional head of state, and he was not expected to involve himself in the politics of the federation. The memorandum states that the executive authority of the federation should be exercised in the name of the *Yang di-Pertuan Besar* by the elected government headed by a prime minister.[87] In the hearing before the constitutional commission, Reid asked if it would not be better if a "deputy" be appointed at the same time the Paramount Ruler was appointed instead of a "successor."[88] The commission felt that such a provision would make it easier for the rulers to make a fresh appointment when the term of the Paramount Ruler ended. Razak argued the idea of having a successor was to enable him to succeed immediately, and it did not matter if he was called a "deputy" or a "successor." Eventually, the constitution provided for the election of a *Timbalan Yang di-Pertuan Agong*.

The rulers made a more complex submission for the rotation of the position of head of state which contained two lists, A and B.[89] The A list contained a list of the rulers in order of accession to their thrones at independence, and the B list contained the names of rulers who had completed their term in the A list. The rulers would assume the office according to the list A, and if any of the rulers had missed a turn for some reason (death, illness or being a minor), their names would go down the A list. As each ruler in the A list completes his term, their names would be inserted in the B list, which would be a permanent rotation list. When the list A was exhausted, the successive *Yang di-Pertuan Agong* would be appointed from list B. In this way, every state would have a turn before they went to the B list.[90] The rulers suggested that the tenure of office of the *Yang di-Pertuan Agong* would be for a term of five years compared to the Alliance's submission of three years, but he would be permitted to resign or could be removed with the concurrence of the Conference of Rulers by a declaration passed by a two-thirds majority of each house of parliament.[91] If he was removed as ruler of his own state, he would automatically vacate the office of *Yang di-Pertuan Agong*. The rulers sought certain special privileges for the position of *Yang di-Pertuan Agong*. These included immunity from the judicial process during his term of office, "to be the fountain of federal awards and honours" and to be "the fountain of temporal justice making appointments of the judges of the Federal Supreme Court on constitutional advice."[92] Federal executive power would be exercised in his name by persons appointed by him upon advice. The rulers' memorandum noted:

> Federal executive power will be exercised in his name by persons appointed by him upon advice, i.e. as to political appointments in the Federation Government on the advice of the Chief Minister, as to non-political appointments in the Federal service upon the recommendation of the responsible body, e.g. the Judicial service, the Public service or Police service commissions.[93]

The *Yang di-Pertuan Agong* would be the "supreme commander" of the defence forces, represent the federation in external affairs and accredit representatives from other countries, exercise the power of pardon in relation to court martial offences or other offences committed outside the territorial control of the rulers of the states and appoint governors to act on his behalf as head of government in the two settlements.[94] Most of the proposals of the rulers in relation to the powers and prestige of the paramount ruler, the *Yang di-Pertuan Agong*, were in fact incorporated in the draft constitution prepared by the Reid Commission and accepted by the Working Party which reviewed the draft constitution later.

Nevertheless, the draft constitution did not provide many functions for the Conference of Rulers mainly because the commission (and the Alliance) felt that the main purpose of the body was to elect the *Yang di-Pertuan Agong* and that they should not be involved in politics. The Alliance's memorandum merely stated that there should be a Conference of Rulers presided over by the *Yang di-Pertuan Besar*.[95] The rulers, however, felt the Conference of Rulers should have broader "consultative and advisory" functions similar to those provided in the 1948 federation agreement. In their memorandum to the commission, the rulers proposed four additional functions for the Conference of Rulers. These were that the Conference of Rulers should be consulted when territorial changes were considered for the federation or the states; in relation to legislation affecting the status, rights and position of Their Highnesses; in relation to federal legislation affecting the Muslim faith; and when constitutional amendments are considered in relation to Malay special position and the rights and position of the states.[96]

The rulers' representatives raised this issue at the second meeting of the Working Party on 25 February 1957.[97] The rulers submitted that a number of additional powers should be conferred on the Conference of Rulers apart from the appointment of the *Yang di-Pertuan Agong* and his deputy.[98] They wanted the agreement of the Conference of Rulers sought in the appointment of the chief justice and judges of the Supreme Court and heads of important commissions such as members of the Election Commission, Public Services Commission and Police Service Commission.[99] In addition, the rulers submitted that their consent should be sought in changes to the constitution on several matters which affected their sovereignty. These were territorial changes affecting the states, changes which could affect the Muslim religion and Malay customs, changes to the entrenched clauses (Article 157 on Malay special rights and Article 82 on Malay land reservations) in the constitution, changes affecting the status or powers of the States and changes affecting the privileges, position and dignities of the rulers.[100] The rulers felt that changes related to these matters impinged on their sovereignty, and they should have the right "to give or withhold concurrence in such changes."[101]

Further, the rulers wanted the Conference of Rulers to be consulted on changes to law affecting immigration, the concurrent list, power of parliament to legislate for states for uniformity (Article 70 of draft constitution) and the formula used to distribute federal funds to the states.[102] In relation to Article 33 (2) of the Reid draft constitution which provided for the *Yang di-Pertuan Agong* to have the exclusive power to grant pardon, the rulers submitted that in relation to offences committed in the states, the ruler of the state should retain the power to grant pardon as provided under existing law.[103] The rulers were unhappy that the draft constitution did not provide for the involvement of the rulers in the ceremony of affirmation of office of the *Yang di-Pertuan Agong*. The draft constitution merely provided for the newly elected *Yang di-Pertuan Agong* to be sworn into office by taking an oath before the chief justice. The rulers submitted that the *Yang di-Pertuan Agong*, the Supreme Head of State, should make an "affirmation" of office and allegiance, and not an oath, and that this should be done in the presence of the Conference of Rulers and not merely before the chief justice.[104]

There was resistance from the Alliance and the High Commissioner Sir Donald MacGillivray to what was viewed as encroachment into politics by the rulers and which was deemed to conflict with their status as constitutional monarchs. MacGillivray thought that to give these additional functions to the rulers would bring them into the "arena of politics" and contradict one of the main recommendations of the constitutional commission that the rulers should become constitutional rulers.[105] The Alliance leader Tunku Abdul Rahman argued that to give these additional powers to the Conference of Rulers could be viewed as an "encroachment" on the powers of the *Yang di-Pertuan Agong*.[106] MacGillivray pointed out that the existing functions of the Conference of Rulers were clearly understood, and they met from time to time with the high commissioner as representative of Her Majesty's Government to discuss matters of major importance. However, after independence this situation would have changed considerably as the *Yang di-Pertuan Agong* would be the representative of the rulers and there would be no high commissioner, and conferring these powers would impinge on the powers of the *Yang di-Pertuan Agong*, he argued.[107]

The rulers' representatives made some concessions in relation to the demands mentioned earlier but in the main held firm on their request for the concurrence of the Conference of Rulers in policy changes of national importance.[108] After further discussions, the meeting agreed that the Conference of Rulers should be consulted on any changes affecting "the privileges, position and dignities of Their Highnesses."[109] It was also agreed that every *Yang di-Pertuan Agong*, before entering upon his office, would take an oath of office and allegiance before the Conference of Rulers and the chief justice as set out in the First Schedule.[110] This was significantly different from the recommendations of the constitutional commission (Article 31) which recommended that the oath of office be taken before a chief justice.[111]

Eventually, the Alliance agreed to the other demands of the rulers to be consulted on changes which affected their prestige and status, the territorial boundaries of the states and matters of major importance. Changes made to Article 33 and Article 34 of the Reid draft constitution provided for the Conference of Rulers to be officially constituted and consulted in the appointment of members of important commissions such as the Election Commission and the Police Service Commission, appointment of judges to the Supreme Court and have the exclusive power in their respective states to grant pardons, reprieves, suspend or commute sentences passed by any court in respect of criminal offences.[112] The strong arguments presented in the Working Party by the rulers' representatives thus conferred considerably more powers to the Conference of Rulers than that provided under the Reid draft constitution.

The prime minister and the Cabinet

One of the most salient features of the constitutions of the independent nations of the Commonwealth is the adoption of the cabinet system. The cabinet ministerial system and collective decision-making principle is a form of government that originally developed in Britain. India, Pakistan, Ceylon and Burma, the earlier of British colonial territories which obtained independence after the Second World War, all embraced the cabinet system led by a prime minister. This was also the case with British colonised territories of Ghana and Kenya in Africa.[113] The cabinet system in England, as Jennings has argued, developed almost accidentally and was related to political developments in Britain. The growing burden of state functions compelled the monarch to rely heavily upon ministers and thus enabling the prime minister to become the centre of decision-making.[114] The cabinet ministerial system that emerged in the Commonwealth nations, on the other hand, was the direct result of the adoption of the Westminster model of cabinet government by these newly independent nations based on the then prevailing practices and conventions. It is not surprising that the Asian and African Commonwealth nations adopted the cabinet system as their elites had received considerable tutelage in the Westminster model of parliamentary governance during the colonial period and were greatly attracted to this system and believed this was the best available system of governance.

During the framing of the Malayan independence constitution, the ruling Alliance Party made it clear that they preferred a cabinet ministerial system based on the Westminster model. The Alliance memorandum to the Reid constitutional commission, for example, stated:

> The executive authority of Malaysia should be exercised in the name of the *Yang di-Pertuan Besar* (the supreme head of state) by the elected government, headed by a Prime Minister to be known as the *Perdana Mentri*. There should be a Council of Ministers to be known as the *Jumaah Menteri*, presided over by the *Perdana Mentri*.[115]

A proto-type of the cabinet system, headed by the chief minister, was introduced in Malaya a month after the Alliance Party won the first federal election in

July 1955 in keeping with the practices elsewhere in the newly emerging Commonwealth nations. The primary constitutional documents indicate that the provisions related to the establishment and powers of the Cabinet (Article 36 of the Reid draft constitution) were largely drawn from the constitutions of India and Pakistan. Justice Abdul Hamid's early draft of the provisions on the Cabinet and the final Reid draft constitution indicate clearly that the provisions of these two constitutions served as the main source.[116] The article on the "Council of Ministers" in Hamid's early draft states: "There shall be a Council of Ministers (to be called the Cabinet) for the Federation with the Prime Minister at the head to aid and advise the *Yang di-Pertuan Besar* in the exercise of his functions."[117] Subsequently, after further discussions in the commission, an additional phrase, "and be charged with the general direction and control of the government of the Federation," was added to the original article which eventually became Article 36 (1) of the Reid draft constitution.[118] Article 36(1) is almost identical to Article 74 (1) of the Indian constitution and Article 37 (1) of the 1956 Pakistan constitution. Article 74 (1) of the Indian constitution states: "There shall be a Council of Ministers with the Prime Minister at the head to aid and advise the President who shall exercise his functions, act in accordance with such advice."[119] The provisions of Article 37 (1) of the 1956 constitution of Pakistan are similar: "There shall be a Cabinet of Ministers with the Prime Minister at its head, to aid and advise the President in the exercise of his functions."[120] The main difference was the use of the term "Cabinet" in the Pakistan constitution. This term was adopted in the Malayan constitution by the Reid Commission.

Similarly, seven sub-sections in Article 36 of Hamid's draft provided for the appointment of a prime minister and ministers and described their terms and conditions of office and the manner of their removal.[121] These are in essence similar in content to the eight sub-clauses in Article 37 in the Pakistan constitution[122] and six clauses of Article 75 of the Indian constitution.[123] Article 36 (2) of the Reid draft constitution provides that the *Yang di-Pertuan Besar* (later the term *Yang di-Pertuan Agong* is used) shall appoint from among the members of the House of Representatives a prime minister who is in his judgement most likely to command the confidence of the majority of the members of that House, and if the prime minister ceases to command such confidence, "the *Yang di-Pertuan Besar* shall either, at the request of the prime minister, dissolve Parliament or remove the prime minister from office."[124] The provision for the dissolution of Parliament, in the event that the prime minister does not command the majority support, is based on Article 37 (6) of the Pakistan constitution.[125] This clause enabled the president of Pakistan to exercise the power to require his prime minister to resign in the event he does not command majority support in Parliament. The framework of the clauses on the Cabinet and the phrasing style of this section in the Malayan constitution are clearly derived from the constitutions of India and Pakistan. The main difference being that the *Yang di-Pertuan Agong* replaced the position of president as head of state. The final Reid draft of Article 36 had eight clauses and was considerably improved by Jennings from the original provisions in the Indian and Pakistan constitutions in terms of the phrasing style and clarity.[126] There were no extended debates on the position of prime minister or the Cabinet evident in the Reid Commission's discussions or in the later stages of the constitutional deliberations. The system of governance inherited in Malaya under the new federal constitution hence was based on the established Westminster model and included considerable borrowings from the provisions found in the constitutions of India and Pakistan.

Principle of national policies

It is interesting that the Alliance recommended that the constitution contain a number of principles of national policies, along the lines of "directive principles of state policy" found in the constitutions of India, Pakistan and Burma. The directive principles of state policy in the Indian constitution, the first constitution among these states, were in itself inspired by the directives principles found in the Irish constitution. These principles were not legally enforceable but were intended as guiding principles for future governments in Malaya. The Alliance's memorandum contained seven such guiding principles. The Alliance memorandum noted that in order for the new nation to be "prosperous and contented" the government should cndcavour to:

> a. promote a sound social order and the welfare of the people; b. remove illiteracy and provide free and compulsory primary education within the minimum period; c. secure just and humane conditions of work; d. secure ownership and control of natural resources, and ensure that their distribution shall subserve to the common weal; e. provide equal opportunities to nationals to acquire land without prejudice to the system of Malay reservations; f. ensure that the economic system shall not result in concentration of wealth and the means of production to the common detriment; g. ensure that all persons shall have the right to an adequate means of livelihood.[127]

These guiding principles were quite similar to those found in the constitutions of India, Pakistan and Burma. They were broad over-arching principles stating political and socio-economic objectives, which reflected the Alliance's long-term goals and the party's ideological roots. These, to an extent, reflected principles that underlay the Alliance's unwritten ideology. The Reid Commission ignored these guiding principles and did not make any provisions in the constitution related to them as they were not legally enforceable.

Notes

1 See Part IV to Part X, Report of the Federation of Malaya Constitutional Commission 1957, London: Her Majesty's Stationery Office, Colonial No. 330.
2 See Part VII and Part X, Report of the Federation of Malaya Constitutional Commission 1957.
3 See Joseph M. Fernando and Ho Hui Ling, "British and Commonwealth legacies in the framing of the Malayan constitution, 1956–1957," *Britain and the World*, Vol. 8, No. 2, 2015, pp. 181–203.
4 Report of the Federation of Malaya Constitutional Commission 1957, p. 6 and p. 24.

5 See Article 138 of Part XI of the Reid draft constitution. This provision enables the *Yang di-Pertuan Agong* to make a Proclamation of Emergency if the federal government believes that the security or economic life of the nation is threatened by war, external aggression or internal disturbance.
6 Alliance memorandum to Reid commission, 27 September 1956, UMNO/SUA 154/56, Arkib Negara Malaysia, pp. 3–4.
7 Paper on "Form of government," by Tunku Abdul Rahman, 21 March 1955, PH/A/008/4, MCA Files. See also Alliance memorandum to Reid Commission, 27 September 1956, UMNO/SUA 154/56, pp. 4–5.
8 See minutes of meeting of Alliance National Council, UMNO/SUA 154/56.
9 Report of hearing of the Alliance Party, 27 September 1956, CO 889/1 (33), C.C. 3003/3. The Alliance's delegation to the hearing before Reid Commission held at the Executive Council Chamber along Maxwell Road in Kuala Lumpur was headed by Chief Minister Tunku Abdul Rahman and included Dato' Abdul Razak, V. T. Sambanthan, Mohamed Khir Johari, Yong Pung How, Ng Ek Teong, K. Ramanathan and Senu Abdul Rahman.
10 See Rulers memorandum to constitutional commission, 12 September 1956, CO 889/8 (22A), p. 44.
11 Ibid., p. 43.
12 See memorandum by People's Progressive Party (PPP), 18 July 1956, CO 889/5 (1), pp. 2–3.
13 Ibid., p. 3.
14 Ibid., pp. 3–4.
15 Ibid., p. 3.
16 Memorandum by Islamic Association of Malaya, CO 889/5 (1), 14 July 1956, p. 7.
17 Ibid., p. 7.
18 Memorandum by the Labour Party of Malaya, 25 September 1956, CO 889/3 (5), p. 5.
19 Ibid., p. 6.
20 See memorandum by Party Negara's Perlis branch to the constitutional commission, 28 July 1956, CO 889/5 (5), p. 2.
21 Alliance memorandum to Reid commission, 27 September 1956, UMNO/SUA 154/56, pp. 3–4.
22 Report of the hearing of the Alliance Party, 27 September 1956, CO 889/1 (33), C.C.3003/3.
23 The term used earlier in the Alliance memorandum and the draft constitution was *Yang di-Pertuan Besar*, to refer to the Paramount Ruler of the federation, but this was later changed to *Yang di-Pertuan Agong* at the suggestion of the rulers as the earlier title was held by the ruler in Negri Sembilan.
24 Report of the Federation of Malaya Constitutional Commission 1957, pp. 29–31. Article 154 of the Reid draft constitution provided for the continuance of the Federal Legislative Council until 1959 when the first post-independence general election would be held.
25 Alliance memorandum to Reid commission, 27 September 1956, UMNO/SUA 154/56, p. 4.
26 Ibid.
27 Ibid.
28 Hearing of the Alliance Party, 27 September 1956, CO 889/1 (33), C.C. 3003/3.
29 Report of the Federation of Malaya Constitutional Commission 1957, pp. 29–31. The Commission's report noted, "We have calculated the number of seats which should be allocated to each State on various assumptions and the results of our calculations confirm us in our view that the subdivisions of each of the existing constituencies into two is the best method of delimitation for the first elections under the new Constitution."
30 Alliance memorandum to Reid commission, 27 September 1956, UMNO/SUA 154/56, p. 5.
31 Ibid.

32 Report of hearing of the Alliance given by the commission, 27 September 1956, CO 889/6 (3), p. 18.
33 Ibid., p. 17.
34 Ibid., p. 18.
35 Ibid. The Alliance in its written memorandum had stated that the maximum life of the lower house would be for a period of five years but "the Yang di-Pertuan Besar may exercise his prerogative to prorogue, dissolve and in the event of national crisis to extend the life of the Dewan Raayat." See Alliance memorandum, UMNO/SUA 154/56, p. 4.
36 Report of hearing of the Alliance given by the commission, 27 September 1956, CO 889/6 (3), p. 18.
37 Ibid., p. 19.
38 Ibid.
39 Ibid., p. 20.
40 Proposals of Their Highnesses the Rulers made to the constitutional commission, September 1956, CO 889/8 (22a), p. 45.
41 Ibid., p. 45.
42 See Article 40 and Article 47 of the Reid draft constitution.
43 See Article 38 of Reid draft constitution.
44 See Article 43 of the Reid draft constitution.
45 Report of the Federation of Malaya Constitutional Commission, 1957, p. 26.
46 Alliance memorandum to Reid commission, 27 September 1956, UMNO/SUA 154/56, pp. 3–4.
47 Ibid.
48 Ibid.
49 Proposals of Their Highnesses the Rulers made to the constitutional commission, September 1956, CO 889/8 (22a), p. 43.
50 Ibid.
51 Ibid.
52 Ibid., p. 44.
53 Ibid.
54 Proposals of Their Highnesses the Rulers made to the constitutional commission, September 1956, CO 889/8 (22a), p. 44.
55 Report of hearing of the Alliance given by the commission, 27 September 1956, CO 889/6 (3), p. 7.
56 Ibid.
57 Ibid.
58 Ibid.
59 Ibid., p. 8.
60 Ibid., p. 9.
61 Ibid., p. 14.
62 Ibid.
63 Report of the Federation of Malaya Constitutional Commission, 1957, pp. 25–26.
64 Report of hearing of the Alliance given by the commission, 27 September 1956, CO 889/6 (3), pp. 10–11.
65 Ibid., p. 11.
66 Summary record of 31st meeting of Constitutional Commission, 12 September 1956, CO 889/1 (34), C.C. 1000, p. 1.
67 Ibid.
68 Report of hearing of the Alliance given by the commission, 27 September 1956, CO 889/6 (3), p. 12.
69 Ibid.
70 Ibid., p. 13.
71 Report of the Federation of Malaya Constitutional Commission, 1957, p. 27.
72 Ibid.

73 Ibid.
74 Ibid.
75 Ibid., p. 26.
76 Ibid., pp. 34–35.
77 Ibid.
78 Report of the Constitutional Commission Working Party, April 1957, CO 941/87, p. 12.
79 Memorandum by the Labour Party of Malaya, 25 September 1956, CO 889/3 (5), p. 6.
80 Alliance memorandum to constitutional commission, 27 September 1956, UMNO/SUA 154/56, p. 2.
81 Proposals of Their Highnesses the Rulers made to the constitutional commission, September 1956, [submitted 12 September 1956], CO 889/8 (22a), p. 8.
82 Report of hearing given to the Rulers, 14–15 September 1956, CO 889/1 (32), p. 26.
83 See Alliance memorandum to constitutional commission, 27 September 1956, UMNO/SUA 154/56, p. 2.
84 Ibid., pp. 2–3.
85 Ibid.
86 Ibid., p. 3. The Alliance memorandum states, "Should a successor not be appointed within 24 hours, provision should be made for the appointment by the Cabinet of a Council of Regency from among the Rulers."
87 Ibid., p. 5. The Alliance memorandum states, "The executive authority of Malaysia should be exercised in the name of the *Yang di-Pertuan Besar* by the elected government, headed by a Prime Minister to be known as the Perdana Mentri."
88 Report of hearing of the Alliance given by the commission, 27 September 1956, CO 889/6 (3), p. 3.
89 Proposals of Their Highnesses the Rulers made to the constitutional commission, September 1956, CO 889/8 (22a), pp. 8–10. See also Report of hearing given to the Rulers, 14–15 September 1956, CO 889/1 (32), p. 27.
90 Report of hearing given to the Rulers, 14–15 September 1956, CO 889/1 (32), p. 27.
91 Proposals of Their Highnesses the Rulers made to the constitutional commission, September 1956, CO 889/8 (22a), pp. 10–11.
92 Ibid., p. 11.
93 Ibid., p. 12.
94 Ibid., p. 13.
95 Alliance memorandum to constitutional commission, 27 September 1956, UMNO/SUA 154/56, p. 3.
96 Proposals of Their Highnesses the Rulers made to the constitutional commission, September 1956, CO 889/8 (22a), p. 42 and p. 54.
97 Minutes of the Second meeting of the Working Party, 25 February 1957, CO 941/85, p. 1.
98 Ibid. See Note of Points to be raised by the Rulers representatives on the draft constitution, 25 February 1957, p. 1.
99 Ibid.
100 Ibid., pp. 1–2.
101 Ibid., p. 2.
102 Ibid.
103 Ibid.
104 Ibid.
105 Minutes of the Second meeting of the Working Party, 25 February 1957, CO 941/85, p. 1.
106 Ibid., pp. 1–2.
107 Ibid., pp. 1–2.
108 Ibid., p. 2.
109 Ibid.
110 Ibid., p. 3. See also Minutes of the Sixth meeting of the Working Party, 4 March 1957, CO 941/85, p. 5.
111 Report of the Federation of Malaya Constitutional Commission 1957, p. 54.

112 CO 941/85, Minutes of the Sixth meeting of the Working Party, 4 March 1957, pp. 5–6. See CO 941/85, Minutes of Eighth meeting of Working Party, 8 March 1957, pp. 4–6. See also CO 941/87, Minutes of the Working Party.
113 Antony Allot, *Essays in African Law* (London: Butterworth, 1960), pp. 3–27.
114 Jennings, *The law and the constitution*, p. 17. See Ivor Jennings, *The British constitution* (Cambridge: Cambridge University Press, 1971), pp. 154–193. See also Ivor Jennings, *The constitution of Ceylon* (London: Oxford University Press, 1949), pp. 78–88.
115 Alliance memorandum to constitutional commission, UMNO/SUA 154/56, 27 September 1956, p. 5.
116 See Hamid's early draft of the provisions on the cabinet (Part IV, The Federation), 22 October 1956, p. 3, CO 889/2, C.C. 2000/43 (4). See also Hamid's paper the list of main heads of the subjects to be included in the draft constitution, 19 July 1956, p. 3, CO 889/2 (1), C.C. 2000/ 6. Item 11 in this list provides for a council of ministers of the federal government to be headed by a prime minister. The subject matters to be covered in this section, which include the appointment of the prime minister and other ministers, the terms of office of ministers and privileges and responsibilities, are clearly taken from the constitutions of India and Pakistan. See also paper by Lord Reid on matters to be considered for inclusion in the constitution, undated, c. July 1956, CO 889/2 (2), C.C. 2000/6.
117 Hamid's early draft of the provisions on the cabinet (Part IV, The Federation) 22 October 1956, p. 3, CO 889/2, C.C. 2000/43 (4).
118 See Article 36 (1) of Reid draft constitution, p. 13. The final Reid draft has eight clauses.
119 See K. Santhanam, *The constitution of India* (New Delhi: Hindustan Press, 1951), p. 62.
120 *The constitution of the Islamic Republic of Pakistan (1956)* (Karachi: Government of Pakistan, 1956). See Article 37, p. 10.
121 See Hamid's early draft of the provisions on the cabinet (Part IV, The Federation), 22 October 1956, p. 3, CO 889/2, C.C. 2000/43 (4). See also Summary record of the 51st meeting of constitutional commission, 12 October 1956, CO 889/1 (54).
122 *The constitution of the Islamic Republic of Pakistan (1956)*, Article 37, p. 10.
123 See Durga Das Basu, *Constitutional Law of India* (New Delhi: Prentice-Hall, 1991), pp. 147–148. See the provisions of Article 75.
124 See Article 36 (2) of Reid draft constitution, p. 135.
125 See Summary record of 51st meeting of Constitutional Commission, 12 October 1956, p. 3, CO 889/2 (54). See also *Constitution of the Islamic Republic of Pakistan* (1956), Article 37, p. 10.
126 See Article 36 of Reid draft constitution, p. 13.
127 Alliance memorandum to constitutional commission, UMNO/SUA 154/56, 27 September 1956, pp. 11–12.

3 Division of legislative and executive powers

Malaya inherited a federal system of governance with the coming into force of the Federation of Malaya Agreement on 1 February 1948. The federation agreement replaced the controversial Malayan Union constitution, a unitary system of government which had been introduced in April 1946, after negotiations between the British colonial administration, the Malay rulers and the United Malays National Organisation (UMNO). The drafting of the independence constitution between 1956 and 1957 provided the political parties, the rulers and the constitutional commission an opportunity to address the inherent weaknesses in the working of the federal system. The Reid constitutional commission was required by its terms of reference to provide for a strong central government while at the same time ensuring that the states enjoyed a measure of autonomy. The federal system was in general working fairly well, but some senior officials of the Malayan administration revealed when giving evidence to the constitutional commission that some aspects of the workings of the system should be improved. In addition, there was the need to provide for the changed political circumstances (in view of, e.g., the absence of the high commissioner as chief executive and arbitrator between the federation government and the states and settlements) in independent Malaya and the functioning of a fully elected parliament. A new approach to wealth and burden-sharing had to be introduced to replace the federal practices which were in force under the colonial constitution of 1948. The constitutional commission drew considerably from the experiences of India, Pakistan and Burma, and, to an extent, Australia, in drawing up the division of legislative and executive powers between the central government and the states, which they felt would be more suited to the Malayan conditions. They also introduced certain innovations of their own to improve the working of the federal system based on the testimonies of Malayan administrators.

The federal system is a commonly used system of government found throughout the world especially from the twentieth century and is characterised by the distinct division of powers between a central government and state governments, each being sovereign in its own sphere. Historically, according to A. V. Dicey, there were two requisite conditions for the formation of a federation.[1] First, there must be a body of states so closely connected by locality, history, race or the like, as to be

DOI: 10.4324/9781003542537-3

capable of bearing, in the eyes of their inhabitants, an impress of common nationality. Second, there must be the existence of a very peculiar state of sentiment among the inhabitants of the state which proposed to unite. They must desire union but not desire unity.[2] In a federal system, the central government generally had jurisdiction over the major subjects of governance such as defence, security, external affairs, finance and taxation and the penal code. The states, on the other hand, had jurisdiction over local government, land, water resources, forestry, health, education and some local taxation. In the Malayan context, the federal state had evolved from the early experiment of a smaller version of a federal state by the British colonial administration with the formation of the Federated Malay States (FMS) in 1896 between the states of Selangor, Perak, Negri Sembilan and Pahang, all of which had accepted a British Resident. The rationale behind the formation of this early federation was to increase the efficiency of administration, to standardise the laws and, equally important, to enable the financially stronger states to assist the weaker ones.[3] After the Second World War, the federation of the nine states and two settlements in the peninsular was formalised under the 1948 Federation of Malaya Agreement following the rejection of the unitary Malayan Union constitution introduced in 1946.[4]

Under the federal system the powers of the central government and the state governments are clearly defined in the constitution. There was, however, no standard formula or model for the division of powers between the federal government and the state governments, and they tended to vary according to the prevailing local political and socio-economic conditions and historical background to the formation of the federation. India, for example, has three lists detailing the distribution of legislative powers (union, state and concurrent) while Pakistan and Burma had two. The division of powers in the Indian constitution, for example, is clear from the federal list and the state list. The centre has enormous powers, but the states nonetheless retain considerable powers.[5] In the case of Pakistan, which is a smaller federation, there are also two lists, but the division of powers is a little different. The residual powers (that is, powers on subjects not stated in the legislative lists) under the Pakistan constitution rest with the provinces.[6]

The federal system of government in Malaya had been working fairly well since 1948, but there was a feeling among the administrators and the political parties that there was a need to improve the workings of the system which was largely reliant on the moderating role of the British high commissioner as the chief executive of the federation to manage the relations between the central government and the states. The Reid constitutional commission, after examining the federal-state division of legislative and financial powers, felt that there was a real need to improve the system and harmonise these elements better, particularly in the context of providing for situations in the post-independence period and the growth of democratic politics where different parties could hold power at the centre and the states.

The governing Alliance Party in its submissions emphasised the importance of providing for a strong central government to ensure political and economic stability while at the same time providing for a measure of autonomy for the states. The Alliance memorandum to the Reid Commission noted:

> The principle underlying the division of powers is that there should be a strong central government with the states enjoying responsible government and having autonomous powers in certain specified matters. Under the existing constitution, the legislative powers of the Federal Government are enumerated in column (1) of the Second Schedule to the Federation of Malaya Agreement. The residuary powers vest in the States/Settlements. It is recommended under the new constitution, the legislative powers of the States should be stipulated and that the residuary powers should be vested in the Federal Government. It is considered necessary, for the smooth and efficient running of the administrative machinery of the country as a whole, especially in times of national crisis, that the central government should have the residuary powers.[7]

The Malay rulers, on the other hand, wanted to ensure that the states were fairly autonomous in their own spheres and, equally important, had independent sources of revenue and were not too dependent on the federal government for development. The commission, therefore, had to reformulate many aspects of the division of executive and legislative powers in the federation agreement in order to achieve a just balance between the central government and the states and at the same time fulfil their terms of reference. The rulers' memorandum to the Reid Commission stated:

> Save as necessarily required to implement the constitutional changes which may be recommended by the Commission Their Highnesses take the view in principle that there should be no further surrender of Their sovereignty in Their respective States beyond the position which is set out in the 1948 Agreement and the Second Schedule thereof. Further adopting the stand-point that Their sovereignty remains intact save in so far as it is agreed to be limited or curtailed, Their Highnesses propose that, as at present, residuary legislative competence should remain vested in Their respective States. Their Highnesses therefore propose that the new Federal Constitution should in form broadly follow that which is set forth in the 1948 Agreement on this subject, i.e. there should be only one list of subjects which should be that containing matters upon which the Federal Legislature is competent.[8]

One of the major changes made by the commission to the 1948 federation agreement was to provide for the executive and legislative powers to go together. Previously, the federal government had the legislative powers and the state governments had the executive powers on many federal subject matters. The commission felt that this arrangement would not be suitable in independent Malaya where there was a possibility of different parties in power at the federal and state levels. During the hearing given to the Alliance when Lord Reid raised the possibility of difficulties arising if the federal government had legislative powers and the states the executive powers, as suggested by the Alliance in their memorandum, the Alliance told the commission that they were subject to advice on the matter.[9] Reid pointed out that in situations where there were different parties in the centre and the states, it could cause great difficulty if the federal government were to try to enforce "compulsory delegation" to the states, which had executive authority on these matters.[10] The commission felt that there was a need to recast the federal-state relationship in the context of the workings of a democratic parliamentary system for the post-independence period. The commission noted in its report:

> We think it would be impractical to continue the present system in so far as, with regard to many matters, it confers legislative powers on the Federation and the executive power on the States. If Malaya is to be a democratic country the Government of each State must be controlled by its elected Legislative Assembly, and we must envisage the possibility that from time to time the party in power in one or more of the States may differ in outlook and policy from the party in power in the Federation. It appears that in such circumstances the present division of powers would probably lead to friction and might well have graver circumstances. We therefore recommend (Art. 75) that in future legislative power and executive responsibility should always go together. We have specified (Schedule VI) those subjects which we think ought to be Federal and those which we think ought to be State subjects.[11]

The Alliance had in fact suggested that the states should have executive powers over matters on which the federal government had legislative powers (as provided in column two of Second Schedule of the 1948 Federation Agreement) with the exception of education.[12] With the coming into force of the 1956 Education Report, the federal government assumed responsibility for secondary and higher education while local authorities were responsible for primary education. This meant that the states had only supervisory powers over education and had to work with the federal government and local authorities.[13]

The commission declared some broad principles which it felt the federation and state governments should observe in relation to the division of legislative and executive powers. They emphasised that in regard to subject matters which appeared in the federal list, the federal parliament should have not only the sole power to legislate but also the "ultimate responsibility for determining policy and controlling administration."[14] In regard to the state list, the commission recommended likewise that in general the state legislature should have the exclusive power to legislate and the state government the responsibility for determining policy and controlling administration. The commission used the term "in general" in the context of state powers because in certain circumstances the federation would still have overriding powers. Nevertheless, there was a compromise in this strict division of legislative powers. The draft constitution provided for the federal parliament (Article 70) to have the power to pass any act on any state matter to promote uniformity "but at the same time provided that such legislation would not come into force until it was adopted by an enactment of the state legislature which was entitled to make modifications."[15] "In this way," noted the commission,

> the supremacy of a State on State subjects would be preserved; if a State Legislature agrees with the policy of such a Federal Act it will adopt that Act, but if it disagrees it will either take no action for the moment or make amendments to meet its own views.[16]

This provision was introduced because the commission recognised that the states did not have the facilities for drafting complicated legislation, and they felt that there was a need for some measure of uniformity in law on state subjects between the states such as land, local government and other areas.

The commission touched on several subjects where they felt there was a need to define more clearly the division of powers while at the same time providing for consultations between the central government and the state governments. Central to the development and progress of the country, the commission noted, was the proper use of land, including conservation of land.[17] The commission noted in its report:

> If the agricultural possibilities of Malaya are to make their maximum contribution to the nation's welfare, a planned policy appears to us to be essential. This policy should involve a complete land survey for the country as a whole, the introduction of a soil conservation programme, the encouragement and expansion of agriculture, and the conservation and development of forests having regard to Malaya's future timber requirements.[18]

The commission felt that the existing situation in Malaya in relation to land was unsatisfactory:

> The present position with regard to law is not the same in all parts of the Federation and is not at all satisfactory. In the settlements the law is substantially similar to the law of England. In the old federated states the law is substantially uniform, subject to certain specialities in Negri Sembilan. In the old unfederated states the law is not uniform.[19]

While the commission observed the need for a more uniform system of law and procedure, they agreed that land must remain a state subject (Schedule VI, List II). The constitutional commission's report noted:

> We think that it would be neither practicable nor desirable to transfer the general administration of land to the Federation, and moreover the States could have no real autonomy if they were deprived of their right to deal with their land.[20]

The commission hoped that a new National Land Code would be drafted and enacted soon and which would then be adopted by the states with some possible modifications.[21] They made some specific recommendations in relation to land particularly to enable national development programs to be implemented smoothly. The draft constitution provided for the federal government to acquire land from the states for federal purposes (Article 78), including for public or statutory authorities, but varied it a little from the Alliance's original proposal to allow the states a greater measure of rights when such land was to be disposed. The Alliance had proposed that the federal government should have the powers to acquire land anywhere in the country "for any purpose of national importance" after consultation with the state government concerned.[22] The coalition further submitted that such land should vest in the federal government which should have full ownership, including the right to sell or lease the land for federal purposes.[23] The draft constitution provided for the federal government to acquire state land at market value. But when the federal government ceased to use the land for federal purposes, the land would revert to the state (Article 80) provided the latter paid market value to repossess the land, failing which the federal government was entitled to sell the land in the open market. The state would be bound in such circumstances to grant a title to the purchaser or lessee accordingly.[24] This was a compromise between the Alliance's demand on access to state land and the states' concerns over federal intrusion into their sphere. The commission suggested the setting up of a Lands Tribunal, headed by a senior judge appointed by the chief justice, to handle disputes which could arise in relation to land valuations between the federal government and the states.[25]

On a broader issue, the commission recommended that research and technical assistance to states should continue to be provided by the federal government, which had more technical and financial resources. They felt this was an important element related to the use of land, including for agriculture, mining and forestry and improvement of land by irrigation and drainage.[26] Under Article 145, the commission recommended that these matters (research and technical assistance) should be federal subjects and that the powers of the federal departments on agriculture, land, forestry and social welfare should be continued.[27] The commission expressed much concern over the problem of soil erosion throughout the country, which they had observed during the course of their travel in Malaya and felt serious attention should be given to address this problem: "We have no desire to exaggerate the effects of erosion but the problem appears to us to be of sufficient importance to require urgent attention."[28] As a sign of their real concern over the problem of soil erosion in the country, the commission recommended that the federal government should have the powers to set up a "soil conservation service" as a central authority to work with the states (Article 145(3)).[29]

It is interesting that the commission made some distinct forward-looking and long-term observations and suggestions in their report about the state of the country's forests and the need to conserve these resources. They felt that the country's forestry resources should be better utilised and that there should be some fore-planning to conserve the valuable resources so that Malaya could continue to rely on its own timber resources in the future. The commission's report noted:

> Some three-quarters of the area of the Federation is covered with forest. Much of this is in areas which are so broken and mountainous that they cannot be worked, and in any case the forest areas must be retained for protective purposes. Today, Malaya meets all its domestic timber requirement and has a surplus for export, but within 50 years, unless there is a change in present policies, Malaya will be unable to meet even its local demands, and will become a heavy importer. This is simply because a sufficient amount of revenue received from timber is not being used for the purpose of regeneration and the establishment of forest reserves.[30]

The commission observed that the federal government had limited powers to make law in respect of forests and all executive authority lay with the states. They recommended (Article 145) that while the states should continue to have these powers over the forests and the income derived from it, they should cooperate with the federal authorities for future development and conservation of the forests.

The commission gave the federal government considerable powers to conserve and to develop the country's water resources, improve its drainage and irrigation, while retaining the executive powers in the hands of the state governments. They recommended that water should be a federal subject, but soil conservation should be retained as a state subject owing to its close connection to the use of land.[31] In the division of powers relating to the use of land, irrigation and drainage, conservation, forestry and agriculture, it appears that the commission was attempting to ensure a fair balance between the powers of the federal government and the states. The federal government was given considerable powers to legislate on many of these state subjects to enable greater national planning for development and to maximise use of the technical resources that the federal government had in its hand, but at the same time ensured that the states continued to retain ultimate control over these resources, in keeping with the terms of reference which required that the states should have a measure of autonomy.

Possibly one of the more contentious issues in relation to the division of legislative powers was the decision of the commission to award residual legislative powers to the states although the Alliance had proposed that these powers should be given to the central government. The Alliance memorandum states: "It is recommended that under the new constitution, the legislative powers of the States should be stipulated and that the residuary powers should be vested in the Federal Government. It is considered necessary, for the smooth and efficient running of the administrative machinery of the country as a whole, especially in times of national crisis, that the central government should have the residuary legislative powers."[32] The rulers had argued strongly that residual powers should rest with the states and that there should not be "any further surrender of their sovereignty."[33] The commission noted that the major subject matters (defence, external affairs, education, health, finance, etc.) had been placed under the federal list and the awarding of residual powers to the states would not make much of a difference to the federal powers. They felt that the residual powers were unlikely to come into operation as most of the subject matters had been covered in the federal and state lists. Nonetheless, the commission felt that if some unforeseen matter arose "which is so peculiar it cannot be brought within any of the items mentioned in any of the Legislative Lists," then it would only be fair that these matters should fall within the state powers.[34]

There was an interesting debate in the commission on the division of legislative powers. Justice Abdul Hamid felt that there should only be one list. That is, there should be a federal list, and the jurisdiction of subjects which were not stated in the federal list should rest with the states. In his note of dissent, Hamid remarked:

> The Commission has come to the decision that there should be three Lists, the Federal, the State and the Concurrent. In my opinion only one list would be enough, either Federal or State and the residue should have been left with the other. This was the recommendation both by the Alliance and the Rulers. That would have been in consonance with the scheme of the Federation Agreement of 1948 which is under work in Malaya and with which the people are well acquainted. In fact in view of the limited number of subjects which have now been placed in the Concurrent List, there appears to be no justification or no Concurrent List at all.[35]

The Alliance in fact suggested two lists. The first list should contain the legislative powers of the federal government, and a second should stipulate the matters in which the states should have legislative powers.[36] Hamid argued that the draft constitution contained provisions under Articles 70 and 71, which enabled the federal government to legislate on state subjects with the consent of the states to promote uniformity. He felt these provisions served the purpose of a Concurrent List:

> In my view there should have been either a Federal List containing the subjects which have been specified in it together with some more transferred to it from the Concurrent List, and the residue should have been left with the States, or there should have been a State List containing subjects which are now included in it together with some more transferred to it from the Concurrent List and the residue should have been left to the Federation.[37]

Hamid felt that the state list was "too narrow" as it only contained 10 subjects and contended that the outcome of the draft constitution was that "the field is subject to easy encroachments by the Federation on various pretexts."[38] Hamid's original working paper on the division of federal-state legislative powers had 35 items on the state list and considerably more sources of local revenue for the states.[39] Interestingly, Hamid's original working paper on the distribution of legislative powers had three lists – a federal list, state list and a concurrent list.[40]

The majority in the commission, however, felt that a three-list division of legislative powers would be more suitable, with the third list (the concurrent list) being matters on which both the federal and state governments shared jurisdiction. The commission in essence appears to have followed the distribution of legislative power in the constitution of India, which had three lists. The provincial list in India though was broader and had 54 items with considerably greater taxing powers on local produce and services while the concurrent list had 36 items.[41] Hamid thus was right in his observation that in the commission's draft constitution the states had very limited powers of taxation and raising local revenue. Many of the ideas and inspiration for the drawing up of the division of powers, which drew considerably from the 1948 federation agreement, came from practices and precedents in India, Pakistan, Burma and Australia.

The prime minister and the Cabinet

The Reid Commission's draft constitution surprisingly does not say much on the position and powers of the prime minister, the qualifications of office, the manner of his election to office or possible grounds for removal from office. It also says little on the organisation and powers of the Cabinet. Article 35 of the Reid draft constitution merely stated that the *Yang di-Pertuan Agong*, the supreme ruler, has the responsibility to appoint the prime minister and could exercise his personal discretion in making the appointment.[42] Nevertheless, the commission pointed out in its explanatory note that the *Agong* was expected to appoint the leader of the majority party in the lower house likely to command the confidence of the House.[43] The notes of the deliberations of the constitutional commission provide a little more clarity and state that the appointment of the prime minister should be made by the head of state and that the person appointed should have the "support of the majority of the members of the house."[44] The commission recognised that there could be occasions when it would be unclear who should be appointed as the prime minister after an election but noted, "we see no practicable alternative to leaving the *Yang di-Pertuan Besar* (later, the term *Yang di-Pertuan Agong* was used) to choose the person whom he thinks most likely to command the confidence of the House of Representatives."[45] Thus, in the event there is no clear majority in the House, the *Yang di-Pertuan Agong* has a personal responsibility in selecting a suitable member as prime minister.

The only other article which elaborated a little on the role of the prime minister was Article 36 of the Reid draft constitution, which stated that there shall be a Cabinet of Ministers presided over by a prime minister which "shall aid and advise the *Yang di-Pertuan Besar* in the exercise of his functions and be charged with the general direction and control of the government of the Federation."[46] While the prime minister is charged with the general direction and control of the government, the Reid draft is unclear on the extent of the powers of the prime minister or prohibitions of any kind on the office holder or grounds for possible removal. The constitutions of India, Pakistan and Burma have more detailed provisions on the appointment of the president, who is the equivalent chief executive in Pakistan and Burma and the nominal head of state in India. The Pakistan constitution is quite detailed on the powers of the chief executive. Articles 41–48 of the Pakistan constitution detailed the election of the president, the qualifications for election as president, the holding of presidential elections, the taking of the oath of office and the conditions of the president's office (he cannot, for example, hold any office of profit), the terms of office and the mode of removal or impeachment of the president.[47] The constitution of India, similarly, has detailed provisions of the position of president (Articles 52–62), although in the case of India, the prime minister is the chief administrator and *de facto* chief executive. The Indian constitutional provisions state clearly the manner of election of the president, qualification for election as president (he must be a citizen of India aged at least 35 years), the conditions of office (that he cannot hold any office of profit) and the powers of president.[48] The constitution of India also details the duties of the prime minister but is silent on the qualifications for prime minister, the conditions of office or mode of removal or impeachment. The constitution of Burma likewise has detailed provisions on the election of the president, the qualifications of office, terms of office and conditions for removal from office (Articles 45–64).[49] The Burma constitution, which borrowed many of the provisions from the Indian constitution, had very detailed provisions (Article 54) on the removal of the president, who may be impeached for high treason, violation of the constitution or gross misconduct. Such charges would be preferred by either chamber of parliament, as is also the case in India and Pakistan. The first constitution of all three countries provided for indirect election of the president by the members of the legislatures.

Considering the centrality of the office of prime minister in the context of Malaya, this lack of detail on the election and conditions of office of prime minister may have been an oversight by the commission. The Reid draft also had no provision in the constitution for the election or selection of a deputy prime minister. Article 36 (3) provides for the appointment of the ministers by the *Yang di-Pertuan Agong* from among the members of parliament, but the role of the prime minister in this process is not clearly stated. The article states that ministers "shall hold office during his (the king's) pleasure."[50] The Alliance memorandum is also very brief, only a single paragraph, on the position of prime minister and states:

> The executive authority of Malaysia should be exercised in the name of the *Yang di-Pertuan Besar* by the elected government, headed by a Prime Minister to be known as the *Perdana Mentri*. There should be a Council of Ministers to be known as the *Jumaah Menteri*, presided over by the *Perdana Mentri*.[51]

The rulers, too, in their memorandum were silent on the position and powers of the prime minister. There is a mere mention in the rulers' memorandum that political appointments in the federation government would be made by the *Yang di-Pertuan Agong* on the advice of the chief minister.[52]

What is clear, however, are the limitations of the powers of the prime minister in relation to the dissolution of Parliament. Under the federal constitution, the power of dissolution of Parliament is the constitutional responsibility of the *Yang di-Pertuan Agong* (Article 35(6)).[53] The Reid Commission noted:

> Experience has shown that there are substantial objections to the Prime Minister or the Government of the day having unrestricted power to insist on a dissolution of Parliament. A Prime Minister may ask for a dissolution in various circumstances and it is not possible to define the circumstances in which his request ought to be granted. Normally, the *Yang di-Pertuan Besar* (later the term "*Yang di-Pertuan Agong*" is used) would accept the advice of his Prime Minister but he should not be bound to do so in all cases. He ought in a critical case to be free to decide what is in the best interests of the country.[54]

If the prime minister ceases to command the confidence of the House, he must either vacate his office or ask for a dissolution. Article 36 (2) of the Reid draft provided that if the prime minister ceases to command the confidence of the House, the *Yang di-Pertuan Agong* shall at the request of the prime minister either dissolve Parliament or remove the prime minister from office.[55] The constitutional documents indicate that there were no extended debates on the position or election of a prime minister. At the same time, the documents reveal that the powers of the prime minister and his cabinet followed in essence the practices and conventions of the cabinet system in Britain. The prime minister of Malaya can be said to occupy the same position in the federal constitution as the British prime minister does in the British constitution.

Conference of rulers

The Reid Commission did not make specific provisions on the constitution and functions of the Conference of Rulers other than providing for the election of the *Yang di-Pertuan Agong* under Article 27.[56] The commission felt that the Conference of Rulers should only have "purely formal or ceremonial functions" and possibly deal with matters of Muslim law and Malay customs.[57] The Conference of Rulers had been formally convened since 1948 and met several times a year to discuss issues of national importance and be briefed by the British high commissioner. Prior to that, a more informal meeting of the rulers in the FMS, called "Durbar," had met infrequently before the war to discuss issues of common importance to the four states chaired by the Resident-General. The commission felt strongly, as did the Alliance Party, that the rulers should not be drawn into the politics of the federation. At the second meeting of the Working Party on 25 February 1957, the rulers' representatives, led by Queen's Counsel Neil Lawson, pointed out that there was no provision in the draft constitution for the establishment and constitution of the Conference of Rulers. The rulers' representatives felt this could give rise to difficulties even in the limited functions conferred on the Conference of Rulers in Article 27.[58]

The rulers' representatives submitted that a number of additional powers should be conferred on the Conference of Rulers in addition to the appointment of the

Yang di-Pertuan Agong and his deputy under Article 27.[59] The rulers contended that the concurrence of the Conference of Rulers should be sought in the appointment of the "Supreme Head of the State of Judges of the Supreme Court," members of the Election Commission and the Public Service Commission.[60] The rulers felt, for example, that if they were to give up their existing right of veto on the residence of a judge in the state, they should be consulted in the appointment of the Supreme Court judges.[61] They argued, similarly, that as the members of the Election Commission in the discharge of their duties would be encroaching into areas of their respective states and impacting their territorial sovereignty, it was only right that they "should have the right to concur in the appointment of such bodies."[62] The rulers submitted that their consent should be sought in changes to the constitution affecting several subject matters which affected their sovereignty. These were: (i) territorial changes affecting the State as at present constituted; (ii) changes which may affect the Muslim Religion and custom of the Malays; (iii) changes in the entrenched clauses (Articles 157 and 82); (iv) changes affecting the status or powers of the States; and (v) changes affecting the privileges, position and dignities of Their Highnesses.[63] The rulers felt that these changes impinged on the sovereignty of the rulers and therefore they should have the right "to give or withhold concurrence in such changes."[64] The rulers proposed further that the Conference of Rulers should be consulted in changes to law affecting: (i) immigration; (ii) proposed Federal legislation on the concurrent list; (iii) Federal legislation under Article 70 of the Draft Constitution (power of parliament to legislate for states for uniformity); and (iv) the formula according to which financial grants will be made from Federal funds to the States.[65] The rulers stressed that the *Yang di-Pertuan Agong* should be required to convene a meeting of the Conference of Rulers and the two governors with their respective constitutional advisers to discuss matters of important national policy.[66] The rulers noted that the Supreme Head of State should make an "affirmation" of office and allegiance, and not an oath, in the presence of the Conference of Rulers and not merely before the chief justice. The rulers also submitted that they should retain their power of pardon relating to offences committed in their respective states.[67]

An interesting discussion ensued following the submission of these additional functions for the Conference of Rulers by the rulers' representatives. There was resistance from the Alliance and the high commissioner to what was viewed as encroachment into politics by the rulers that conflicted with their status as constitutional monarchs. High Commissioner Donald MacGillivray pointed out that to give these additional functions to the rulers would bring them into the arena of politics and would be contrary to one of the main recommendations of the constitutional commission that the rulers should become constitutional rulers.[68] The Alliance leader Tunku Abdul Rahman added that to give these powers to the Conference of Rulers could be regarded as an "encroachment on the powers of the *Yang di-Pertuan Besar*."[69] It was pointed out that the then existing functions of the Conference of Rulers were clearly understood, and they met from time to time with the high commissioner as representative of Her Majesty's Government to discuss matters of major importance. However, after independence this situation would have changed considerably as the *Yang di-Pertuan Agong* would be the representative of the rulers and there would be no high commissioner and conferring these powers would impinge on the powers of the *Yang di-Pertuan Agong*.[70] The rulers' representatives made some concessions in relation to the demands above, but in the main held firm on their request for the concurrence of the Conference of Rulers in changes to policies of national importance. In the ensuing discussion, the representatives of the rulers said they were prepared to waive their demand that the approval of the Conference of Rulers should be obtained before the appointment of the chief justice by the *Yang di-Pertuan Agong*.[71] They were also willing to drop their demand that the rulers' approval be sought before the stationing of a judge in a state, if the Conference of Rulers could be associated with the appointment of members of the Judicial and Legal Service which would be responsible for recommending the appointment of judges to the Supreme Court.[72] After some further discussions, the meeting agreed that the Conference of Rulers should be consulted on any changes affecting, "the privileges, position and dignities of Their Highnesses."[73] The meeting agreed that the Supreme Head of State would be termed *Yang di-Pertuan Agong* rather than *Yang di-Pertuan Besar* as the latter title was held by the head of state in Negri Sembilan.[74] In the discussion, it was agreed that every *Yang di-Pertuan Agong*, before entering upon his office, would take an oath of office and allegiance before the Conference of Rulers and the chief justice as set out in the First Schedule.[75] This was significantly different from the recommendations of the constitutional commission (Article 31) which recommended that the oath of office be taken before a chief justice or in his absence the next senior judge of the Supreme Court.[76] In a sense, the rulers were able to obtain their demand that the oath of office for the *Yang di-Pertuan Agong* should be taken in their presence. Eventually, the Alliance agreed to the other demands of the rulers to be consulted on changes which affected their prestige and status, the territorial boundaries of the states and matters of major importance. Changes made to Articles 33 and 34 provided for the Conference of Rulers to be officially constituted and consulted in the appointment of members of important commissions such as the Election Commission and the Police Service Commission changes; appointment of judges to the Supreme Court; and have the exclusive power in their respective states to grant pardons, reprieves, suspend or commute sentences passed by any court in respect of criminal offences.[77] These provisions provided for a clearer position on the role of the Conference of Rulers than that which had been recommended by the Reid Commission mainly on the advice of the Alliance Party. It also provided stronger safeguards in the constitution to protect the status, position and privileges of the rulers. Nevertheless, the role of the Conference of Rulers remained largely advisory.

There were also other areas where the rulers put up a tough fight to gain more concessions and recognition in the new constitution. The rulers' representatives opposed Article 66 of the draft constitution which gave the federal government considerable powers to make laws for the states and wield executive authority on matters enumerated in the state list in the event the state constitutions do not include "essential provisions" or contained provisions which were inconsistent with the federal constitution in line with Lord Reid's objections.[78] Reid in his note of dissent contended that Article 66 provided considerable authority automatically to the federal government to take executive action to legislate on behalf of the states in the event certain essential provisions had not been promptly adopted by the states after independence. He argued that there was no need for such automatic provision:

> I am of the opinion that it might be embarrassing to the Federal Government if they were compelled to undertake responsibility in this way for the whole administration of a State, that there is no need for any such automatic provision, and that if a sanction is necessary it should be in general terms similar to those of article 65 which deals with habitual disregard by a State of its Constitution.[79]

He felt that in accordance with the principles of democracy in such a situation the choice of remedy should be left to the elected representatives of the federation rather than being imposed on them by law.[80] The composition of the state legislatures in the initial phase after independence also drew some attention. The rulers agreed that there should be an elected majority in the state legislatures but argued that in the earlier phase there should not be any limit on the number of non-elected members of the state legislatures, this being determined by the states themselves.[81] The states, as discussed earlier, felt that in the initial phase after independence the states should be allowed to have nominated members in the state executive council, including the *Mentri Besar*.

At the third meeting of the Working Party, the rulers' representatives proposed that there should be a provision in Section 2 of the Fifth Schedule (which contained provisions to be inserted in the state constitutions) which stated that the *Mentri Besar* should be a Malay and should profess the Muslim religion.[82] The Alliance's representatives, however, pointed out that it was possible that in certain states in future there may be a situation where a Malay may not command the confidence of the majority of the elected members. In such a situation, the Alliance argued, if the ruler could not exercise his discretion under Section 1 of the Fifth Schedule to appoint a non-Malay as *Mentri Besar*, there could be a constitutional crisis.[83] The Alliance was also not happy with the decision of the constitutional commission to confer residual powers (Article 73) to the states, and in the third meeting of the Working Party proposed together with the attorney general that residual powers of legislation should rest with the federal government.[84] The rulers' representatives, however, did not agree with the Alliance's proposal. Eventually, the Working Party agreed that the residual powers should lie with states, as recommended by the Reid Commission.[85] The rulers' representatives suggested that in regard to Article 150 of the Reid draft, the concurrence of the rulers should be obtained before the constitution could be amended. The Working Party, however, did not agree to this suggestion and accepted the Reid draft. The only change being that the constitutional amendment now required a two-thirds majority of the "total" members in both houses present and voting.[86] It would be clear from the discussion above that the provisions related to the division of legislative and executive powers between the federal government and the state governments entailed considerable compromises between the two main parties in the constitutional negotiations, the Alliance government and the rulers, with the Reid Commission playing a moderating role.

Notes

1 G.N. Joshi, *The constitution of India* (London: Macmillan, 1950), pp. 26–27.
2 Ibid., pp. 26–27.
3 See Eunice Thio, *British policy in the Malay Peninsula, 1880–1910* (Singapore: University of Malaya Press, 1969), pp. 120–189.
4 Fernando, *The making of the Malayan constitution*, pp. 9–20.
5 See *The constitution of India, 1949.*
6 See *The constitution of Pakistan, 1956.*
7 See Alliance memorandum to Reid Commission, 27 September 1956, UMNO/SUA 154/56, p. 7.
8 See Rulers' memorandum to the Reid Commission, 12 September 1956, CO 889/8 (22), p. 24.
9 Report of hearing given by the commission to the Alliance, 27 September 1956, CO 889/6 (3A), p. 22.
10 Ibid., p. 22.
11 Report of the Federation of Malaya Constitutional Commission 1957 (London: Her Majesty's Stationery Office, Colonial No. 330), p. 36. See also Article 75, p. 24, of the Reid draft constitution.
12 Alliance memorandum, 27 September 1956, UMNO/SUA 154/56, p. 8.
13 Ibid., p. 8.
14 Report of the Federation of Malaya Constitutional Commission 1957, p. 36.
15 Ibid., p. 37.
16 Ibid.
17 See Summary record of the 37th meeting of the Constitutional Commission, 3 October 1956, CO 889/1 (40), C.C. 1000, for a discussion on the issue of land.
18 Report of the Federation of Malaya Constitutional Commission 1957, pp. 37–38.
19 Ibid., p. 38.
20 Ibid., pp. 38–39.
21 Report of the Federation of Malaya Constitutional Commission 1957, p. 39.
22 Alliance memorandum, 27 September 1956, UMNO/SUA 154/56, p. 9.
23 Ibid., p. 9.
24 Report of the Federation of Malaya Constitutional Commission 1957, p. 42.
25 Ibid.
26 Ibid., pp. 42–43.
27 Ibid., p. 43.
28 Ibid.
29 Report of the Federation of Malaya Constitutional Commission 1957, p. 44.
30 Ibid.
31 Ibid., pp. 44–45.
32 Alliance Memorandum, 27 September 1956, UMNO/SUA 154/56, p. 7.
33 Rulers' memorandum to the constitutional commission, 12 September 1956, CO 889/8 (22), p. 24.
34 Report of the Federation of Malaya Constitutional Commission 1957, pp. 52–53.
35 Hamid's Note on State Autonomy in Sir Ivor Jennings' Papers B/X/6, p. 11.
36 Alliance memorandum, 27 September 1956, UMNO/SUA 154/56, p. 17.
37 Hamid's Note on State Autonomy in Sir Ivor Jennings' Papers B/X/6, p. 11.
38 Ibid., p. 2.

4 Federal-state financial relations

The financial relations between the federal government and the states were an important element of the constitution-making process, and the Reid constitutional commission gave considerable attention to the financial provisions in the draft constitution to ensure smooth federal-state relations. The commission's terms of reference required the commission to ensure that the states had a "measure of financial autonomy" while providing for a strong central government. The federal-state financial relations were defined by the 1948 Federation of Malaya Agreement, and allocations to the states and settlements were determined according to the provisions stated in Part III of the Fifth Schedule of the agreement. Some improvements were made periodically after consultation with the states. The financial relations between the federal government and the states had evolved over time through trial and error, and while it had worked fairly well there were considerable weaknesses and the constitutional commission paid much attention to this area in an effort to improve the existing financial arrangements and procedures in Malaya. While the high commissioner, as the chief executive of the federation, was empowered to moderate the demands of the states under the federation agreement, financial relations between the centre and the states in the post-independence period would be dictated by political parties and this required a thorough reconsideration of the existing financial arrangements in view of the changing situation.[1]

The financial procedure in the federation and the states was regulated by the 1948 Federation of Malaya Agreement and General Orders and accorded with the general colonial adaption of British practice.[2] The high commissioner had power under Clause 123 of the federation agreement to make General Orders, and these would be binding on the States and Settlements.[3] Typically of the federal system, the federation had separate budgets for the federal government and the state governments. There were taxes which were levied by the federal government and some local taxes levied by the state governments. Under the existing financial arrangements, estimates of expenditure were prepared by the heads of departments and submitted to the relevant treasury at the federal or state levels. After the departmental estimate was agreed at the respective state or federal levels, it was submitted to the finance committee or budget committee of the appropriate legislature (state or federal). Following a report from the finance or budget committees, a decision is made by the High Commissioner in Council, the Ruler in Council or the High

DOI: 10.4324/9781003542537-4

Commissioner in Nominated Council. The estimates were then discussed in the executive council or nominated council and laid before the legislature by the high commissioner or the president of the Council of State.[4] On expenditure related to education, medical and health, drainage and irrigation services, there was prior consultation between the heads of these departments at the state and federal levels. The heads of the federal departments for these services had considerable influence in determining the approved expenditure. Under the existing financial system, the Director of Audit was required under Clause 122 of the federation agreement to audit the accounts of the states and his reports were published.[5]

The commission was keen to ensure that apart from the states having a real measure of financial autonomy, they could also have access to supplementary grants with greater ease than the cumbersome procedure under the existing system. The commission drew on the experiences of the federal systems in India, Pakistan and Australia and the financial procedures in the United Kingdom to draft the provisions relating to the division of federal-state financial powers. The financial arrangements in the various federations in the Commonwealth differed from one another, and there was no commonly accepted model, and while the commission drew from their experiences, they had to adapt their proposals to the Malayan conditions and peculiarities. Many of the financial practices under the federation agreement were retained with some modifications and improvements. After much deliberation and consultation with the Malayan administrators, the Alliance government and the rulers' representatives, the commission made significant changes to the provisions on financial relations between the federal government and the states in order to improve the working of the system. They sought to create a better balance between the federal government and the states in the distribution of financial powers while providing for a strong central government and a measure of autonomy for the states.

In the main, the commission sought to create a strong central government financially and provided for most of the taxing powers in the constitution to be reserved to the federal government. This was much more than that provided under the 1948 federation government. At the same time, through an intricate set of grants guaranteed to the states annually from the federal government, the commission tried to provide for a greater degree of financial autonomy to the states. As we will see later, the states were not happy with the scheme of distribution of financial grants from the federal government and the sharing of levies from the export of tin and fought strongly to further strengthen the states' financial position when the Working Party, which reviewed the recommendations of the Reid Commission, met to discuss the draft constitution.

The ruling Alliance Party had merely included a bare general statement in their memorandum to the Reid Commission stating that the states should have financial autonomy while the power to raise revenue and the system of allocation of funds between the state and federal governments should follow the Third Schedule and Part III of the 1948 Federation of Malaya Agreement.[6] The record of the Alliance meeting with the constitutional commission on the issue of finance barely covers ten lines of the report. At the meeting Lord Reid remarked that in order for the states to be made financially autonomous they would have to get more revenue as of right than they did under the 1948 federation agreement. Turning to the Alliance leader Tunku Abdul Rahman, Reid asked if he agreed that the states should be financially autonomous "as is reasonably practicable?"[7] Tunku merely agreed to Reid's remarks. The Alliance further agreed that they did not want to continue the present financial arrangement.[8] This was not much to work on for the commission and they had to study in depth the complex and sometimes ad hoc financial arrangements in Malaya and consult senior officials in the Malayan administration before formulating the section on federal-state financial powers. Sir Ivor Jennings, Justice Abdul Hamid and Sir William McKell had considerable experience in dealing with constitutional provisions on federal-state financial relations and the commission could draw on their knowledge. Jennings and Hamid had drafted the Pakistan constitution and McKell had been a member of the Australian cabinet and was familiar with the workings of the Australian financial arrangements.

The rulers' memorandum to the constitutional commission on financial relations, on the other hand, was more detailed and emphasised the need for greater financial autonomy for the states.[9] A contest between those seeking a stronger federal government and those seeking a more autonomous state government, not unlike the debates between the federalists and anti-federalists in the drafting of the United States constitution, is evident during the constitutional deliberations.[10] The rulers sought further improvements on the provisions of the federation agreement on financial relations between the federal government and the states. They wanted certain revenues to be specifically allocated to the states based on Schedule Three of the 1948 federation agreement with the possibility of addition of other new sources of revenues for the states.[11] They felt new sources of revenue should not be automatically allocated to the federal government but should be the subject of discussion between the parties. The states wanted a per capita allocation for the states based on a sliding scale depending on the size and concentration of the population in a state.[12] The rulers proposed that a fixed proportion of the substantial revenues collected by the federal government (e.g. revenue from the import duty on petrol) be allocated to the states.[13] They demanded special allocations should be given to the states where much federal revenue was derived from the exploitation of "assets of a wasting character" (such as tin and other minerals) to compensate for the depletion of these state resources.[14] On certain items of expenditure on which the federal government had over-riding policy control such as education, medical services and new villages, the states wanted 100% federal grants.[15] The rulers' memorandum sought special federal grants to finance "major development projects" in the states, and wanted provisions in the constitution for "transitional grants" if required by the states to meet special contingencies.[16] As in the case of the Alliance Party, the rulers suggested a National Finance Council be set up to discuss financial policy issues.[17] The states wanted to be empowered to raise loans for development purposes but with prior consultation with the federal government and other states, and the approval of a Federal Loan Board.[18] The states emphasised that the autonomy of the states with regard to expenditure and revenue should be retained and that they should be permitted to retain any surplus of revenue.[19] In the hearing before the constitutional commission, the rulers' counsel Neil Lawson did not spend too much time on federal-state financial relations, being preoccupied with several other issues, and merely explained some of the main demands of the rulers contained in their detailed memorandum.[20] The counsel nevertheless stressed the need for the states to find new sources of revenue to enable them to be more financially autonomous. The states felt it was not practicable to depend on the per capita allocation from the federal government. As an illustration of a potential future scenario, the counsel pointed out that if the states' expenditure and revenue continued at the current level, the state governments would have to find new sources of revenue to raise an additional $150 million for the next financial year.[21] The rulers emphasised the importance of establishing a National Finance Council which could enable the states to make their case for development projects financing from the federal government. If the decision on the priority of a project was left solely to the federal government, then projects of vital importance to certain states such as new roads or drainage and irrigation projects may not get any support, they argued.[22]

The commission noted at the outset of its report that the existing financial relations between the federal government and the states were "not based on any consistent principle," and observed the lack of financial security for the states, and for long term economic planning.[23] The advent of an elected majority in the legislatures was expected to complicate further the financial relations between the federal government and the states. Jennings remarked in his paper on a proposed new financial scheme that the present grant system was unsatisfactory and would be unworkable when democratic majorities were installed in the states.[24] He suggested that this could be overcome by increasing the independent revenues of the states. Under the existing financial arrangements outlined in Part III of the 5th Schedule of the 1948 Federation of Malaya Agreement, the states received several types of grants from the federal government. Since 1 January 1956, this comprised: a capitation grant based on the number of persons in the state above the age of 19 years; a petrol allocation under which 30% of the year's proceeds from the import duty on petrol was distributed to the states according to the amount spent on petrol in each state; a development grant which amounted to about a quarter of the capitation grant (mainly for the states of Kelantan, Pahang, Perlis and Terengganu and determined by the high commissioner); and a special transitional grant which would be paid to the states if the high commissioner was of the opinion that the state would otherwise not have a surplus (the amount not exceeding $500,000).[25] The federal government also provided grants for expenditures related to education, medical services and drainage and irrigation, the major items in the budgets, based on the projected expenditure to be incurred for such services in the state.[26] In addition, the federal government provided (under Clause 119 of federation agreement) for supplementary allocation to the states to meet expenses related to "exceptional and unforeseen circumstances," on application from the states.[27] The high commissioner in this instance had to obtain the approval of the Federal Legislative Council for the special grants. The Treasury in its memorandum on finance submitted to the commission noted that the ad hoc allocations had not proved satisfactory as it did not enable forward planning, hindered financial autonomy and compelled an "annual wrangle" between the federal government and the states.[28] Sir Ivor Jennings in his paper on the existing financial arrangements noted of several weaknesses in the existing financial system. He observed that the various grants benefited the states "in a rather haphazard fashion."[29] At the same time, he felt that a 100% grant to the states had usually been found to be unsatisfactory because it discouraged administrative economy as the states had to surrender any savings made in any financial year.[30] He pointed out the basis for calculating the capitation grant, that is, on the number of persons in the state above the age of 19 years, could hardly be regarded as, "determining the relativity of the need."[31] Jennings felt that the states could be made financially autonomous through three approaches. First, if adequate sources of revenue were assigned to the states; second, if the federal government distributed revenue in accordance to a formula; and third, if the federal government made, in addition, grants-in-aid.[32]

Under the existing financial arrangements, the states depended on federal grants to meet most of their annual expenses which in 1955, for example, ranged from between 60% in Johore and 83% in Perlis. In 1956, the federal grants to the states amounted to $193 million of the total $292 million expenditure (66%) by the states.[33] The federation also paid most of the state expenditure on education, health services and the capital cost of drainage and irrigation. Under the existing system there was continued haggling each year between the federal government and the states to cover the latter's expenses and need for development funds. The commission also found some weaknesses in the way in which capitation grants were calculated based on the number of persons in the state above 19 years. The commission wondered, as observed by Jennings, why those below that age had not been taken into consideration in calculating the capitation grant.[34] The federation government determined the rate of capitation grant per head after consultations with the states but no clear principles were laid down as to how this rate was determined.[35] Jennings felt that the distribution of allocations of petrol duty based on expenditure on roads maintenance was uneven.[36] A major weakness in the existing financial system was the absence of a "Consolidated Fund" in the federation or in the states from which money would be disbursed legally by a vote of the legislatures. Jennings felt this, weakened the system considerably and drew a parallel with the British government's financial system[37]:

> There is, too, one important consequence of not having a Consolidated Fund. In the British system the produce of all loans has to be paid into the Consolidated Fund and voted out by the Appropriation Act. In the Federation loans are "below the line." Estimates of expenditure from loan funds are set out in great detail in an Appendix to the Estimate, but they are not actually voted by the Legislative Council. The same problem does not arise in the States and Settlements, since they have no power to borrow. Loans are sometimes made to them (e.g. for water supplies) by the Federal Government. The justification for vesting borrowing powers solely in the hands of the Federation is, no doubt, that it would be undesirable for the States and Settlements to compete

> with the Federation for the limited savings of the people of the Malaya. On the other hand, the States and Settlements claim that in consequence they are last in the queue for funds for capital expenditure and that the Federal Treasury in effect takes control of the expenditure by requiring full details to be supplied.[38]

He felt the states faced difficulty in meeting additional expenditure or a transfer of a grant-aided service.[39] Under the present system, Jennings noted, the "annual wrangle" had not been avoided and only Johore, Penang, Perak and Selangor had any real financial autonomy.[40]

The commission, in its report, noted that the existing financial system (which came into force on 1 January 1956), while it was an improvement to the system in existence before 1954, was still not very satisfactory and felt it could pose difficulties after independence when political parties would determine the finances. The commission also took note of criticisms by the Malayan administrators and the states over the system of allocation of finances and particularly over capitation grants when gathering evidence during the oral hearings.[41] The rulers' representatives had also in their written and oral submissions noted weaknesses in the existing financial system.[42] In its report the commission noted:

> The present system of grants had not been operation for a full year when we left Malaya, and it is perhaps too early to express any definite opinions about it, but our general impression is that, while it is an improvement on the old system, it is not entirely satisfactory even in the present circumstances, and that after independence further difficulties may well emerge if it is continued unaltered for any long period.[43]

The commission felt the existing financial system did not give real financial autonomy to the states. The states did not have any assurance as to their total income from federal grants in future years which made it difficult for them to plan ahead.[44]

One major change that the commission made to ease the states' financial situation was to make education, medical and health services federal subjects.[45] This meant that the states would not be burdened by these large expenses and, consequently, be dependent on large federal grants. Taxation was a very contentious issue in the federal system and varied considerably in the Commonwealth and other federal systems. There was no cut-and-dried formula that could be used as economic conditions varied in each country. Malaya provided some unique challenges to the commission. The majority in the commission did not want to extend the powers of the states to levy taxes. Any extension of states' powers of taxation, they argued, would be wasteful causing duplication of staff, hamper the conduct of business on a national scale and retard the development of unity in the nation.[46] Beneath these words, they were concerned that it might weaken the central government. The federation was dependent on four main sources of revenue and in 1956 they were export duties on rubber (22.2% of federal revenue), export duties on tin (7.1%), income tax (19.5%) and import duties (31.8%). The commission felt that these sources should not be allocated to the states as it would weaken the central treasury.[47] Justice Abdul Hamid, however, disagreed with the majority in the commission and felt that the states should be allowed to levy taxes in respect of all matters in the state list.[48] He was of course drawing on the experience in Pakistan where the states had more sources of tax revenue. The commission had considered the possibility of enabling the states to raise further revenue through levy from land planted with rubber and royalties from tin mining, but eventually decided against allowing for such levies. They felt it would hamper the development of these industries on which the national economy greatly depended.[49] In addition, they were also against taxation by two independent taxing authorities. Nevertheless, the commission felt that the states should be entitled to a share of the export duty of tin. They pointed out that tin mining involved "the permanent removal of valuable assets from a state" and the states should thus be entitled to receive some compensation, suggesting at least 10% from the export duty on tin should go to the states.[50] The rulers had raised this issue of "assets of a wasting character," in their memorandum and had proposed that the states concerned should receive a portion of the taxes raised from these sources.

The commission provided for the setting up of a national fund called the "Consolidated Fund" (Article 89) out of which "moneys cannot be paid except under the authority of the law."[51] This enabled an organised collection of federal revenue into a consolidated fund and for distribution of funds to the states. The commission was concerned over the uncertainty in the federal-state finances and wanted the states to be assured of a fixed amount in grants to meet their annual expenditure over a longer period and provided a simple formula for this purpose.[52] The commission noted:

> In our view it is of primary importance that the basis of calculation of the amount of grants to meet annual expenditure should be fixed for a period of at least five years, subject only to alteration if there is some general change of circumstances such as substantial alteration of wage or salary scales or of the price of materials. The states would then have an incentive to make economies, a basis for planning for the future and a responsibility for keeping their expenditure within their income.[53]

In this way, the commission provided for certain guaranteed grants to the states from the Federal Consolidated Fund and sought to accord a certain level of financial security. The commission provided for three main sources of grants to the states under Article 103.[54] These were grants-in-aid of general revenue; the assignment of certain amounts from federal taxation and licence fees and other fees of a local character. The commission provided for a simple formula for the calculation of the grants-in-aid which drew on the provisions of the federation agreement but with further improvements. The commission had worked out specific state revenue proposals but did not include them in their report and advised that these details be worked out in the proposed National Financial Council.[55] To consolidate the financial planning, the commission recommended (Article 102) the establishment of a National Finance Council, comprising the prime minister, one other minister and the chief ministers of the states to discuss matters of finance, including the state expenditures, capitation and other federal grants.[56] The commission provided for some limited rights for the states to take commercial loans. The commission enabled the state governments (Article 105) to borrow from the proposed central bank or local banks for a period not exceeding 12 months, but with the approval of the federal government.[57] The commission was well aware of the potential for a national debt problem arising if the states were allowed to borrow freely without sufficient regulatory controls and the competition that would ensue for limited local funds and provided for very conservative provisions for the state to secure commercial loans. They felt that this measure would be in line with their terms of reference requiring them to provide for a degree of autonomy to the states.[58] In essence, the commission sought to provide better financial safeguards for the states and a greater degree of financial security to enable the states to make longer term plans for economic development. But the recommendations of the commissions did not rest entirely well with the states and the Alliance government and considerable negotiations took place in the Working Party which reviewed the recommendations of the commission between February and April 1957. There was much debate, horse-trading and even a sense of crisis at a particular juncture when the Working Party, comprising the Alliance Party representatives, the rulers' representatives and the high commissioner, discussed the various aspects of the financial relations between the federal government and the states as we will see next.

The Working Party deliberations on federal-state financial relations

When the Working Party met in February 1957 to discuss the Reid Commission's recommendations, the representatives of the rulers expressed dissatisfaction with the provisions relating to the division of federal-state financial powers and raised several issues. The rulers' counsel said they were not satisfied with the limited taxing powers, sources of state revenue and grants provided in the draft constitution and felt that this would negate efforts to achieve a greater degree of financial autonomy. At the eleventh meeting of the Working Party on 12 March 1957, the rulers' representative raised four issues: the taxing powers of the states; state revenues; state rights to grants; and the issue of the disposal of surpluses (In the existing financial system the state's surpluses reverted back to the federal government.).[59] The rulers' representatives noted that the constitutional commission had intended that the states should have limited taxing powers but that this was not reflected in the draft constitution.[60] They suggested that taxes on which the federal government had power to levy taxes should be as those set out under the Second Schedule of the 1948 Federation Agreement under the head "Banking, Customs and Revenue, Public Debt."[61] If this was done, they said, the states could take action under the provisions of the proposed Section 17 in the State constitutions to levy taxes.[62]

The rulers' representatives also submitted that there should be an assignment to the states, as a matter of right, of revenues from the sources mentioned in the Third Schedule of the federation agreement.[63] These included revenues from lands, mines and forests, revenues from licences, entertainment duty, fees in courts, fees and receipt from services provides by state governments, revenues from municipal and town boards, rents from state property and a share in surplus from the Malayan Currency Fund.[64] There was a proviso to their submission, a kind of concession to the federal government. The rulers' representatives submitted that any of the sources of revenue could be removed by the federal parliament after consultation with the states if alternative sources of revenue of equivalent value were offered as a replacement.[65]

The Alliance representatives did not accept these proposals as they felt the federation government should be free to make any adjustment necessary after consultation with the National Finance Council.[66] The Alliance argued that revenues of the state should be authorised by Act of Parliament and that it would be difficult to lay down in the constitution that the states should receive any specific items of revenue.[67] The rulers' representatives disagreed with the Alliance's argument, pointing out that under the provisions of Article 156 of the draft constitution the states would in fact continue to receive revenue during the transitional period from sources cited in the Third Schedule of the 1948 Federation of Malaya Agreement, indicating that it would not be a great departure from the existing practice.[68] On another point, the Alliance submitted that the period of five years proposed in Article 104 (2) by the constitutional commission for the assignment of taxes or fees levied by the federal government to the states was too long. They preferred a period of three years for such assignments in view of the fluctuating economic circumstances.[69] In regard to the question of state surpluses, the Alliance was more conciliatory and agreed with the rulers' representatives' suggestion that states should be permitted to accumulate surpluses. Previously, any surplus remaining at the end of the financial year reverted back to the federal government.[70]

After further discussion the Alliance made some concessions on finance to the rulers' representatives. At the thirteenth meeting of the Working Party on 25 March 1957, the Alliance agreed to the rulers' proposal that the states should be entitled to certain revenues "as a matter of right."[71] The Alliance proposed that Clause 112[72] of the federation agreement should be reproduced in the new constitution and that an additional schedule similar to the Third Schedule in the federation agreement should be included in the new constitution to enable this change to be implemented.[73] It was proposed in the meeting that a Central Bank should be established, as suggested by the constitutional commission. With the establishment of the Central Bank, the Alliance pointed out, any currency surplus (a share of which went to the states under the federation agreement) would go to the Central Bank rather than to the federal government.[74] It was also agreed by the Working Party that the item "education" should be included in the federal legislative list, as suggested by the commission, to ease the financial burden of the states.[75] The revenue from education fees would thus go to the federation government or local authorities and would not be considered as state revenue.[76] The Alliance further proposed as a concession that states should receive allocations from the import duty on petrol as presently provided in Part III of the Fifth Schedule of the federation agreement.[77] The meeting agreed that a new article should be inserted after Article 102 similar to the wording contained in Clause 112 of the federation agreement. It was agreed that a new schedule would be inserted in the constitution containing items 1 to 13 in the Third Schedule, taking into consideration the changes that were due to take place in independent Malaya as, for example, the fact that the Currency Board would be replaced by the Central Bank.[78]

On the issue of the states' receiving as of right a portion of revenues from the exploitation of their assets such as minerals, the rulers' representatives proposed that the states should receive at least 15% of the export duty on tin without any conditions attached.[79] They disagreed with the federation government's proposal that the states should receive only 10% of the export duty on condition that the states do not raise royalties on tin, and that the states established a mines committee to "facilitate the availability of land for mining."[80] The rulers' representatives observed that the states had the power to raise royalties but had not done so "because they had no occasion to exercise the power."[81] The Alliance countered this argument by saying that the federal government's offer to give 10% of the export duty on tin was without prejudice to the negotiations on the formation of an organisation to assist in the rehabilitation of old mining land.[82] This implied that there were no conditions attached to the offer.

The rulers' representatives also proposed that 25% of the national revenue from customs import duties and excise should be paid annually to the states, based on a formula that would be decided by the states, instead of the general grants suggested by the constitutional commission.[83] The Alliance argued that this proposal would be difficult to implement because the national revenue from customs import duties and excise could vary considerably annually. The rulers' representatives, however, argued that the states were willing to put up with the risk of a possible reduction from import duties.[84] To persuade the Alliance, the rulers' representatives offered to accept a fixed ceiling set by the federal government beyond which the states would not receive additional revenue. The Alliance leader Tunku noted that many countries were now lifting import duties to provide for free trading and if the federal government were to adopt this principle the revenues from import duties and excise would be reduced considerably.[85] The Alliance, as we will see next, eventually agreed that the states should be given as of right a certain percentage of the export duty on tin produced in the respective states.[86]

In regard to taxing powers, the rulers' representatives argued that taxing powers should follow the legislative powers as provided in the Sixth Schedule of the federation agreement.[87] The Alliance, however, argued that it would be wrong for the states to have the power to raise taxes on all matters included in the state list.[88] Justice Abdul Hamid, a member of the Reid constitutional commission, had argued in his note of dissent that the states should have power to levy taxes on items in the state list to give them greater financial autonomy.[89] This issue was only resolved later after further negotiations.

In the ensuing discussions, the Working Party agreed that a new article would be included in the constitution to enable states to accumulate state surpluses.[90] On the question of federal surpluses, the rulers' representatives suggested that the states should have a share of the federal surpluses as of right periodically. The Alliance,

states were not advancing towards financial stability and self-sufficiency, the federal government "would give the matter most careful consideration."[116] The rulers' representatives then tried a different tack. They suggested that a "Reserve Fund" could be created to assist states which were facing financial difficulties.[117] If the proposals were accepted in principle, they noted, it would not be too difficult to work out a formula for the allocation of funds to the states based on a percentage basis.[118] They said that if this was agreed the states would give up the percentage of petrol import duty, the development grant, the transitional grant and the currency surplus (on which they were earlier adamant).[119] The meeting agreed that the rulers' representatives would prepare a memorandum outlining their new proposals and this would be discussed at the eighteenth meeting of the Working Party on 18 April 1957.[120] The rulers' representatives also submitted that they were willing to forego their proposal that the states should be entitled to raise new taxes if the states were given the grants contained in their new proposals as of right.[121]

The rulers' proposals received a positive response from the Alliance Finance Minister Lee who attended the twentieth meeting of the Working Party on 18 April on invitation. Lee said he was prepared to accept the proposals of the rulers' representatives subject to further consideration of details.[122] Lee agreed that the proposal that Class 1 of the state revenues should be revenues derived from sources one to 12 as contained in the Third Schedule of the 1948 federation agreement.[123] He also agreed that none of these items should be removed without an equivalent replacement.[124] In regard to the proposed Class II sources of revenue contained in the memorandum of the rulers' representatives, Lee felt that the figures were too high, noting the average cost of state road were $4,200 per mile.[125] He suggested that state roads should be defined as the length of non-federal roads in a state that was maintained by the Public Works Department and the basic figures for calculation should be the length of state roads as at 31 December 1956 (4,366 miles).[126] Any additions should be subject to the agreement of the federal government. Lee felt that the federal government could not accept the rulers' representatives' proposal that the capitation grant should not be revised for five years, except in the event of a serious fall in federal revenue.[127] On the allocation of a percentage of the export duty on tin revenue, Lee said it would be better to reach a separate agreement for such payment than to include provisions dealing with this in the constitution as references would have to be made as to the conditions on which the payment was to be made.[128] He referred to the offer made by the federal government before the report of the constitutional commission was published, noting that the offer was an inducement for the state to open up more land for mining rather than a general allocation for the states. Eventually, the Working Party agreed that the states should receive not less than 10% of the export duty on tin produced in the states as determined by parliament after consultation in the National Finance Council.[129] Lee suggested that a small committee could examine the new proposals in detail as to the rate for the new capitation grant.[130]

High Commissioner MacGillivray felt that the new proposals of the rulers' representatives were "too rigid," and he expected that as a result some states would suffer.[131] He suggested instead that a percentage of the capitation grant could be paid into a reserve fund which could be used to assist the undeveloped states and be used for development in general.[132] The rulers' representatives said that their main intention was to ensure that the states were given sufficient revenue "to maintain their present services and to provide for reasonable expansion."[133] They were agreeable to changes in the calculation of the figures contained in their proposals. After further discussion, it was agreed that there should be a capitation grant formulated along the lines proposed by the rulers' representatives.[134] The meeting also agreed that there should be a grant to meet the cost of maintenance of state roads and that a portion of the annual capitation grant should be set aside in a reserve fund for the states.[135] At the twenty-second meeting of the Working Party on 27 April, an agreement was reached on the rate of capitation grants for the states.[136] The Working Party agreed that the capitation grant would be based in a sliding scale at the rate of $15 per head for the first 50,000 persons, $10 per head for the next 200,000 and $4 per head for the remainder. The road grant was agreed at $4,200 per mile.[137]

At a later meeting, however, the rulers' representatives contended that if the amount for the reserve funds came from the capitation grant, the states would need to apply each year for this funds and argued that this special fund was actually intended to supplement the existing revenues of the state.[138] This meeting then agreed that funds for the reserve fund would not be deducted from the capitation grants but would be additional funds provided by the federal government.[139] This reserve fund would only be disbursed with the authority of parliament after discussion in the National Finance Council.[140] It was agreed that the new financial arrangements would come into force in 1959 and that the total sum involved in the new financial arrangements would not exceed the combined total of the capitation grant and road grant under the previous proposals.[141] This brought to a close the very difficult and complex discussions on the finance relations between the federal government and the states. The states, through the rulers' representatives,[142] fought hard to ensure that the states received adequate allocations annually to meet their expenses and to plan their development programmes. Both the federal government and the state governments had sound and strong reasons for their demands. The federal government wanted to ensure that the financial relations were an improvement on the existing slightly ad hoc arrangements to ensure a strong central government financially. The states, on the other hand, wanted to ensure that they had a reasonable measure of autonomy to meet the annual expenditures and development programs. It took a small crisis at one stage of the discussions which were nearing an impasse to get the Alliance federal government to be more flexible in relation to the distribution of financial powers to the states.

The discussions in relation to the financial provisions in the constitution show that there were considerable differences of opinion between the Alliance and the rulers' representatives, which at one stage threatened to disrupt the discussions. Some intelligent manoeuvring by the High Commissioner MacGillivray and generous concessions made by the Alliance enabled these complex financial provisions to be resolved quickly and amicably. What is also clear from this episode is that there were significant differences over the working of the concept of federalism in Malaya between these two parties and their understanding of the terms of reference of the constitutional commission which required the commission to provide for a strong central government and a measure of autonomy to the states. The Alliance wanted to ensure a strong central government, a key feature of the federal system, that could determine the financial relations with the states, while the states fought hard to preserve, if not to increase, the financial autonomy which was also a central element of the federal system.

Notes

1 See Paper on financial arrangements in the Federation of Malaya by Sir Ivor Jennings, 29 August 1956, CO 889/2 (5), p. 10. See also Memorandum by federal government on financial relations with states and settlements, CO 889/7 (6), 10 October 1956; and Paper titled, "New financial scheme," by Ivor Jennings, 31 August 1956, CO 889/2 (6).
2 See Paper on financial arrangements in the Federation of Malaya by Sir Ivor Jennings, 29 August 1956, CO 889/2 (5), p. 10. Jennings notes that from the provisions of Part I and II of the Fifth Schedule, which are considered General Orders under the clause, no General Orders had been made. See also Paper titled, "New financial scheme," by Ivor Jennings, 31 August 1956, CO 889/2 (6).
3 Paper on financial arrangements in the Federation of Malaya by Sir Ivor Jennings, 29 August 1956, CO 889/2 (5), p. 10.
4 Ibid., pp. 10–11.
5 Ibid., p. 10.
6 Alliance memorandum to constitutional commission, 27 September 1956, UMNO/SUA 154/56, p. 9.
7 Record of hearing given to Alliance Party by Reid Commission, 27 September 1956, CO 889/6 (3), p. 24. Report of hearing given to Alliance Party, 27 September 1956, CO 889/1 (33), C.C. 2167, p. 4.
8 Record of hearing given to Alliance Party by Reid Commission, 27 September 1956, CO 889/6 (3), p. 24.
9 Proposals of Their Highnesses the Rulers made to the Constitutional Commission, September 1956, CO 889/8 (22A), pp. 29–34.
10 See Joseph M. Fernando, *Federal constitutions: A comparative study of the constitutions of the United States and Malaysia* (Kuala Lumpur: University of Malaya Press, 2007).
11 Proposals of Their Highnesses the Rulers made to the Constitutional Commission, September 1956, CO 889/8 (22A), p. 30.
12 Ibid.
13 Ibid., p. 31.
14 Ibid.
15 Ibid., pp. 31–32.
16 Ibid., p. 32.
17 Ibid., pp. 32–33.
18 Ibid., p. 33.
19 Ibid., p. 34.
20 Report of hearing of counsel on behalf of Their Highnesses the Rulers, 14–15 September 1956, CO 889/1 (32), pp. 52–57.
21 Ibid., p. 53.
22 Ibid., pp. 54–55.
23 Report of the Federation of Malaya Constitutional Commission 1957, London: Her Majesty's Stationery Office, Colonial No. 330, p. 57. See also paper on Present Financial Arrangements by Sir Ivor Jennings, 29 August 1956, CO 889/2 (5).
24 See Jennings paper titled, "New financial scheme," 31 August 1956, CO 889/2 (6), C.C. 2000/3, p. 5.

25 Memorandum on finance by federation government, CO 889/2 (1), C.C. 2000/3, June 1956. Paper on Present Financial Arrangements by Sir Ivor Jennings, 29 August 1956, CO 889/2 (5), C.C. 2000/3, pp. 2–6. See also Federation of Malaya Agreement, 1948.
26 Memorandum on finance by federation government, June 1956, CO 889/2 (1), C.C. 2000/3. Paper on Present Financial Arrangements by Sir Ivor Jennings, 29 August 1956, CO 889/2 (5), C.C. 2000/3, p. 5.
27 Paper on Present Financial Arrangements by Sir Ivor Jennings, 29 August 1956, CO 889/2 (5), C.C. 2000/3, p. 6.
28 Memorandum on finance by federation government, June 1956, CO 889/2 (1), C.C. 2000/3, p. 4.
29 Paper on Present Financial Arrangements by Sir Ivor Jennings, 29 August 1956, CO 889/2 (5), C.C. 2000/3, p. 6.
30 Jennings' paper titled "Present financial arrangements," 29 August 1956, CO 889/2 (5), C.C. 2000/3, p. 6. Jennings noted that the present system was tolerable because federal officers seconded to the states exercised some control over the finances and had a sense of responsibility to their federal department heads. But he felt the situation could become uncontrollable if the expenditure was controlled by political leaders.
31 Paper on Present Financial Arrangements by Sir Ivor Jennings, 29 August 1956, CO 889/2 (5), C.C. 2000/3, p. 6.
32 Summary record of 30th meeting of Constitutional Commission, 12 September 1956, CO 889/1 (33), p. 2.
33 Report of the Federation of Malaya Constitutional Commission 1957, p. 57.
34 Ibid., p. 58.
35 Ibid.
36 Paper on Present Financial Arrangements by Sir Ivor Jennings, 29 August 1956, CO 889/2 (5), C.C. 2000/3, p. 6.
37 Ibid., p. 11.
38 Ibid., p. 12.
39 Ibid., p. 13.
40 Ibid., p. 7.
41 Jennings' paper titled "Present financial arrangements," 29 August 1956, CO 889/2 (5), 2000/3, p. 6.
42 See Rulers' memorandum, 12 September 1956, CO 889/8, pp. 29–35, and oral submissions by the Rulers' representatives, 14–15 September 1956, CO 889/8.
43 Report of the Federation of Malaya Constitutional Commission 1957, p. 59.
44 Ibid., p. 60.
45 Ibid.
46 Ibid.
47 Paper on Present Financial Arrangements by Sir Ivor Jennings, 29 August 1956, CO 889/2, C.C. 2000/3, p. 1.
48 Report of the Federation of Malaya Constitutional Commission 1957, p. 60.
49 Ibid., pp. 60–61.
50 Ibid., p. 61.
51 Report of the Federation of Malaya Constitutional Commission 1957, p. 65. See also CO 889/2 (5), C.C. 2000/3, Paper on Present Financial Arrangements by Ivor Jennings, 29 August 1956, pp. 11–13.
52 Report of the Federation of Malaya Constitutional Commission 1957, pp. 61–62. See also Summary record of the 55th meeting of the Constitutional Commission, 16 October 1956, CO 889/1 (58), and Summary record of the 56th meeting of the Constitutional Commission, 16 October 1956, CO 889/1 (59).
53 Report of the Federation of Malaya Constitutional Commission 1957, pp. 61–62.
54 Ibid., pp. 62–63.
55 See CO 941/86 (E15C) for a tabulation of the Reid Commission's state revenue proposals.

56 Report of the Federation of Malaya Constitutional Commission 1957, pp. 61–64.
57 Ibid., pp. 63–64.
58 Ibid., pp. 63.
59 Minutes of Eleventh meeting of the Working Party, 12 March 1957, CO 941/85, p. 1.
60 Ibid., p. 1.
61 Minutes of Eleventh meeting of the Working Party, 12 March 1957, CO 941/85, p. 1. Federal powers of taxation under the Second Schedule include corporation tax, customs duties including export duties, duties of excise, taxes on remittances, stamp duties, taxes on capital value of assets of individuals and companies and taxes on income.
62 Minutes of Eleventh meeting of the Working Party, 12 March 1957, CO 941/85, p. 1.
63 Minutes of Eleventh meeting of the Working Party, 12 March 1957, CO 941/85, pp. 1–2. See also Memorandum by federal government on financial relations with states and settlements, CO 889/7 (6). Part III of the federation agreement provides for 30% of customs duty on petrol to be divided by the states; a capitation grant for each adult who has attained the age of 20 years; a grant to cover all expenditure on education, medical and health services and capital expenditure on drainage and irrigation works; a development grant determined by the High Commissioner for the states of Kelantan, Pahang, Perlis and Terengganu; and a transitional grant to ensure there was a surplus over expenditure, not exceeding $500,000. See Memorandum on financial relations between federal government and states, 10 October 1956, CO 889/7 (6).
64 Third Schedule, Federation of Malaya Agreement, 1948.
65 Minutes of Eleventh meeting of the Working Party, 12 March 1957, CO 941/85, p. 2.
66 Ibid.
67 Ibid.
68 Ibid.
69 Ibid.
70 Ibid.
71 Minutes of Thirteenth meeting of the Working Party, 25 March 1957, CO 941/85, p. 2.
72 Clause 112 of the 1948 Federation of Malaya Agreement provides that the revenues of the states shall be derived from the sources set out in the Third Schedule of the agreement and from sums to be allocated for each of them by the federal legislative council.
73 Minutes of Thirteenth meeting of the Working Party, 25 March 1957, CO 941/85, p. 2. The Alliance also suggested that items 13 (share in the Malaya and British Borneo Currency Surplus Fund) and 14 (receipts in respect of education rate imposed under any written law) of the Third Schedule of the federation agreement should not be included in the new schedule.
74 Minutes of Thirteenth meeting of the Working Party, 25 March 1957, CO 941/85, p. 2.
75 Ibid.
76 Ibid.
77 Minutes of Thirteenth meeting of the Working Party, 25 March 1957, CO 941/85, p. 3. See also CO 889/7 (6), Memorandum by federal government on financial relations with states and settlements, 19 October 1956. Part III of the federation agreement provides for 30% of customs duty on petrol to be divided by the states; a capitation grant for each adult who has attained the age of 20; a grant to cover all expenditure on education, medical and health services and capital expenditure on drainage and irrigation works; and a development grant determined by the High Commissioner for the states of Kelantan, Pahang, Perlis and Terengganu and a transitional grant to ensure there was a surplus over expenditure, not exceeding $500,000.
78 Minutes of Thirteenth meeting of the Working Party, 25 March 1957, CO 941/85, pp. 2–3.
79 Ibid., p. 3.
80 Minutes of Thirteenth meeting of the Working Party, 25 March 1957, CO 941/85, p. 3. See also Federal government memorandum on mining, 18 October 1956, CO 889/7 (4).

81 Minutes of Thirteenth meeting of the Working Party, 25 March 1957, CO 941/85, p. 3.
82 Ibid., p. 3.
83 Ibid., p. 3. The rulers' representatives produced a table of estimated figures to show how the revenue from the proposed 25% share of customs duties would help the states manage their budget expenditures. See attachment to the minutes of this meeting.
84 Minutes of Thirteenth meeting of the Working Party, 25 March 1957, CO 941/85, p. 4.
85 Ibid., p. 4.
86 Minutes of Sixteenth meeting of the Working Party, 2 April 1957, CO 941/85, p. 3.
87 Minutes of Thirteenth meeting of the Working Party, 25 March 1957, CO 941/85, pp. 4–5.
88 Ibid., pp. 4–5,
89 See Justice Abdul Hamid's note of dissent in Sir Ivor Jennings Papers, B/X/6 (Second Draft), pp. 20–21.
90 Minutes of Thirteenth meeting of the Working Party, 25 March 1957, CO 941/85, p. 5.
91 Ibid., p. 5.
92 Ibid., p. 6.
93 Ibid.
94 Minutes of Sixteenth meeting of the Working Party, 2 April 1957, CO 941/85, p. 2. See also Treasury memorandum, 5 April 1957, commenting on the Reid proposals, CO 941/86 (E13).
95 Minutes of Sixteenth meeting of the Working Party, 2 April 1957, CO 941/85, p. 2.
96 Ibid. In one large state, he noted, the surplus would amount to $4.8 million and in a small state it would amount to $2.4 million.
97 Minutes of Sixteenth meeting of the Working Party, 2 April 1957, CO 941/85, pp. 2–3.
98 Ibid., p. 2.
99 Ibid.
100 Ibid., p. 4.
101 Minutes of the Working Party of the Constitution of the federation 1957, CO 941/86 (E/14).
102 Minutes of Sixteenth meeting of the Working Party, 2 April 1957, CO 941/85, p. 1. The ruler's representatives at this meeting were Dato Panglima Bukit Gantang, Tuan Haji Mustapha Albakri bin Haji Hassan, Shamsuddin bin Nain and Tunku Ismail bin Tunku Yahya.
103 Minutes of Sixteenth meeting of the Working Party, 2 April 1957, CO 941/85, p. 4. See also Note of discussion in Conference of Rulers, 10 April 1957, CO 491/86. At the meeting of the Conference of Rulers on 10 April 1957, the High Commissioner informed the rulers of the progress made in the Working Party and the difficulties in relation to some of the issues. Their Highnesses while appreciating that some of the issues posed difficult problems were confident that with "goodwill and understanding on the part of all" these problems could be resolved.
104 Minutes of Sixteenth meeting of the Working Party, 2 April 1957, CO 941/85, p. 1.
105 Minutes of Seventeenth meeting of the Working Party, 9 April 1957, CO 941/85, p. 1.
106 Ibid., p. 1.
107 Ibid.
108 Minutes of Seventeenth meeting of the Working Party, 9 April 1957, CO 941/85, p. 1. The provisions of the Fifth Schedule of the Federation Agreement allowed the states additional funds, after consultation with the financial secretary and the high commissioner, to cover special circumstances, to provide for additional appointments in the state civil service, to make use of savings on expenditure as supplementary expenditure and to receive special allocations for expenditure for "unforeseen circumstances." See Fifth Schedule of Federation Agreement.
109 Minutes of Seventeenth meeting of the Working Party, 9 April 1957, CO 941/85, p. 2.
110 Minutes of Eighteenth meeting of the Working Party, 16 April 1957, CO 941/85, p. 1.

111 Ibid., p. 4.
112 Ibid.
113 Ibid.
114 Ibid., p. 5.
115 Minutes of Eighteenth meeting of the Working Party, 16 April 1957, CO 941/85, p. 4. See also Memorandum on financial relations between the federal government and the states, 19 October 1956, CO 889/7 (6).
116 Minutes of Eighteenth meeting of the Working Party, 16 April 1957, CO 941/85, p. 5.
117 Ibid.
118 Ibid.
119 Ibid.
120 Ibid.
121 Ibid., p. 6.
122 Minutes of Twentieth meeting of the Working Party, 18 April 1957, CO 941/87, p. 1.
123 See Third Schedule, Federation of Malaya Agreement, 1948. These included revenue from Toddy shops; lands, mines and forests; issuing of licenses; entertainment duties, fees in courts; fees and receipts in respect of specific services rendered by state departments; revenues of local authorities (town and municipal councils, etc.); receipts in respect of water supplies; rents on state and Settlements properties; interest on state and Settlement balances; receipt from land sales; and fines in courts.
124 Minutes of Twentieth meeting of the Working Party, 18 April 1957, CO 941/87, p. 1.
125 Ibid.
126 Ibid.
127 Ibid., p. 2.
128 Ibid.
129 Minutes of Twenty-second meeting of the Working Party, 27 April 1957, CO 941/87, p. 2. It was agreed that a new clause would be added to Article 104 to enable the states to receive this payment to be made.
130 Minutes of Twentieth meeting of the Working Party, 18 April 1957, CO 941/87, p. 2.
131 Ibid.
132 Ibid.
133 Ibid.
134 Minutes of Twentieth meeting of the Working Party, 18 April 1957, CO 941/87, p. 2. Minutes of the Twenty-second meeting of the Working Party, 27 April 1957, CO 941/87, pp. 2–3. The rate of the capitation was eventually agreed at the Twenty-second meeting of the Working Party on 27 April 1957.
135 Minutes of Twentieth meeting of the Working Party, 18 April 1957, CO 941/87, p. 2.
136 Minutes of Twenty-second meeting of the Working Party, 27 April 1957, CO 941/87, p. 3.
137 Ibid., p. 3.
138 Ibid., p. 2.
139 Ibid.
140 Minutes of Twentieth meeting of the Working Party, 18 April 1957, CO 941/87, p. 2.
141 Minutes of Twenty-second meeting of the Working Party, 27 April 1957, CO 941/87, p. 2.
142 Minutes of Twentieth meeting of the Working Party, 18 April 1957, CO 941/87, p. 1. The rulers were represented in the discussions on financial relations mainly by Tuan Haji Mustapha Albakri bin Haji Hassan, Samsuddin Nain, Tunku Ismail bin Tunku Yahya and Abdullah bin Ibrahim.

5 Citizenship

Citizenship is one of the basic foundations of the modern nation-state. A legally formulated citizenship in the modern nation-state identifies those who are entitled to protection of the state and certain inherent rights and privileges in return for their loyalty and obligations to the state. Most modern constitutions clearly identify the groups of people who are entitled to such protection, rights and privileges as against others who are not. The use of the term "citizen" in the British Commonwealth, however, was a post-Second World War novelty that was created to describe the new status of the peoples in colonial territories that were becoming independent. During the period of decolonisation in the post-1945 period, citizenship became a widely contested issue in the British colonial territories, particularly those with plural societies, where the colonised people were known either as British subjects or as British Protected Persons (in the case of those who originated from territories which were not British colonial territories). In India, Pakistan, Ceylon and Burma as well as emerging nation-states in Africa such as Ghana, Kenya, Nigeria, Uganda and Tanzania citizenship posed a vexed issue for the withdrawing colonial power and the national leaders of these states.

In the British Commonwealth, traditionally those who would be described as "citizens" or "nationals" of their respective countries in other jurisdictions were referred to as "subjects" of the King (or Queen later), who was the monarch for the whole of the Commonwealth, or "British subjects."[1] In the Commonwealth, prior to the gaining of independence in Asian and African colonial territories, the phrase "British subject" implied a wider common citizenship. Citizenship in this context meant a relationship towards a king, an "allegiance," and not a relationship towards a country. Thus, all persons who were born in the British colonial territories can be said to be born "within the King's allegiance."[2] This accorded them certain rights such as protection under the law, right to employment, the right to vote or to be elected to a legislature. In other words, it bestowed all the benefits of a modern post-war citizenship. The introduction of "citizenship" after the Second World War in many British colonial territories caused considerable dislocation of communities, including many who were rendered stateless, who previously were "British subjects" or "citizens" in the modern sense of the term. Prior to the introduction of new nationalities and citizenships in the post-war period, the legal

DOI: 10.4324/9781003542537-5

status of peoples in the colonial territories was defined by the British Nationality and Status of Aliens Act, 1914.[3] Under this Act, any person born in British dominions (such as Canada and Australia) or territories annexed by the British (such as India, Ceylon and Hong Kong) was deemed as a British subject. Ivor Jennings has observed that under British law, a person born in a Malay state whose father was a British subject by birth was a British subject by birth and passed on his British nationality to his children and grandchildren.[4] He noted further that according to the United Kingdom law no British subject can renounce that status.[5] The new concept of citizenship introduced in the colonial territories, including in Malaya, altered this historical position and status of many domiciled peoples. Many who were previously British subjects and citizens of the colonial territories in a wider sense, particularly the Indians and Ceylonese in Malaya and a smaller group of Chinese who originated from the British territory of Hong Kong, became stateless as a result, unaware of their inherent rights to automatic federal citizenship as British subjects.[6] Where previously in the colonial territories there was a free flow of people from one country to another to meet the manpower needs of the modern colonial economy, the situation was altered considerably when at decolonisation new constitutions were being drawn up for these emerging states and new categories of citizens and residents were formulated.

In the Federation of Malaya, citizenship was an issue of much debate during the drafting of the Malayan independence constitution (1956–1957) as was also the case when a Malayan citizenship was introduced with the Malayan Union constitution in 1946. The Federation of Malaya at independence in 1957 had a multiracial population comprising mainly of Malay, Chinese and Indian communities with their distinct cultures and languages. The population was divided almost evenly between Malays and non-Malays. From the 1870s till the early part of the twentieth century, Britain had gradually gained control of the Malay states after a reversal in its previous non-interference policy following internal strife in some of the Malay states and a disruption in economic activities with the Straits Settlements comprising Penang, Singapore and Malacca.[7] Apart from the Straits Settlements, which were Crown Colonies under the full jurisdiction of Britain, four of the Malay states which had a British Resident with enormous powers of administration (Perak, Selangor, Negri Sembilan and Pahang) were unified under a federation called the Federated Malay States in 1895. Britain, further, had considerable influence over the remaining five Unfederated Malay states which had British advisers. With a strong rein over the Malay states and in its endeavour to exploit the rich natural resources of the territory, the British administration encouraged mass immigration from the last quarter of the nineteenth century to the early decades of the twentieth century from India and China to meet the labour needs of the tin and rubber industry, to build the rail and road infrastructure for these export industries and to fill the lower administrative positions in the civil service. Thus, in the process a plural society was created.[8]

The Reid constitutional commission's terms of reference required them to provide for a single common nationality for the whole federation. The rationale behind the creation of a common nationality was to provide for the development of a sense of national identity, loyalty and community for the citizens of the future independent federation.[9] This requirement in the terms of reference invariably meant that the commission had to sort out the different types of citizenship and state nationalities which co-existed in the federation and decide who was entitled to citizenship in the independent federation. The constitutional documents reveal that the issue of citizenship proved a difficult and vexed issue for the Reid constitutional commission, as it did to the ruling Alliance Party and the Malay rulers. There were considerable differences of view on the subject of citizenship in the federation among the Alliance parties, the Malay rulers and other political and socio-economic organisations. Almost every memorandum from the total of 131 submitted to the constitutional commission touched on the issue of federal citizenship.

Ever since the concept of citizenship was introduced in Malaya in 1946 under the Malayan Union Plan, the issue had been mired in political controversy.[10] The general intention of the British government in their effort to introduce local citizenships in the colonies and protectorates in the post-war period was to provide for the development of a national political community and a sense of national consciousness and belonging in the long term for the peoples of these territories. Equally important, Britain was considering changes to its British Nationality Act between 1946 and 1947 with the imminent transfer of power in India, Burma, Ceylon and potentially several other colonial territories, which would produce separate citizenships and which would affect those holding British nationality or the status of British subjects in these countries.[11] The British response to these political changes was, after much discussion with representations from the colonial territories, eventually to appear in the amendments made to the British Nationality Act, 1948, which created a category of citizenship called "citizens of the United Kingdom and Colonies," in addition to the category of "British subjects"[12] or "Commonwealth citizens."[13] Other persons in colonial territories such as protectorates, protected states or trust territories were defined as "British protected persons" under these changes. In this context, the populace of the nine Malay states were considered as "British protected persons," although a sizeable proportion would legally be "British subjects" of the earlier pre-1948 kind by virtue of the connection with Penang and Malacca (and who would have migrated to the other nine states in search of employment, etc.), or their links to previous British colonial territories such as India, Pakistan and Ceylon, and Hong Kong which remained a British colony.[14] The residents of Penang and Malacca which were Crown colonies, on the other hand, were considered as "citizens of the United Kingdom and Colonies."

The Malayan Union citizenship had sought to create a broader national Malayan polity with a common citizenship that would incorporate all the inhabitants in the 11 states and settlements and develop a sense of national consciousness and belonging. The divisions caused among the three main communities, the Malays, Chinese and Indians, during the Japanese occupation of Malaya and, more importantly, Britain's long-term plans for decolonisation necessitated these radical changes. The Malayan Union scheme, however, met with much resistance from the Malay political organisations and the Malay community who were opposed to the transfer of sovereignty of the nine Malay rulers to the British crown. They were also opposed to the perceived liberal provisions in the grant of citizenship to the non-Malays under the Malayan Union.[15] Malay organisations mobilised protests throughout the country and the Malay rulers were urged to boycott the inauguration of the first Malayan Union Governor, Sir Edward Gent, in Kuala Lumpur on 1 April 1946. Stunned by these protests, the colonial administration began discussions with the main political organisation representing the Malays, the newly formed United Malays National Organisation (UMNO). After a few months of discussion in the second half of 1946, agreement was reached on changes to certain aspects of the Malayan Union constitution.[16] The rulers regained their sovereignty, and the citizenship requirements for non-Malays to acquire Malayan citizenship stipulated in the Malayan Union constitution was tightened. This resulted in counter-protests from the non-Malays led by the All-Malaya Council of Joint Action (AMCJA) headed by the venerable Malayan Chinese leader Tan Cheng Lock whose family roots in Malaya went back a few hundred years.[17] A special committee, the Cheeseman committee, then attempted to obtain the views of the various communities on the proposed changes to the Malayan Union scheme which had been agreed with the rulers and UMNO.[18] After some minor amendments to the previously agreed draft of the 1948 Federation of Malaya Agreement between the Malay rulers, UMNO and the British administration, wherein the provisions for acquisition of Malayan citizenship had been made more stringent, the new constitution came into force on 1 February 1948.[19]

Under the 1948 Federation Agreement, citizenship could be obtained by three main modes: through operation of law automatically, by registration on application by those born in the federation after fulfilling a period of residence and, by naturalisation on application which required a longer period of residence in the federation and an oath of allegiance.[20] Under the federation agreement, any Malay or aboriginal born in one of the states was a subject of the ruler and automatically became a citizen by virtue of that status. British subjects born in the Settlements of Penang and Malacca automatically became federal citizens if they were permanent residents in the federation.[21] The federation agreement via Clause 125 also enabled citizenship to be acquired by registration through application for those born in the federation if they had lived there for 8 of the previous 15 years. Clause 125 also enabled those who were not born in the federation to acquire citizenship by application if they had lived there for 15 of the previous 20 years. Applicants for this category needed to be of good character and have "adequate knowledge" of Malay or English.[22] This, nevertheless, left a considerable number of domiciled non-Malays,[23] especially those born outside the federation and their children, stateless, and further efforts were made by political leaders to liberalise the requirements of federal citizenship between 1949 and 1952, particularly through the Communities Liaison Committee (CLC) discussions.[24] As a result, in 1952[25] there was created a state nationality[26] in each of the nine states which enabled non-Malays who had resided in the federation for a certain number of years to become the subjects of the rulers and to obtain these state nationalities, and which then enabled them to acquire federal citizenship. Thus, in 1952, federal citizenship could be obtained in three ways: by operation of law, by registration on application and by naturalisation on application.[27] Citizenship of the federation, through the operation of law, was automatic for those who held a state nationality and for citizens of the United Kingdom and the Colonies, if they were permanently resident in the federation. Others could acquire by registration the federal citizenship if they had lived there for eight years (for those born in the federation) and 15 years (for those not born in the federation). Citizenship of the federation could also be obtained by the process of naturalisation, which required a longer period of residence. The underlying British policy in the citizenship legislation, according to the Colonial Office, was to make the citizenship of the federation available to those "who may now reasonably be assumed to be assimilated to Malayan life and ready to give their undivided loyalty to the Federation."[28] According to the federation government, in June 1953 the total number who were citizens of the federation was 4,139,000 of whom 2,227,000 were Malays; 1,157,800 Chinese; 222,000 Indians, Pakistanis and Ceylonese; and 33,050 others.[29] It was also estimated that there were 647,300 persons who possessed the qualifications to be registered as citizens of the Federation.[30] In December 1955, from the total population of 6,151,000 of the federation, the total number of citizens was 5,273,000, comprising Malays, 2,967,000; Chinese, 1,840,000; Indians, 412,000; and Others, 54,000.[31] Among the Malays, 98.8% were federal citizens; Chinese, 79.1%; Indians, 56.5%; and Others, 57.9%.[32] Thus, when the Reid Commission began drafting the new constitution, there was a federal citizenship, nine state nationalities, a special category of citizens from the Settlements of Penang and Malacca who were also citizens of the United Kingdom and Colonies and a category of "British protected persons." This wide range of citizenship and nationalities were, as noted earlier, the result of various constitutional developments in Britain and Malaya since 1914.

In view of this complex and contentious background to the issue of citizenship in Malaya, the Reid Commission thus had to find a delicate balance between the differing views and demands of different sections of the population in addition to consolidating the various categories of citizenship into a common citizenship. The commission, in the main, relied on the agreements reached between the component parties of the Alliance Party – UMNO, Malayan Chinese Association (MCA) and Malayan Indian Congress (MIC) – which they felt represented the views of the majority of Malayans and was a reasonable compromise between the communities reached after inter-party negotiations in 1956. They also took note of the rulers' views which were quite similar to those of the Alliance but which were a tad more liberal. Almost all the organisations which submitted a memorandum to the commission had a view on the issue of citizenship, often with a particular inherent bias. The commission tried to find a middle ground between the views in the Malayan polity while adhering to their terms of reference and practices in international law governing citizenship. The other political and socio-economic organisations in Malaya made more general recommendations on citizenship which were often divided on a Malay and non-Malay continuum, and the commission merely took note of their views. In the context of residents of the Settlements of Penang and Malacca, the commission took extra pains to ensure this group of people did not lose their rights accorded under the British Nationality Act 1948 and argued strongly for the recognition of dual citizenship. Commission Chairman Lord Reid wrote a long section in the commission's report to explain the rationale behind the provision for dual citizenship which was generally recognised in international law. This was largely influenced by a strong memorandum on nationality submitted by the British government to the constitutional commission, which asked the commission to ensure that the rights of the British subjects in the Settlements were adequately protected in the new constitution.[33]

Alliance Party's proposals on citizenship

The Alliance Party's proposals in general were quite accommodating in their approach to addressing the issue of a common nationality and sought to find a middle ground between the demands of the three component parties: UMNO, MCA and MIC. Essentially, the Alliance proposed that those who were already citizens under the 1948 federation agreement, those who were born in the federation and those who had lived in the federation but who were born outside Malaya should be able to acquire citizenship, some automatically by operation of law while others would need to apply to register as nationals. A certain period of residence was required in the case of the latter groups. The Alliance had reached their compromises contained in their joint memorandum to the constitutional commission after considerable discussions in Alliance National Council in 1956.[34] There were, however, some areas where there were differences between UMNO, MCA and MIC, and these disagreements were stated in the memorandum. In some of these contentious areas, the coalition essentially left it to the constitutional commission to find a common ground acceptable to all the parties. The Alliance agreements included the acceptance of the principle of *jus soli* (right by birth) for those born in the federation on and after Merdeka Day. The principle of *jus soli*, an internationally accepted principle for conferment of nationality, had been a source of much debate previously in the federation right from the time the Malayan Union citizenship proposals were discussed in 1945–1946. UMNO had then opposed the provision. Subsequently, UMNO had entered in an electoral partnership with MCA (and later MIC) in the local council elections in 1952, and in the run-up to the federal elections in July 1955, UMNO, MCA and MIC had agreed that the principle of *jus soli* would be accepted in independent Malaya. The Alliance's election manifesto for the July 1955 federal elections had stated that the principle of *jus soli* was accepted, but this agreement was not revealed in the published version to avoid opposition particularly among the Malay opposition groups.[35] Among the Alliance elites, there was a realisation that most of the non-Malays were born in Malaya and others who were not would in due time be entitled to become citizens after fulfilling a certain period of residence. They thus wanted to provide for these people to acquire citizenship without undue difficulty. The Alliance proposals were reached after considerable negotiations in the Alliance National Council and its sub-committees which drafted the

Alliance memorandum. A spirit of compromise prevailed among the Alliance leaders as they reached compromises on a range of issues in order to put forward a joint memorandum. UMNO nevertheless was able to carry more weight on the final shape of the memorandum compared to the MCA and MIC, being the dominant party in the coalition. In their memorandum, the Alliance stated that they hoped that the nationality laws would create greater unity and provide for a peaceful and stable independent federation.[36] The Alliance memorandum noted:

> The constitution should provide for nationality laws that would build a peaceful and stable independent federation, with a contented and unified people whose loyalty is unquestioned and undivided, so that, in due course, the country can take its proper place in the comity of nations. To achieve this end, it is essential to have a nationality law which provides for a common nationality, to the exclusion of all others.[37]

The Alliance nevertheless was aware that there was opposition from certain groups and sections of the population on the further liberalisation of citizenship, and the coalition had to toe a fine line in crafting their citizenship proposals.

There were several categories of citizens and others who were entitled to be citizens in the federation following the coming into force of the 1948 Federation of Malaya Agreement, and the Alliance sought to address this in their memorandum. The first proposal in the Alliance's memorandum stated that all existing federal citizens should be accepted as citizens of the federation.[38] This was a recognition of the existing rights of those who were already federal citizens under the federation agreement and the enactments introduced in 1952. The memorandum noted: "We would, therefore, wish that all those who are Federal citizens by operation of law, registration or naturalisation on the date of the declaration of independence should be accepted as the first nationals of Malaysia."[39] This included British subjects in the Settlements of Penang and Malacca (who were automatically federal citizens under the 1948 federation agreement), but this latter group, as we will see next, was given a choice to choose between the federal citizenship and their existing status as British subjects within a year after independence. If they chose to retain their status as British subjects, they would have to renounce their Malayan nationality.[40] The Alliance was strongly opposed to the concept of dual nationality which they felt would create divided loyalties. And, as we will see next, the subject was vigorously debated in the constitutional discussions as the British government had recommended in their memorandum that these British subjects should be entitled to retain both nationalities. The constitutional commission, too, felt that dual nationality was an accepted international practice and should be recognised by the independent federation.

The Alliance proposed that those born in Malaysia (the term used for the independent federation in the memorandum) on Merdeka Day and thereafter should be nationals of the federation.[41] The Alliance memorandum stated: "To ensure a common nationality, we would want the constitution to provide that those born in Malaysia on and after the declaration of independence should be nationals of Malaysia."[42] This essentially meant that the Alliance accepted the principle of *jus soli* or right by birth. However, in the case of nationals born in the country of alien parents on or after the date of independence, UMNO suggested that they should be free to choose their nationality on reaching the age of 21 years. UMNO wanted the constitution to contain a provision stating that such persons should cease to be nationals after attaining the age of 21 years unless they made a declaration of retention of nationality within a year.[43] The MCA and the MIC, however, did not agree with the UMNO colleagues on this proviso.[44] In addition, the Alliance proposed that anyone born outside the federation after the declaration of independence, whose father at the time of the child's birth was a national, "should be eligible to become a national."[45] The Alliance discriminated a little against women as they proposed that a woman who was a legal wife of a national "should be entitled" on making an application to be registered as a national; it was not an automatic right. This meant that the state had greater discretion and their application could be rejected. The provisions for acquisition of citizenship in post-independent Malaya were more stringent. The interested person had to be 21 years of age, of good character, take an oath of allegiance and abjure allegiance to any other country, declare their intention to reside in Malaya permanently, must have resided in Malaya for 10 of the following 12 years preceding their application and have a reasonable knowledge of Malay.[46] The constitutions of several Commonwealth nations allowed for the acquisition of citizenship after a period of residence of five years.

The Alliance recognised the existence of a substantial "alien population problem" in Malaya and felt this could affect national unity and sought to provide for these groups to acquire the federation citizenship under a separate section on "transitional provisions."[47] The Alliance memorandum noted:

> However, we recognise the fact that a large alien population exists in the Federation of Malaya, and that the continued existence of such an element will not be in the interests of national unity. We consider it is vital to such unity that the nationals of the independent Federation should comprise all those who genuinely desire to make the Federation their home and the object of their undivided loyalty. We, therefore, consider it imperative as a step towards solving our alien population problem in the interests of national unity, that in the case of these existing aliens there should be some relaxation of the qualifications to encourage those who genuinely desire to be the nationals of this country to make this their home and the object of their undivided loyalty.[48]

Under these "transitional provisions," the Alliance proposed that those born in the country before independence "should be entitled" on registration to become nationals provided that they were 18 years of age, of good character, took an oath of allegiance, declared their intention to stay permanently, had resided in Malaya for five of the preceding seven years and had a simple knowledge of Malay. The language qualification was to be waived for a year (but the MIC felt two years would be preferable).[49] Under these provisions an alien who was not born in the country but was a resident there before independence would be "eligible" to become nationals if he was 18 years of age, of good character, took an oath of allegiance, declared his intention to reside permanently, had resided in Malaya for eight of the 12 years preceding the application and had a simple knowledge of Malay.[50] The language requirements would be waived for those above 45 years for a year (but the MIC felt that two years would be preferable).[51] The Alliance's proposals were a compromise between the Alliance parties, but, as we have seen earlier, the MCA and MIC had some misgivings on some elements of the proposals.

The rulers' proposals

The Malay rulers were quite liberal in their proposals on citizenship. The rulers' representatives, led by Queen's Counsel Neil Lawson, submitted that on and after the date of independence, anybody who is born in the federation, or born outside the federation whose father is at that date a federal citizen, except by descent only, "should automatically acquire citizenship of the federation."[52] This was a recognition of the principle of *jus soli*. Secondly, the rulers agreed that the then existing status of a subject of a ruler to be acquired by either operation of law or naturalisation "should be continued in the overall framework of Federal nationality."[53] The rulers also submitted that acquisition of citizenship by registration, whether it was a state or federal citizenship, should be discontinued, except for residents of the federation on the date of independence who should be given a further period in which to be registered as citizens.[54] The rulers did not stipulate any time-frame in which this should be done, except that the applicants should be given "sufficient time."[55] On the language test, the rulers felt that the test for those intending to acquire citizenship should be a simple Malay spoken test, without a written test.[56]

The rulers, however, were strongly against the idea of dual nationality. They felt those who had acquired federal citizenship should not retain the status of citizens of the United Kingdom and the Colonies.[57] This mainly affected the residents in the settlements of Penang and Malacca who enjoyed the status of "citizens of the United Kingdom and Colonies" as these states were Crown colonies under the direct jurisdiction of the Crown. The British government had wanted the new constitution to make provisions for these subjects to continue to enjoy their status as "citizens of the United Kingdom and the Colonies" and had stressed this in a memorandum addressed to the constitutional commission.[58] The memorandum stated:

> As it has already been agreed that the Federation of Malaya will remain within the Commonwealth, the United Kingdom consider it to be of greatest importance that the form of citizenship law recommended for the Federation should be one which would accord with the Commonwealth citizenship scheme. This would mean that the citizenship law of the Federation of Malaya would provide that citizens of the Federation and of the other Commonwealth countries should have common status.[59]

Britain urged the commission to ensure that the inhabitants of the Settlements of Penang and Malacca were not deprived of any rights or facilities which they presently enjoyed when acquiring the citizenship of the federation.[60] The memorandum reminded the constitutional commission that the qualifications for the inhabitants of the Settlements to acquire the federal citizenship should not be stricter than those required for citizenship of the United Kingdom and the Colonies.[61]

The commission was in favour of the continuation of this status which they felt did not contradict with existing international practices in regard to dual nationality. Justice B. Malik asked the counsel for the rulers, Neil Lawson, why they objected to this as the principle of "dual nationality" was an internationally well-recognised principle. Lawson said the rulers felt that this position was inconsistent with the terms of reference creating a common nationality for the whole federation if some people were to hold two citizenships and spoke of the "loyalty problem." Lawson explained:

> Now if one is endeavouring to build up a loyalty to the country and get over difficulties which do undoubtedly exist, one of the ways of doing it is to establish a Federal Citizenship which is the political expression of the ideal of loyalty to the country. Now in our view the status of State subjects is within that framework, and the status of citizens of the United Kingdom and the Colonies falls outside that framework.[62]

The rulers, however, noted that they were not against the concept of "Commonwealth citizenship" which accorded Malayans, as long as Malaya remained in the Commonwealth, certain rights and privileges as Commonwealth citizens.[63]

Dual nationality

The Alliance was also against the continuation of a dual nationality as they felt that this would raise the question of loyalty of the new citizens of the federation. In the hearing before the commission, the Alliance made it clear that those who were British subjects, particularly from the Settlements of Penang and Malacca, should declare themselves as nationals of independent Malaya. If they wanted to remain as British subjects, they would not be considered as nationals of independent Malaya.[64] But the Alliance accepted that they could continue to be "Commonwealth citizens," a looser category of citizenship which, particularly in countries such as Britain and Canada, afforded certain rights to citizens of other Commonwealth countries. Reid, however, told the Alliance that dual nationality should not pose a problem because it was accepted international practice:

> There are many people with dual nationality and it does not cause much trouble. Of course anybody who is a Federal citizen is, in the eyes of international law, a Malayan or a Malaysian. There is no question as to his nationality in international law. It is possible to have two nationalities both within the Commonwealth, or maybe one within and one outside.[65]

The Alliance, however, maintained that this could give rise to divided loyalties and would not be suitable for a new nation. The Tunku explained the Alliance's position:

> For a new nation, it will be rather troublesome later. It is all right for an established or old nation; it can make all sorts of laws. But, at this moment, our main interest is to try and bring these people towards one common nationality and that is the reason why we have provided in our terms of reference that there shall be common loyalty, so that the loyalty of the people shall not be divided. They shall be for Malaya alone. We made no provision that those in Malacca shall be British subjects and at the same time citizens or subjects of Malaya. We will find that their interest, loyalty and everything else will be rather divided and that, we fear, will create different feelings among the people in this country. A person in Malacca will say that he is a British subject, so he can claim all the rights of a British subject, and at the same time enjoy all the rights that a Federal citizen can have. There is bound to be a little feeling of jealousy from the side of the Federal citizen who is entitled to what is given to Federal citizens.[66]

Reid then noted that the Alliance had made its position quite clear and their views would be given due consideration. In the commission's report, largely written by Reid, the constitutional commission chairman explained at length why they thought that the Alliance arguments were misconceived.[67] The report stated:

> It has been represented to us that dual nationality within the Commonwealth is undesirable in that it may lead to divided loyalty. We do not agree, and we think that this view is based on some misunderstanding. It is well recognised in International Law and custom that a person who has dual citizenship owes undivided loyalty to the country in which he is residing, and that the Government of the other country of which he is also a citizen should not seek to interfere between him and the Government of the country in which he is residing. In the same way we think that, in the case of dual territorial citizenship within the Commonwealth, the person with such dual citizenship owes undivided loyalty to the country in which he is residing, and that the Government of the other Commonwealth country of which he is a citizen ought not to seek to come between him and the Government of the country in which he is residing.[68]

In the hearing given to the Alliance, Reid raised the question of "aliens" who were born in Malaya being free to choose their nationality on attaining the age of 21 years (proposed by UMNO), noting that one could not effectively renounce such rights and some countries (such as Britain) would not allow their subjects to renounce their citizenship:

> All you can say is that you won't do anything to rely on this – you won't take advantage of any right which may be given by these foreign countries. Can

> you really do more effectively than that, because that would apply and that would seem to meet the point you have in mind, I think – I am not sure.[69]

Razak replied that the Alliance would be satisfied once these persons had declared their allegiance.[70] On the question of language test, UMNO felt those who applied within a year need not undergo a language test, but the MIC argued that a two-year period would be more adequate. When Reid asked why such a longer period was needed, the MIC representative in the Alliance, K. Ramanathan, explained: "Because most of them [Indians] are in the estates, they might find it difficult to go through the process. It was thought a longer period would be most satisfactory; it would be difficult to organise them."[71] Ramanathan noted that there would be thousands of applicants, and they would have to travel twice: first, for the application and second, for the test, and a two-year period would make the process easier. The MCA representative Ng Ek Teong in supporting his colleague noted of the practical difficulty for the Indians to get referees to support their application. Tunku, however, maintained that one year was preferred and that UMNO felt strongly on this issue: "We feel, politically, it is untenable because the objection is very strong. If a real effort is made to be citizens of this country, it can be made very quickly indeed."[72] UMNO was under considerable pressure from within the party ranks and from Malay opposition parties not to concede much ground on the citizenship provisions.

The other organisations that submitted on citizenship, with the exception of some political parties, were aligned along communal lines. Chinese and Indian groups sought the recognition of the principle of *jus soli* retrospectively and for a shorter period of residence to enable the acquisition of federal citizenship, and that the language test should be waived. Many Malay organisations, on the other hand, requested that the principle of *jus soli* should not be recognised and wanted a longer period of residence before a person could qualify to apply for federal citizenship.[73] The other political parties such as the People's Progressive Party, the Labour Party and the Pan-Malayan Islamic Party proposed something close to these proposals, and their suggestions were to an extent influenced by the communal or non-communal make-up of these organisations. In general, it can be said that these groups proposed a period of residence of between five and ten years for the acquisition of federal citizenship by the non-Malays. There was very limited debate within these organisations and hardly any lengthy discussion when they were given a hearing by the Reid Commission. The constitutional documents indicate that it was the Alliance Party, as the ruling party, which set the tone on the issue of citizenship in the constitutional deliberations.

Reid Commission's recommendations

The Reid Commission viewed the Alliance proposals as the best possible compromise between the communities and adopted almost wholly the Alliance's recommendations. In their report, the commission noted:

> Many different proposals have been submitted to us in memoranda and in evidence with regard to qualification for citizenship of the Federation. We

have carefully considered them all and we have come to the conclusion that the best proposals for dealing fairly with the present situation are those put forward by the Alliance. The parties of the Alliance have given full consideration to this matter and apart from a few minor points they have reached agreement. We are satisfied that this agreement is a reasonable and proper compromise between the views of the parties, each of which has the most widespread support from the race which it represents, and we are further satisfied that this agreement is a better way of doing justice between the races than any other that has been suggested or has occurred to us.[74]

The main exception in the Reid Commission's recommendations was their acceptance of dual citizenship which the Alliance strongly objected. They sought to provide adequate protection in the constitution to cover all affected groups. Through Articles 14 and 15, the commission recommended that all those born in the federation on or after Merdeka Day should be citizens by operation of law, but they rejected appeals by some groups to apply the principle of *jus soli* retrospectively.[75] The commission noted:

We received many representations that the principle which has come to be known generally in Malaya as *jus soli* should be given retrospective effect. We are not entirely satisfied that it is entirely possible or desirable to provide that all those born in Malaya, whatever be the date of their birth, wherever they may be now, and whatever their present nationality, should be retrospectively made citizens of the Federation by operation of law.[76]

Under Article 15 (1) the commission provided for those who were entitled to be registered as citizens before Merdeka Day to be registered as citizens on application. Article 15 (1) was essentially for those British subjects who were entitled to be registered as citizens of the federation under the 1948 federation agreement but who had not yet registered to continue to be accorded this right. The commission felt that this group should be entitled to this right.[77]

In respect of acquisition of citizenship by registration, the commission, under Article 16 and Article 18, provided for those born in the federation before Merdeka Day to be registered as citizens if they intended to reside permanently in the federation and were willing to take an oath of allegiance and had resided in the federation for five of the preceding seven years, besides having an elementary knowledge of Malay (although the language requirement would be waived for the first year).[78] The Commission felt that the applicants should not be required to renounce any foreign citizenship, despite the Alliance's request, as we have seen earlier, for two reasons.[79] First, they felt that the principle of dual nationality was an accepted principle in international law and were not convinced of the Alliance's claim that it would create divided loyalties. Second, the Commission observed that in some countries it was not possible to renounce their nationality (as, for example, in Britain) and it would not be fair to expect such persons to renounce their nationality. The practice of holding two nationalities in Britain was quite normal as many locals held Canadian, Irish and Australian nationalities. Thus, Reid, Jennings and McKell regarded dual nationality as an accepted international norm. Justice Abdul Hamid and Justice Malik, too, agreed with their colleagues on dual nationality as both Pakistan and India provided for recognition of dual nationality on independence.

Under Article 17, the commission provided, in line with the Alliance's proposal, that residents who were not born in Malaya but who had made Malaya their permanent home and had shown their loyalty should be entitled to be eligible to be registered as citizens if they had resided in the federation for eight of the preceding 12 years. This provision, the commission said, was to enable a common nationality to develop. The commission's report noted:

> Those to whom this recommendation applies [Article 17] are very numerous, and, in order, that a sense of common nationality should develop, we think that it is important that those who have shown their loyalty to the Federation and have made it their permanent home, should participate in the rights and duties of citizenship.[80]

Article 19 provided for acquisition citizenship by naturalisation. The applicant should be 21 years of age, of good character and must have resided in the federation for 10 of the preceding 12 years.[81]

Justice Abdul Hamid differed a little on some of the commission's recommendations and noted his objections separately in a dissenting note. Hamid's first objection was in relation to Article 15 (1) of the commission's draft constitution which he felt favoured persons in the Settlements of Penang and Malacca over the residents of the other states and said that the Alliance had not requested this.[82] Hamid felt Article 15 (1) conferred rights of citizenship on persons who were merely "entitled" to be registered as citizens of the federation under Clause 126 of 1948 Federation of Malaya Agreement. Hamid noted:

> A demand for a provision of this kind was not made by anybody. Right of citizenship under Clause 126 of the Federation of Malaya Agreement 1948 is claimable as of right by persons who are citizens of the United Kingdom and Colonies, and were born in the Federation. On applications alone such persons are, as of right, entitled to become citizens of the Federation, provided that they have been in residence in the Federation for five years or if resident outside they are certified to have maintained substantial connection with the Federation. Under the Federation Agreement of 1948 they enjoyed certain privileges which were not available to other persons born in the Federation. In the presence of Article 16 in the new Draft there is no need for a provision of this kind because that Article covers a person born in the Federation whether they are citizens of the United Kingdom or not. If Clause 126 of the Federation of Malaya Agreement 1948 be imported into the new Constitution Citizens of the United Kingdom and Colonies will continue to remain in position of advantage over other persons born in the Federation who are not citizens of the United Kingdom and Colonies.[83]

Hamid felt that Article 15 should be omitted.[84] The majority in the commission, however, felt that all who enjoyed rights of citizenship before Merdeka Day "should continue to have such rights."[85] Sir Ivor Jennings, in his response to Hamid's note of dissent, said Article 15 (1) was unanimously inserted in the draft constitution at its first reading in early December 1956 and only affected a small number of people. Jennings remarked:

> The number of persons to whom it applies is small, since the great majority of persons to whom Clause 126 of the Federation Agreement might have applied are citizens by operation of law under Clause 125 (6), (c), (d) and (e), and their rights are protected by Article 14, not article 15 (1).[86]

The commission thus did not think that Hamid's differences of view on Article 15 (1) were significant, but they felt that those who were entitled to citizenship should not be deprived of this right.

Referring to Article 17, Hamid noted that citizenship by registration which was permissible under this article should be given at the discretion of the Federal Government and should not be claimable as of right.[87] Hamid argued that Articles 16 and 17 were based on the recommendations made by the Alliance and should be closely followed:

> Persons falling within the ambit of Article 16 are those born in the Federation and by reason of birth have been allowed to claim citizenship as of right. This Article in fact confers right of *jus soli* retrospectively if birth is accompanied by at least five years residence. But under Article 17, eight years' residence alone has been made the foundation for the claim. If the claim is founded on residence alone citizenship should not ensue as of right but should be within the discretion of the Federal Government. The Alliance Memorandum clearly distinguished between the two cases. It said with respect to persons born in the Federation that they shall be entitled on application to become nationals. But in respect of persons born outside the Federation and depending on residence alone, the recommendation was "Those aliens who have not been born in this country but have been residents here before and up to the date of the Independence, should also be eligible to become nationals." The language used in the [Alliance] Memorandum in my view clearly means that registration in the case of persons born outside the Federation should be in the discretion of the Federal Government.[88]

Jennings in response to Hamid's criticism of Articles 16 and 17 said both these articles were in line with the "transitional provisions" suggested by the Alliance, adding that in that part of the memorandum the Alliance was dealing with registration and not naturalisation.[89]

The constitutional commission did not include any reference in the draft constitution to subjects of the Malay rulers, a category of citizenship that was introduced in 1952 under an amendment to the 1948 Federation Agreement. The majority in the commission felt that to retain this provision would be inconsistent with the creation of a common nationality for the federation. The report of the commission noted:

> Under the Federation Agreement all subjects of a Ruler are citizens of the Federation by operation of law. We think that to allow this provision to remain would be inconsistent with the creation of a common nationality for the whole Federation, because citizenship of the Federation must depend on, and be conferred by, Federal law and not State law. Accordingly we do not include in our proposed qualifications for citizenship any reference to being a subject of a Ruler.[90]

But the majority in the commission nevertheless did not have any objection to persons who were federal citizens being also subjects of a ruler. They left it to state law to define subjects of the ruler. Sir William McKell and Justice Abdul Hamid did not agree with the majority on this as they felt it would be inconsistent with the principle of a common citizenship and work against national unity for each of the nine rulers to have subjects of his own.[91]

The commission also recommended (under Article 23) that the federation recognise the status of "Commonwealth citizenship."[92] The British government had under the British Nationality Act, 1948, introduced the category of "Commonwealth citizenship," and this created the status of "Citizen of the United Kingdom and Colonies," which provided that every citizen in the Commonwealth should have the status of Commonwealth citizen. This Act had been adopted by most Commonwealth countries so that Commonwealth citizens would not be considered "aliens" in any other Commonwealth country and would have certain rights and privileges. The commission felt that the status of Commonwealth citizen was a valuable link within the Commonwealth and recommended that the federation should recognise this category of a broader territorial citizenship.[93] In countries such as Britain, Commonwealth citizens have greater rights than persons outside the Commonwealth. This nevertheless remained a thorny issue when it was discussed in the Working Party which reviewed the commission's draft constitution and at the final constitutional talks in London in May 1957.

The commission was very cautious in the provisions for termination of citizenship to prevent any abuse by the state and only made provisions for such deprivation of citizenship in extraordinary circumstances. The deprivation of citizenship was largely reserved to cases in which the federal citizen had taken up another citizenship or in the case of those who acquired federal citizenship through naturalisation and who had committed acts of disloyalty. It also provided for voluntary renunciation of citizenship (Article 21). The commission recommended that a citizen, by operation of law or by registration under Articles 15 and 16, should not be deprived of his citizenship unless the person becomes a citizen of another country.[94] To protect the country against disloyalty by any citizen who voluntarily acquires a foreign citizenship and takes advantage of it, the commission recommended, under

Article 22, that the person should be deprived of that citizenship.[95] The commission also provided for the deprivation of citizenship if a person obtained his citizenship by fraud or concealment (Article 23).[96] The draft constitution provided for the deprivation of citizenship for a person who had not obtained his citizenship by birth or descent "if he is also a citizen of another country and he has shown himself by act or speech to be disloyal or disaffected towards the Federation," or had been imprisoned for not less than two years within five years of naturalisation, or had traded with the enemy in any war.[97] Citizens deprived of citizenship would have legal recourse to defend themselves. The commission provided for any citizen against whom action is to be taken to deprive him of his citizenship (Article 23 (6), (7) and (8)) to be informed of the grounds for such action and to be given the opportunity to have his case referred to a committee of inquiry headed by a chairman with judicial experience.[98]

The Working Party and the London discussions

The Working Party, comprising representatives of the Alliance government, the rulers and the High Commissioner Sir Donald MacGillivray, which met between February and April 1957, made some changes to the provisions relating to citizenship, but on the whole left intact most of the compromises which had been reached between the Alliance parties. These changes mainly related to acquisition of citizenship by registration (Articles 15, 16 and 17), where UMNO insisted that the state should have some discretion in the award of citizenship, and provisions which recognised dual citizenship. In the first Working Party meeting on 22 February chaired by MacGillivray, the UMNO representatives said that they preferred if Article 17 could be drafted such that persons to whom it applied could not claim citizenship as of right.[99] This was in line with the suggestion made by Justice Hamid (see earlier) who had argued in his note of dissent that the government should have the discretion to confer citizenship on this category of people to whom this applied. The rulers representatives, however, said they preferred the draft of Article 17 as it stood.[100] After further discussion, the Working Party eventually agreed that citizenship under this category would be awarded at the discretion of the government.[101]

In regard to Article 18 of the draft constitution which provided for an oath of allegiance for those acquiring citizenship by registration under Articles 15, 16 and 17, the Alliance suggested that persons who obtained citizenship through registration (Article 18 (1)(b)) should be required to "abjure or renounce foreign nationality."[102] The Alliance was concerned that this clause implied that the federation recognised dual nationality. MacGillivray pointed out in the committee that if the Alliance proposal was accepted, the federation government would then not be able to deprive a person of his citizenship, if he had been compelled to abjure his foreign nationality.[103] It was also noted that it was doubtful if the country whose nationality the person had been forced to renounce would be prepared to accept such a "stateless" person.[104] It would be mean that such a person would become stateless, having renounced his other nationality. In regard to Article 18 (1)(b), the Colonial

Office felt that the Alliance's objection was misconceived as some countries did not allow their nationals to renounce their citizenship. "A person can only effectively renounce a foreign nationality if the law of the country allowed him to do so," replied the Colonial Office to MacGillivray's note on the issue, pointing out the case of the United Kingdom.[105] When Article 18 was discussed at the eighth meeting of the Working Party, the rulers' representatives said they were willing to accept the article but the Alliance was adamant that those who obtained citizenship through Article 15, 16 or 17 should be required to renounce all loyalty to any foreign country in their oath of allegiance.[106] At the last meeting of the Working Party on 27 April 1957, the Alliance reiterated their objection to Article 18. Tunku told the Working Party that the Alliance was in doubt as to the implications of the Article 18 and as to whether the provision meant the law of the federation permitted dual nationality.[107] It was then agreed that the question of dual nationality should be discussed in London.[108] At the London constitutional talks, the Alliance eventually conceded some ground on this and agreed that those who enjoyed dual nationality would be given a year to decide if they wanted to retain their federal citizenship or the other nationality. The form of oath of allegiance to be taken was varied a little to emphasise that all federal citizens owed undivided loyalty to the federation.[109] The Alliance also recognised the status of "Commonwealth citizens" which provided certain rights and privileges for Malayan citizens in Commonwealth countries.

Article 15 also drew some debate in the Working Party. The Alliance suggested that the first clause in Article 15 should be omitted as had been pointed out by Justice Hamid.[110] MacGillivray, however, pointed out this clause was "merely continuing a right which at present existed."[111] Hamid had argued that Article 15 (1) conferred rights of citizenship on persons who were merely "entitled" to be registered as citizens of the federation under Clause 126 of 1948 Federation of Malaya Agreement, and that it privileged this category of persons compared to others.[112] Hamid suggested that Article 15 should be omitted.[113] The secretary of state was very much opposed to the Alliance suggestion, stating that no persons should be deprived of existing citizenship rights. In a telegram to MacGillivray, the secretary of state noted: "Article 15. We think it of cardinal importance that persons should not be deprived of existing citizenship rights under C1.126 of the Federation Agreement and therefore this Article should stand."[114] The majority in the constitutional commission felt that all who enjoyed rights of citizenship before Merdeka Day should continue to have such rights.[115] The Working Party eventually decided to remove the first clause of Article 15 from Part III of the constitution and to include it in Part XIII (Temporary and Transitional Provisions) which enabled those who were entitled to this right to make a choice within a year if they wanted to acquire the federal citizenship.[116] The proviso would cease to have effect one year after independence. In regard to the Alliance's earlier proposal on Article 14 that a person born in the federation after Merdeka of alien parents should be required to make a declaration of intention in regard to his nationality on reaching 21 years of age, the Alliance's representatives informed the last meeting of the Working Party that they had decided not to proceed with their proposed change.[117]

The Alliance objected to Article 142 which provided for a "Commonwealth citizenship" that conferred some rights and privileges for citizens of the federation in another Commonwealth country.[118] The Alliance viewed it as a form of dual citizenship and argued that it would create divided loyalties in the federation. The Colonial Office, however, felt this provision would not create such difficulties and were particularly concerned that persons in the Settlements of Penang and Malacca who would most benefit from this provision, being citizens of the United Kingdom and Colonies, should not be deprived of such a right.[119] That is, they should continue to enjoy their rights as British subjects while embracing the new federal citizenship. The Alliance eventually conceded on this article and recognised the status of "Commonwealth citizens."

At the London constitutional talks in May 1957 the Alliance repeated their disapproval of provisions in the draft constitution relating to dual citizenship. The Alliance deputy leader, Dato' Abdul Razak, told the meeting that if dual citizenship was recognised, those having dual citizenship would "enjoy the best of both worlds" and he feared that this could lead to dual loyalties.[120] The Colonial Office, however, thought that it was inconsistent with Commonwealth practice to require that a person who acquired a Commonwealth citizenship should lose the citizenship of the federation.[121] The Colonial Office pointed out that there was a distinction between exercising another citizenship rights in a foreign country and in a Commonwealth country.[122] The Alliance also raised some dissatisfaction with Article 24 which was redrafted by the Commons parliamentary draftsmen. Tunku, for example, told the meeting that the Alliance was not happy with the latest draft of Article 24(2) prepared by the parliamentary draftsmen which contained the phrase "any citizen who is also a citizen of any foreign country." He said he did not want the constitution to indicate that a citizen could possess dual citizenship.[123] While the Alliance accepted the "Commonwealth citizenship," they did not wish citizens of other Commonwealth countries to have extra rights beyond those enjoyed by virtue of Commonwealth citizenship. The Malayan delegation asked that the word "foreign" be deleted.[124] Eventually, the Alliance conceded on the main outstanding issue at the London constitutional talks, that of dual nationality and the issue of "Commonwealth citizenship." The Alliance agreed to enable federal citizens to continue to enjoy the citizenship of the United Kingdom and Colonies for a year after independence, after which the persons concerned would have to choose either the federal citizenship or United Kingdom citizenship. The Alliance also agreed to recognise the status of "Commonwealth citizens" when they realised that this provision was more symbolic in nature and that it mainly enabled Commonwealth citizens to enjoy certain privileges and rights while in the United Kingdom.[125]

The citizenship provisions in the new constitution were essentially based on the Alliance's compromises that had been reached between the three component parties of the coalition and which were deemed by the Reid constitutional commission as the best proposals for "dealing fairly with the present situation."[126] The complex Alliance compromises on citizenship were viewed by the commission as being reflective of the wishes of the majority of the communities in

Malaya. The main departure by the commission from the views of the Alliance, as we have seen earlier, was on the issue of dual citizenship which the Alliance strongly opposed.

Notes

1 Ivor Jennings, *The constitution of Ceylon* (London: Oxford University Press, 1953), p. 37. See also Daniel Gorman, *Imperial citizenship* (Manchester: Manchester University Press, 2006), pp. 9–28.
2 Jennings, *The constitution of Ceylon*, p. 37.
3 Ibid., pp. 38–39.
4 See Note on British subjects by Sir Ivor Jennings, 2 October 1956, CO 889/2 (1), C.C. 2000/27, p. 1. See also Paper on British subjects in the Federation of Malaya by Ivor Jennings, 15 October 1956, CO 889/2 (268), C.C. 2000/40, pp. 1–2.
5 Note on British subjects by Sir Ivor Jennings, 2 October 1956, CO 889/2 (1), C.C. 2000/27, p. 1.
6 This point that Indians were British subjects by virtue of the British Nationality Act and hence automatically federal citizens, as the residents in Penang and Malacca which were Crown colonies, was noted by Sir Ivor Jennings (see Summary record of 47th meeting of Constitutional Commission, 10 October 1956, CO 889/1 (50), p. 1) and Justice Abdul Hamid (see Summary record of 19th meeting of Constitutional Commission, 21 August 1956, CO 889/1 (23), p. 4.) when the Reid constitutional commission was deliberating the new Malayan federal constitution in 1956. Renowned Malayan lawyer R. Ramani also made this point when the 1952 State Nationality Bill was discussed in a select committee of the federal legislative council in 1952.
7 Cowan, *Nineteenth-century Malaya*, pp. 99–212.
8 K.G. Tregonning, *A history of modern Malaya* (Singapore: Eastern Universities Press, 1964), pp. 162–207.
9 See Memorandum to Federation of Malaya Constitutional Commission by the United Kingdom government, 1 August 1956, CO 1030/134 (6).
10 See Albert Lau, *The Malayan Union controversy, 1942–1948* (Singapore: Oxford University Press, 1991); and A.J. Stockwell, *British policy and Malay politics during the Malayan Union experiment, 1942–1948* (Kuala Lumpur: Malayan Branch of Royal Asiatic Society, Monograph 8, 1979).
11 See Memorandum by secretary of state on question of nationality in India and Burma, 1 April 1947, CO 537/1910 (194). See also Memorandum to Federation of Malaya Constitutional Commission by the United Kingdom government, 1 August 1956, CO 1030/134 (6).
12 The status of "British subject" has the same meaning as the status of "Commonwealth citizen" under United Kingdom legislation. See Memorandum to Federation of Malaya Constitutional Commission by the United Kingdom government, 1 August 1956, CO 1030/134 (6).
13 The countries which recognised this status of "Commonwealth citizens" or "British subjects" as defined under Section 1 of the British Nationality Act, 1948, were Canada, Australia, New Zealand, South Africa, India, Pakistan, Southern Rhodesia and Ceylon. The term "Commonwealth citizen" is the same as "British subject" as defined in the 1948 British Nationality Act. The British Nationality Act, 1948, came into force on 1 January 1949. Citizenship of the United Kingdom could be obtained through birth, descent (a child born to a father who is a citizen of the United Kingdom and Colonies), registration (a citizen of the Commonwealth has the right to acquire citizenship of the United Kingdom and the Colonies if ordinarily resident in the United Kingdom and the Colonies for a year), married women (a woman who marries a citizen of the United Kingdom and Colonies has the right to be registered as a citizen) and naturalisation (this

is discretionary and requires a period of residence in the United Kingdom or colonies for five years). See Memorandum to Federation of Malaya Constitutional Commission by the United Kingdom government, 1 August 1956, CO 1030/134 (6).

14 See Memorandum to Federation of Malaya Constitutional Commission by the United Kingdom government, 1 August 1956, CO 1030/134 (6). See also Note on British subjects by Sir Ivor Jennings, 2 October 1956, CO 889/2 (1), C.C. 2000/27; and Paper on citizens of the United Kingdom and Colonies in Penang and Malacca by Justice B. Malik, CO 889/2, C.C. 2000/18.

15 Lau, *The Malayan Union controversy*, pp. 123–145; and Stockwell, *British policy and Malay politics*, pp. 17–73.

16 Lau, *The Malayan Union controversy*, pp. 152–209.

17 Ibid., pp. 212–249.

18 Ibid., pp. 219–229. The committee was headed by H.R. Cheeseman, the Director of Education in Malaya.

19 The federal citizenship is outlined in Part XII of the Federation of Malaya Agreement, 1948.

20 See Note on Citizenship of the Federation of Malaya, September 1952, CO 1022/175 (8).

21 Ibid.

22 Ibid.

23 It was estimated that 350,000 Chinese and 225,000 Indians were eligible for citizenship by operation of law under the federation agreement. As of May 1952, about 350,000 citizenship certificates had been granted. See note on Citizenship of the Federation of Malaya, September 1952, CO 1022/175 (8).

24 The Communities Liaison Committee was an unofficial but influential body made up of Malayan community leaders such as Dato' Onn Jaafar, Sir Tan Cheng Lock, E.E.C. Thuraisingham and Panglima Bukit Gantang and held many confidential meetings between 1951 and 1952 to discuss inter-communal issues such as citizenship, education, Malay economic problems, local elections and others. Its discussions were guided by the commissioner-general for Southeast Asia Malcolm MacDonald. While the body was informal, its recommendations were well received by the federation government. For more details, see Joseph M. Fernando, "Elite inter-communal bargaining and conflict resolution: The role of the Communities Liaison Committee in Malaya, 1949–1951," *Journal of Southeast Asian Studies*, Vol. 43. No. 2, June 2012, pp. 280–301.

25 See Note on Citizenship of the Federation of Malaya, September 1952, CO 1022/175 (8). The Federation of Malaya Agreement (Amendment) Ordinance 1952 was passed by the federal legislative council in May 1952 and the related state enactments by September 1952. The new citizenship code came into force on 5 September 1952. See also Memorandum to Federation of Malaya Constitutional Commission by the United Kingdom government, 1 August 1956, CO 1030/134 (6). The changes made in 1952 were contained in a new Part XII of the Federation of Malaya Agreement (Amendment) Ordinance, 1952) which came into effect from 15 September 1952.

26 See Memorandum by the United Kingdom government to Federation of Malaya Constitutional Commission, 1 August 1956, CO 1030/134 (6). State nationality could be obtained by *operation of law* (subjects of the rulers included a member of an aboriginal tribe in the state, a Malay born in the state or any person born in the state or one of whose parents was born in the state), *registration* (subject to certain exceptions, a person born in the state is entitled to be registered as a subject of a ruler if he can speak Malay or English, is of good character and has taken an oath of allegiance) and *naturalisation* (the ruler may grant a certificate of naturalisation to a person if he has resided in the federation for 10 out of the preceding 12 years, is of good character, speaks Malay or English and intends to settle permanently in the federation). See also Note on federal citizenship by Justice Abdul Hamid, 27 June 1956, CO 889/2, C.C. 2000/2.

27 See Note on Citizenship of the Federation of Malaya, September 1952, CO 1022/175 (8).

28 Ibid.
29 See "Note on citizenship of the Federation of Malaya and subjects of the Rulers of the Malaya States," by Justice Abdul Hamid, 27 June 1956, CO 889/2, C.C. 2000/2, p. 6.
30 Ibid., p. 6.
31 Memorandum on citizenship by Sir Ivor Jennings, 31 July 1956, CO 889/2, C.C. 2000/7, p. 1.
32 Ibid., p. 1.
33 See Memorandum to Federation of Malaya Constitutional Commission by the United Kingdom government, 1 August 1956, CO 1030/134 (6). See also Summary record of 29th meeting of Constitutional Commission, 11 September 1956, CO 889/1 (32), pp. 1–3, for the commission's discussions on dual citizenship.
34 Alliance memorandum, 27 September 1956, UMNO/SUA 154/56, pp. 11–16.
35 See Memorandum by Tunku Abdul Rahman, 1 March 1955, MCA Files, PH/A/008/4.
36 Alliance memorandum, 27 September 1956, UMNO/SUA 154/56, p. 11.
37 Ibid.
38 Ibid.
39 Ibid.
40 Ibid., p. 12.
41 Ibid.
42 Ibid.
43 Ibid.
44 Ibid., p. 13.
45 Ibid.
46 Ibid., p. 14.
47 Ibid.
48 Ibid.
49 Ibid., p. 15.
50 Ibid.
51 Ibid.
52 Report of hearing given to the Rulers, 14–15 September 1956, CO 889/1 (32), p. 32.
53 Ibid., p. 33.
54 Ibid.
55 Ibid.
56 Ibid.
57 Report of hearing given to the Rulers, 14–15 September 1956, CO 889/1 (32), p. 34. See also Memorandum by rulers to the constitutional commission, 6 September 1956, CO 1030/134 (16).
58 See Memorandum to Federation of Malaya Constitutional Commission by the United Kingdom government, 1 August 1956, CO 1030/134 (6).
59 See Memorandum to Federation of Malaya Constitutional Commission by the United Kingdom government, 1 August 1956, CO 1030/134 (6), p. 18. See also minute by R.W. Newsam, 24 July 1956 in CO 1030/134.
60 See Memorandum to Federation of Malaya Constitutional Commission by the United Kingdom government, 1 August 1956, CO 1030/134 (6), p. 20.
61 Ibid., p. 20.
62 Report of hearing given to the Rulers, 14–15 September 1956, CO 889/1 (32), p. 35.
63 Ibid., p. 34.
64 Alliance hearing before the commission, 27 September 1956, CO 889/6, pp. 35–36.
65 Ibid., p. 36.
66 Ibid.
67 Report of the Federation of Malaya Constitutional Commission 1957, London: Her Majesty's Stationery Office, No. 330, pp. 21–24.
68 Ibid., p. 23.

69 Alliance hearing before the commission, 27 September 1956, CO 889/6 (2A), p. 36.
70 Ibid., p. 36.
71 Ibid., pp. 35–36.
72 Ibid., p. 36.
73 See, for example, memoranda submitted by The Federated Teochew Association of Malaya, 14 July 1956, CO 889/5; Perak Chinese Association, 26 September 1955, CO 889/5 (1); Federation of Kwan-Tung Association of Malaya, 16 July 1956, CO 889/5 (1); Malay Society of Great Britain, 10 July 1956, CO889/5 (1); Persatuan Melayu Semenanjong, 15 July 1956, CO889/5 (1)(b); All Malaya Tamils Conference, 24 September 1956, CO 889/6 (1); and Malayan Sikhs' Representative Committee, 14 July 1956, CO 889/5 (1).
74 Report of the Federation of Malaya Constitutional Commission 1957, London: Her Majesty's Stationery Office, No. 330, p. 16.
75 Ibid., p. 17.
76 Ibid.
77 Ibid.
78 Ibid.
79 Report of the Federation of Malaya Constitutional Commission 1957, London: Her Majesty's Stationery Office, No. 330, p. 17. See also Alliance hearing before the commission, 27 September 1956, CO 889/6 (2a), pp. 35–36.
80 Report of the Federation of Malaya Constitutional Commission 1957, p. 18. Alliance hearing before the commission, 27 September 1956, CO 889/6 (2a), pp. 35–36.
81 Report of the Federation of Malaya Constitutional Commission 1957, p. 19. Alliance hearing before the commission, 27 September 1956, CO 889/6 (2a), pp. 35–36.
82 See Justice Hamid's Note of dissent (second draft) in Sir Ivor Jennings Papers, 28 January 1957, B/X/6, p. 2. See also Hamid's note of dissent in Report of the Federation of Malaya Constitutional Commission 1957, pp. 95–96.
83 See Justice Hamid's Note of dissent (second draft) in Sir Ivor Jennings Papers, 28 January 1957, B/X/6, p. 2.
84 Ibid., p. 3.
85 Report of the Federation of Malaya Constitutional Commission 1957, p. 17.
86 See Jennings response to Hamid's note of dissent in Sir Ivor Jennings Papers, B/X/6, p. 2.
87 See Justice Hamid's Note of dissent (second draft) in Sir Ivor Jennings Papers, 28 January 1957, B/X/6, p. 4.
88 Ibid., p. 4.
89 See Jennings note of response to Hamid's "Note of dissent," in Sir Ivor Jennings Papers, 28 January 1957, B/X/6.
90 Report of the Federation of Malaya Constitutional Commission 1957, p. 20.
91 Ibid.
92 Ibid., pp. 20–21.
93 Report of the Federation of Malaya Constitutional Commission 1957, p. 21. See also Summary record of 23rd meeting of the Constitutional Commission, 25 August 1956, CO 889/1 (25), pp. 1–2.
94 Report of the Federation of Malaya Constitutional Commission 1957, p. 19.
95 Ibid.
96 Ibid.
97 Ibid., p. 20.
98 Ibid.
99 Minutes of First meeting of Working Party, 22 February 1957, CO 941/85, p. 4.
100 Ibid.
101 See Report of the Working Party, CO 941/87.
102 Minutes of First meeting of Working Party, 22 February 1957, CO 941/85, p. 4.

103 Ibid., pp. 4–5.
104 Ibid., p. 5.
105 Outward telegram, Secretary of State to MacGillivray, 28 February 1957, CO 1030/524 (4).
106 Minutes of Eighth meeting of Working Party, 8 March 1957, CO 941/85, p. 3.
107 Minutes of Twenty-third meeting of Working Party, 27 April 1957, CO 941/87, p. 7.
108 Ibid.
109 Report of the Working Party, see CO 941/87.
110 Minutes of First meeting of Working Party, 22 February 1957, CO 941/85, p. 5.
111 Ibid. See also Minutes of Eighth meeting of Working Party, 8 March 1957, CO 941/85, p. 2. The Alliance at this meeting said they wanted the Clause 1 of Article 15 deleted but agreed to discuss it further.
112 See Justice Hamid's Note of dissent (second draft) in Sir Ivor Jennings Papers, 28 January 1957, B/X/6, p. 3.
113 Ibid., p. 3.
114 Outward telegram, Secretary of State to MacGillivray, 28 February 1957, CO 1030/524 (4).
115 Report of the Federation of Malaya Constitutional Commission 1957, p. 17.
116 See Report of the Working Party, CO 941/87.
117 Minutes of Twenty-third meeting of Working Party, 27 April 1957, CO 941/87, p. 1.
118 Minutes of First meeting of Working Party, 22 February 1957, CO 941/85, p. 5. Article 142 (1) states: "Where the law in force in any other part of the Commonwealth confers upon citizens of the Federation any right or privilege it shall be lawful, notwithstanding anything in this Constitution, for Parliament to confer a similar right upon citizens upon citizens of that part of the Commonwealth who are not citizens of the Federation."
119 Outward telegram, Secretary of State to MacGillivray, 28 February 1957, CO 1030/524 (4).
120 Summary record of First Plenary Meeting, 13 May 1957, CO 1030/496 (1), p. 6.
121 Summary record of Fourth Plenary Meeting, 21 May 1957, CO 1030/496 (23), p. 7.
122 Ibid., p. 7.
123 Summary record of Fourth Plenary Meeting, 21 May 1957, CO 1030/496 (23).
124 Ibid.
125 Ibid.
126 Report of the Federation of Malaya Constitutional Commission 1957, p. 16.

6 The other voices

Constitutions reflect a compromise between diverse and often competing interests. Some voices, particularly those of political elites representing major political parties, are more dominant and influential in the constitution-making process. Others, while less visible, are nevertheless significant as they represent particular sectional interests whose electoral support can be vital. The major influence on the drafting of the 1957 Malayan federal constitution was invariably the ruling Alliance Party and the Malay rulers. The Reid constitutional commission gave considerable attention to the submissions of these two major actors in Malaya in formulating the draft constitution because of their influence and status in Malayan society. The Alliance Party, comprising the three communal parties, the United Malays National Organisation (UMNO), the Malayan Chinese Association (MCA) and the Malayan Indian Congress (MIC), was the ruling party which was viewed as representing the voice of the three major communities in the peninsula by the commission.

After the overwhelming victory in the July 1955 federal elections, the Alliance demanded a firm date for independence and the setting up of an independent constitutional commission to draft a new constitution for independent Malaya. The British government after some dithering conceded to the coalition's request, and the constitutional commission was initiated. Hence, the Alliance Party was the *de facto* dominant political force at the time of the framing of the constitution. The Malay monarchy, on the other hand, was historically an important institution. The Malay rulers were the primary political power before the intervention of the British in the nineteenth century. British intervention in the Malay states was the result of treaties between the Malay rulers and Britain. Hence, the rulers were also important stakeholders in the future of the country. After the Second World War, they remained a pivotal institution and a source of legitimacy of the government of the states in Malaya and an integral part of the modern political and administrative system. The constitutional reforms invariably would affect the rulers' historical position and status, and their views had to be seriously considered.

There was at the same time a diverse collection of socio-economic and political interests in Malaya, the "other voices," that represented a cross section of community interests which sought to influence the constitution-making process through their memoranda and letters and in their oral presentations before the commission.

DOI: 10.4324/9781003542537-6

These included political organisations, socio-cultural organisations, trade union movements, chambers of commerce, clan associations, labour movements and individuals. These voices were given fair hearing by the Reid Commission, judging from the deliberations of the commission and the record of their interactions with the commission during the oral hearings given to these organisations during the commission's tour of the country. A total of 131 memoranda were submitted to the commission by a wide range of interest groups.[1] These voices represented a wide cross section of Malayan society and provide a deeper insight into the constitution-making process and the hopes and concerns of Malayans in a broader sense and in that critical period of time when the country was undergoing phenomenal changes. Existing studies on the Malaysian constitution have not examined these other voices and their roles in the constitution-making process. The collective concerns of these voices are to an extent reflected in the compromises embedded in the constitution particularly on the issues of fundamental rights, citizenship, language and education. The commission sought to address the concerns and fears of these groups.

A close examination of the constitutional records indicates that the majority of these organisations and individuals were concerned with several issues in particular which had been a source of much debate and even controversy in the post-war period. These included the issues of citizenship, the protection of basic fundamental liberties, language, education, Malay special position and religious freedom. There was an interesting convergence on some of the issues that were raised by these organisations and which often had an ethnic orientation or basis. But there was considerable divergence of views on these issues as well. The issues of citizenship and fundamental liberties were among the most popular in the submissions of the groups. On the hotly debated issue of *jus soli* in relation to the grant of federal citizenship, for example, 33 organisations and 12 individuals made submissions in their memoranda and during the oral hearings.[2] On the subject of a single Malayan nationality, 13 organisations and 5 individuals submitted. On the citizenship-related issue of revised tests for naturalisation, 19 organisations and 3 individuals made submissions. The subject of fundamental freedoms and rights received the second highest attention; 31 organisations and 9 individuals raised the issue in the memoranda and oral submissions. Representation in the legislature was also an issue of much interest; a total of 15 organisations and 4 individuals made submissions on the issue of nominated members of legislature. Table 6.1 gives an idea of some of the main issues that were raised by various groups.

On the issue of the special position of the Malays, 13 organisations and five individuals raised the issue with the commission. The subject of multilingualism in legislature also attracted much attention – 15 organisations and one individual made submissions on the issue.[3] Other issues which attracted significant attention from the various organisations and interest groups were the issues of the retention of status of British subjects (mainly for those living in the Settlements of Penang and Malacca) – nine organisations and two individuals submitted; protection of racial minorities – 12 organisations and three individuals submitted; vernacular

Table 6.1 Major issues raised with Reid constitutional commission

Subject	*Organisation*	*Individual*	*Total*
Jus soli	33	12	45
Fundamental freedoms and rights	31	9	40
Nominated members of legislature	15	4	19
Single Malayan nationality	13	5	18
Special position of Malays	13	5	18
Multilingualism in legislature	15	1	16
Protection of racial minorities	12	3	15
Retention of English as official language	9	5	14
Retention of status of British subjects	9	2	11
Vernacular education	9	1	10

Source: Summary record of the main points submitted by individuals and organisations in memoranda and at the hearings, 5 September 1956, CO 889/8/1 (1), C.C. 1003/5.

education – nine organisations and one individual submitted; and retention of English as official language – nine organisations and five individuals submitted.[4]

The constitutional documents indicate that communally based organisations, both political and socio-economic, were focused on championing issues that they felt were important to the preservation of the cultures and languages of their respective communities and the basic rights as citizens. Malay organisations, for example, were focused primarily on safeguards for Malay special position, elevating Islam as a state or official religion, establishing Malay as the national language and wanting restrictive conditions on the grant of federal citizenship.[5] The Chinese and Indian organisations, on the other hand, wanted citizenship requirements to be made less restrictive compared to the existing conditions and particularly the adoption of the principle of *jus soli* (right of citizenship by birth).[6] They were also concerned that the vernacular languages (Chinese and Tamil) and vernacular schools would be given recognition and protected in the new constitution to preserve their distinct cultural identities. They urged strong safeguards for civil and political liberties, particularly religious freedom, and wanted the constitution to ensure equality of citizenship and non-discrimination in job opportunities in the civil service. At the same time, while they generally accepted the premise that Malays needed to be assisted economically, they felt that Malay special privileges should be temporary and only continued for a specified period of time. Most of these organisations supported the use of Malay as the national language but wanted official recognition for their own languages, some seeking official language status for these vernacular languages, and the retention of English as an official language and the English-medium schools.[7]

Interestingly, on closer examination of the constitutional documents, it is evident that within the communally based organisations there were different shades of opinion on these communal demands. Some organisations were very narrow in their outlook and emotional in their demands while others were more open, flexible and inclusive in the demands and proposals. The quality and quantity of the memoranda submitted also varied considerably, reflecting the lack of political awareness and political literacy at the time of the framing of the constitution. The Chinese organisations were more numerous and better organised in their submissions to the constitutional commission compared to the Malay and Indian organisations which were fewer in numbers and less well organised. The quality of the memoranda also varied. Some of the memoranda submitted by the Chinese organisations were quite similar and sometimes used a standard format of presentation, essentially focusing on citizenship, particularly *jus soli*, education and language. This was partly because some of the leaders served in more than one organisation which made representations to the constitutional commission and they held similar views on the core issues raised. The challenge for the Commission was to find a fair balance between the wide-ranging and sometimes conflicting communal demands. If there was a common thread that bound the various groups together, it is that all of them favoured a parliamentary system of governance with a bicameral legislature and a constitutional monarchy.

An examination of these "other voices" provides an important insight into the broad-ranging and diverse voices that sought to be heard during the constitution-making process in 1956 and their concerns and hopes for the emerging nation-state. It was a microcosm of the myriad voices of the Malayan people. It indicates that the constitution-making process was a fairly wide consultative process that enabled all sectors of the population an opportunity to put forward their views. In the following section, we examine a selection of submissions made by political parties, socio-cultural organisations, chambers of commerce, trade unions and individuals to give an idea of the range of issues and concerns raised by different groups during the constitutional consultations between June and October 1956.

Political organisations

Apart from the Alliance Party, several other political parties submitted memoranda to the constitutional commission. These included the People's Progressive Party (PPP), the Labour Party of Malaya, Party Negara and the Parti Islam Sa-Malaya which was also known as the Pan-Malayan Islamic Party (PMIP). These memoranda covered a wide range of issues and while having much in common with the Alliance Party, also had some interesting and even radical proposals. There was clearly much in common between these parties on ideas of a parliamentary system of government, bicameral legislature and constitutional monarchy along the lines of the Westminster model. There was also considerable common ground on the contentious inter-communal issues such citizenship, language, religious freedom and education, particularly between the Alliance Party, the PPP, the Labour Party of Malaya and Party Negara. Parti Islam Sa-Malaya's memorandum reflected several substantive differences, yet they had much more in common with the other parties than differences.

The PPP submitted a memorandum to the commission on 20 July 1956.[8] The eight-page memorandum was signed by the PPP President Dr S. Kanapathipillai, Treasurer Choy Kok Kuan and General Secretary D.R. Seenivasagam. The PPP's memorandum which was well-crafted raised some substantive issues of concern to Malayans and the party's supporters. The memorandum was critical of the fact that the Malayan constitution was being drafted by a group of legal experts from outside the country and a subject of agreement between Her Majesty's Government and the rulers unlike the drafting of the constitutions of India and Pakistan which were done by the constituent assemblies. The party felt that the local legislators should have been given a bigger role in the formulation of the draft constitution. The memorandum notes:

> As the terms of reference of the Constitutional Commission do not call for recommendations for the convening of a Constituent Assembly it would appear that unlike India and Pakistan, the people of Malaya cannot adopt, enact and give to themselves a Constitution but can only be granted one by agreement between Her Majesty the Queen and Their Highnesses the Rulers.[9]

The party wanted the commission to provide for a federation of nine Malay states and two Settlements.

The PPP suggested that fundamental rights were the most important part of the constitution and that Part III of the Indian constitution and Part II of the Constitution of Pakistan which dealt with fundamental rights should be adapted and incorporated in the Malayan constitution. The Reid Commission in fact drew considerably from the constitutions of India and Pakistan for the elaborate section on fundamental rights. The party wanted the majority in the second legislative chamber to be appointed and not elected. PPP felt that members elected to the second chamber would in all probability be from the ruling party, and if further nominations were made and filled by supporters of the ruling party, the second house would fail to fulfil its purpose. The PPP proposed that not more than five members of the second chamber should be elected and the rest should comprise the *Mentris Besar* of each state, a number of territorial chiefs from each state and a number of representatives of each Settlement. The memorandum noted:

> There will, of course, be no pretence that this is a democratically constituted body but it is more likely to discharge its duty effectively than would one which is packed with members whose seats depend on the goodwill of the Party in power.[10]

The PPP felt that Malay should be made the national language as was the desire of the Malays, but at the same time it wanted English to be made the second official language.

> In view of the fact, however, that considered from an international point of view the Malay language is spoken by a very small minority of the peoples of the world, it is clear that if the Malays are to advance in their study of law, medicine, arts and sciences a second language is essential and we feel that the English language will serve this purpose.[11]

The party felt that an immediate change from English to Malay was not practicable and that English could be dispensed with as an official language after 25 years when Malay may be adopted as the only official language.[12] The party wanted the judiciary to be separate from the executive. It suggested a reorganisation of the courts and the creation of a Supreme Court: "The Supreme Court will have to assume the role of guardian of the Constitution."[13] Interestingly, the party proposed that a member of the legislature should be able to speak in the language of his choice. This was subject to the speaker providing an interpreter at his own expense to translate his speech into Malay or English. The party felt this was necessary as there were several leaders in the Chinese community who could not speak well in English or Malay.

The PPP was against the reservation of seats for minorities in the legislature as they felt that this would "perpetuate a feeling of communalism."[14] The memorandum noted:

> Special seats for minorities do not in practice serve any useful purpose but on the contrary will retard the process of integration of the various races. Experience has shown that no special benefit has accrued to any minority community through this form of representation in the Legislatures.[15]

The party felt that the best safeguard for the minority community was through an adequate declaration of fundamental rights. The party proposed a very stringent procedure for any amendment to the constitution. Constitutional amendment would require a majority of not less than four-fifths of the total membership of the house. The party felt that a majority of four-fifths of those present and voting was insufficient "as a reactionary Government could cause the absence of opponents by exercising powers of arrest or detention."[16] The party suggested that as the constituent assembly did not have an opportunity to debate the specific articles of the draft constitution, the commission should ensure a draft of the commission's proposals should be published for public comments, and only after receipt and consideration of such comments should the commission submit the proposals in their final form to the Queen and the Conference of Rulers.[17]

The Labour Party of Malaya submitted a ten-page memorandum to the commission dated 25 September 1956 and signed by its President D.S. Ramanathan and General Secretary Tan Phock Kin. The party sought some interesting and also radical changes.[18] The memorandum first provided some background to the party, claiming that it was the only party which was completely non-communal and admitted to its membership "all those who believe in democracy and socialism."[19] The party felt that a written constitution for Malaya at that juncture would only be temporary and thought the constitution should be flexible to meet the changing socio-economic and political demands in order to build "a peaceful, progressive and democratic nation."[20] The Labour Party felt that the commission's terms of reference were "unduly restrictive," adding that the party's recommendations thus went beyond the commission's terms of reference.[21] The party recommended that the independent state be known as "Malaya" and not "Lankasuka" as had been suggested in some circles.[22] It urged the creation of a common nationality, noting that at present there were nine state nationalities and one federal citizenship.[23] On citizenship, the party recommended that those born in Malaya and were domiciled there should automatically be a national. In the case of those not born in the federation but who were domiciled there and had resided there for five years, it recommended that they should be eligible to acquire Malayan nationality by registration by taking an oath of loyalty.[24] The party objected to dual nationality and felt that this amounted to "political dishonesty."[25] It regarded fundamental rights as a central issue and recommended that all Malayan nationals "should enjoy equal rights and share equal responsibilities."[26] The party argued that safeguarding the special position of the Malays would not benefit them in the long run.[27] On language, the party recommended that Malay should be made the national language while English should be a second language. The memorandum noted: "The Labour Party feels that the continued use of the English language, especially in higher education, is an absolute necessity if Malaya is to progress as a modern state."[28] The party recommended multilingualism in the legislative councils and the schools: "It is recommended that, besides the national language, the English, Chinese and Indian languages be taught in schools and spoken in the Councils."[29] Unlike most of the other parties which supported a federal state, the Labour Party recommended that Malaya should be a unitary state.[30] This was beyond the commission's terms of reference which required the commission to provide for a federal system of government. It wanted a merger with Singapore, noting that "neither strategic arguments from Imperial interests, nor narrow racial arguments from extreme communal elements should be allowed to prevent the unification of the two territories."[31] The party recommended that Malaya should be a secular state: "The Labour Party wishes to emphasise that only by the creation of a secular State can religious peace, and consequently, civic harmony, continue to flourish in Malaya."[32] The party favoured a republican system of government, arguing that the general tendency in Southeast Asia was towards republicanism.[33] In line with its preference for a republican system of government, the party recommended that the head of state should be called "the President of Malaya," who would be elected by an electoral college consisting of elected representatives of the federal parliament and the state legislatures.[34] The party felt that constitutional heads of the various states should also be eligible for election as President of Malaya.[35] The party urged the commission to insert a provision declaring the legislative supremacy of parliament so that the people's aspirations could find adequate expression.[36] The commission was urged to provide for a strong central government, a bicameral legislature, independence of the judiciary and separation of powers, and for specific provisions on fundamental human rights.[37] On constitutional procedure, the party recommended a two-thirds majority in both houses of the parliament.[38]

The Islamic Association of Malaya (*Persatuan Islam Sa-Malaya*), also known as the Pan-Malayan Islamic Party (PMIP), submitted a wide-ranging eight-page memorandum dated 14 July 1956.[39] This party, which was formed in 1951, was a small but leading opposition party. It was the only opposition party that won a seat in the July 1955 federal elections and had worked closely with Party Negara and Party

Raayat to form an opposition bloc to challenge the dominant Alliance Party. The association began its memorandum by asserting that Malaya belonged to the Malays and thus "Malay special position" should be safeguarded in the constitution. Not to do so, it argued, would be contradictory to human rights and the principle of law.[40] The party blamed British imperial policy for the poor economic position of the Malays and their lack of political power. The memorandum was critical of the demands of the non-Malays for recognition of the principle of *jus soli* and felt these demands were motivated by a desire for political power.[41] The party sought the creation of a single nationality to be called *Melayu*.[42] On citizenship, the party felt that the principles established in the 1948 Federation of Malaya Agreement should be maintained.[43] It wanted a period of 15 years residence before an alien could qualify to apply for citizenship, opposed the principle of *jus soli* and urged that a Malay language test should be required for citizenship.[44] The party submitted that the education system should be in the Malay medium from primary to university levels and that Malay should be made the official language.[45] English, it added, should be maintained as an official language for a period not exceeding five years. It wanted Islam to be made the official religion.[46] The party proposed that a bicameral legislature should be established and that Malaya should be a federation as provided in the terms of reference.[47] The party submitted that the sovereignty of the Malay rulers should be vested in a Council of Malay Rulers and that a *Yang di-Pertuan Besar* should be regarded as the constitutional monarch of the federation.[48] The party wanted the states of Penang and Malacca to be made Malay states again.[49]

The non-communal Party Negara's Perlis state branch submitted a brief two-page memorandum to the constitutional commission and presented oral evidence on 28 July 1956.[50] This memorandum is interesting because the party's leader Dato' Onn Jaafar had declined to submit a memorandum to the commission and refused to appear before the commission. It showed that some of the party leaders disagreed with Onn's position on submissions to the constitutional commission. Onn had initially agreed to appear before the commission when approached by commission member Justice Abdul Hamid who had been tasked to persuade Onn to appear before the commission. Onn had said that he did not agree with the terms of reference of the commission.[51] The memorandum was signed by three state leaders, Dr Syed Mahmood bin Syed Hussain, Syed Mahadzer bin Syed Hussein and Benedict J. Vong and is very brief and sketchy. Its main focus was the issue of nationality. The Party Negara Perlis branch wanted the existing federal citizenship and state nationality replaced by a Malaysian nationality law.[52] According to the memorandum, those eligible to become nationals were all those who were already federal citizens and state nationals under the existing legislation, those born and bred in the federation who were conversant in Malay and who would forfeit on oath any rights or obligations to the countries of origin of their ancestors and those not born in the federation but who had lived there for ten years and who were conversant in Malay.[53] Party Negara's conditions for eligibility for federal citizenship were more liberal compared to the hardline stand taken by the Islamic Association of Malaya. The party felt that all those who obtained the status of Malayan national should be given equal treatment before the law in all respects. It suggested that the head of state should be a "Paramount Ruler" chosen from members of the Rulers' Conference according to their seniority and should hold the office for life.[54] The powers of the Paramount Ruler should be that of a constitutional monarch. They wanted the Conference of Rulers to be retained. The party felt the public services should be open to all nationals and selection should be based on qualifications and ability.[55] Public servants should not be active in politics. Interestingly, the party suggested a single-chamber legislature with a fully elected membership.[56]

Socio-cultural organisations and minority groups

The numerous memoranda submitted to the constitutional commission by socio-cultural organisations and minority groups provide another interesting window into the views of a wide cross section of the population on the historical constitution-making process. It also reflected the hopes and concerns of the smaller other voices for the emerging nation-state. Many of these socio-cultural organisations had been in existence in Malaya for long periods and were umbrella organisations that sought to protect the interests of the various cultural groups and workers. They were in essence a reflection of the undercurrents prevalent in Malayan society when the constitution was framed.

The Straits Chinese British Association, Penang, (SCBA) submitted a well-drafted 10-page memorandum on 14 July 1956 to the commission discussing a wide range of issues.[57] It was signed by its President Heah Joo Seang, vice president, secretary and two past presidents. The memorandum first provided a background to Malaya and its peoples before emphasising certain points that the association wanted included in the constitution. It pointed out that about 200,000 or about 70% of the Chinese population in Penang were Straits-born and that they had a British and Malayan outlook:

> They have cultivated a British and Malayan outlook and are deeply rooted to this country and consider themselves to be sons of the soil with Penang as their only home. Whilst preserving their Chinese culture and traditions they have always been to the fore in rendering public service to this country and to the Crown and are second to none in their loyalty, love and affection to their Sovereign.[58]

The association urged the commission to ensure that British subjects or subjects of their Highnesses the Rulers be allowed to retain their status after they acquired the proposed federal citizenship.[59] This request reflected the unease of the Straits Chinese about their future status and position in Malaya and some concern over the potential for the rise in extreme nationalism. The association urged that the principle of *jus soli* be recognised in the new federal citizenship.[60] The memorandum stressed the importance of safeguards for fundamental liberties:

> At no time in our history do we appreciate the value, the need of the importance of a guarantee for our fundamental liberties and rights and safeguards

> for minorities not only in reference to legislation but also in the field of executive action.[61]

The SCBA advocated the recognition of multilingualism. Besides Malay, the association wanted English to be made an official language and the Chinese language allowed in the councils.[62] They suggested the federation be known as "the United States of Malaya."[63] The SCBA wanted the position of the Queen recognised in the Settlements of Penang and Malacca and sought representation in the two legislatures for the Straits Chinese. The association proposed that the four major languages, Malay, English, Chinese and Tamil, be recognised as official languages.[64] It urged that the special position of the Malays be defined in the constitution so as not to create conditions detrimental to the interests of the other communities.[65] The organisation wanted the commission to make provisions in the constitution to give landless citizens a stake in the country through a suitable system of land tenure for the purpose of achieving self-sufficiency for the country.[66] In an additional memorandum presented to the commission on the day of the oral hearing, the SCBA asked that if the rights of the people of Penang could not be protected in the new constitution, the state should be allowed to secede.[67] Lord Reid, however, told the SCBA at their oral hearing on 10 August 1956 that the issue of secession was not within the commission's terms of reference and that they were bound to consider Penang as an integral part of the new federation.[68]

The Malay Society of Great Britain sent a wide-ranging memorandum to the commission dated 10 July 1956 and signed by Mohd. Azmi, its honorary secretary.[69] This was a London-based society representing Malay students in Britain that at one time was headed by the Chief Minister Tunku Abdul Rahman in the 1940s. The seven-page memorandum was well-drafted and quite detailed in some aspects of constitutional issues. The society appointed a committee in March 1956 to draft a memorandum which was intended to "incorporate various shades of Malay opinion in the society on the Constitution of independent Malaya."[70] At the outset of the memorandum, the society stated that the submission of the memorandum did not mean that the society unanimously agreed completely with the terms of reference of the commission:

> Some of us do not agree that the Constitutional Commission should have been limited by its terms of reference recommending a federal form of government for our country, and are in favour of the formation of a unitary state. Of this group, some would like the unitary state to take the form of a constitutional monarchy, while others would like to see a republic.[71]

The memorandum begins by stating the society wanted Malaya to remain in the Commonwealth but as a sovereign independent state. The society suggested that the head of state should be a Paramount Ruler chosen from among the Malay rulers and be titled, *Yang di-Pertuan Besar Negara*.[72] The society felt three methods could be used to elect the Paramount Ruler: first, by direct referendum among the nationals; the second, by selection of the federal legislature; and the third, selection by the rulers themselves. The society felt the first method would encourage parochial loyalty, and the third would give rise to differences among the rulers, which it wished to avoid. Thus, the society preferred the second method in which the Paramount Ruler would be elected by the federal legislature through a simple majority, which would mean that the people of Malaya, through their elected representatives, will have a say in the choice of the *Yang di-Pertuan Besar Negara*. The committee was split over giving the Paramount Ruler a one-year term in office to enable all the rulers to hold the office but, on the other hand, some in the committee felt that the Paramount Ruler should hold office for life. As a compromise, the committee decided that the Paramount Ruler should hold office for a term of five to seven years.

The society suggested a bicameral legislature with the lower house to consist of only elected members for a term of four or five years.

> We recommend that the lower house total number of members of the Federal Lower House should be made up on the basis of one member to 50,000 heads of population. Thus the first Federal Lower House will have a membership of about 120 and this total we regard as satisfactory for a start.[73]

The society recommended that the prime minister of the independent state be styled *Perdana Mentri*, who would be appointed by the *Yang di-Pertuan Besar Negara* from among the members of the lower house who commanded a majority in the house.[74] The society suggested an upper house which would be able to check the excesses of the lower house and protect the interests of the states.[75] The upper house was to comprise equal representatives from each state. The membership of the upper house was for a term of six years.[76]

The memorandum proposed a fully elected State Council for each state and a *Mentri Besar* was to be chosen from among the elected members.[77] They wanted the existing division of powers in the federation agreement to continue. Penang and Malacca should recognise the *Yang di-Pertuan Besar Negara* as the constitutional head. They emphasised that the judiciary should be independent of the executive. The society recommended a complex method of making constitutional amendments. Any legislature in the country, federal or state, could recommend an amendment to the constitution, provided that for an amendment to be accepted, it should have the support of two-thirds of the members of every state council in the federation.[78] It wanted the Supreme Court to be the sole arbiter in any dispute regarding the interpretation of the constitution. The society recommended the recognition of the principle of *jus soli* from the date the constitution was promulgated.[79] Nationality, it felt, should be termed *Melayu*.[80] The society wanted Malay privileges to be continued to assist the Malays "to raise their cultural and living standards."[81] The society suggested that Malay reservations should be retained for at least 100 years to allay Malay fears for their future.[82]

The Pan-Malayan Federation of Chinese Associations sent a five-page memorandum to the constitutional commission dated 20 July 1956 and signed by its three-man presidium comprising Lau Pak Khuan, Cho Yew Fai and Lim Lian Geok.[83] The main focus of the association, headquartered at the Chinese Assembly Hall in Kuala Lumpur, was the issue of citizenship and especially the call for the recognition of the principle of *jus soli*.[84] The association said that its memorandum represented the views generally of the Chinese community in Malaya. A total of 1,094 Chinese-based associations from all the states signed the memorandum. The association said the first federal election of July 1955 showed the real need for reform of the citizenship laws. It pointed out that 84% of the voters were Malays and suggested that had there been no pre-arranged agreement between UMNO, MCA and the MIC, no non-Malay member would have been returned.[85] The association felt it was ironic that in the Settlements of Penang and Malacca the principle of *jus soli* had been recognised and British subjects in these territories automatically became citizens of the federation, but it was not recognised beyond the Settlements.[86] The association argued that the principle of *jus soli* was internationally recognised and it would be against international ethics to reject the recognition of the principle in the new constitution.[87] The memorandum noted that before the Second World War Chinese born in the Malay states were regarded as British Protected Persons and granted British passports when they travelled aboard, but that this was no longer the case under the 1948 federation agreement.[88] The memorandum referred to the assurance in the Alliance election manifesto for the 1955 federal election, which stated that a special independent commission should recommend measures to "resolve satisfactorily" the position of the large alien population.[89] The association urged the commission to provide for all foreign-born Chinese who had lived in the country for five years to be eligible to apply for citizenship without having to take a language test.[90]

The association felt that there was a strong case for multilingualism in the legislatures because of the historical development of the educational system. It noted that for generations vernacular education had been encouraged by the colonial system of government without aiming to produce a Malayan outlook.[91] As a result, the association said, the number of students in the English schools was far less than vernacular schools, noting that as of end September 1954 out of a total enrolment of 803,753 pupils for all schools, only 158,485 attended the English schools.[92] Hardly 10% of the 2.4 million Chinese population, constituting 40% of the total population, could speak effective English or Malay, it said.[93] The use of only English or Malay in the councils, the memorandum noted, would drastically restrict the choice of suitable representatives and nullify the benefits of popular elections.[94] On this issue, the memorandum pointed out the promise made in the Alliance election manifesto which had agreed to ensure that all the communities had "a legitimate and fundamental right to preserve their own language and culture."[95] The association urged that the Chinese language be made an official language and be allowed to be used in the legislatures.[96] The association was against the provisions for preferential treatment for the Malays provided in the federation agreement, stressing that this would breed distrust and resentment.[97] It felt that rather than discriminatory legislation, the Malays should be assisted through willing cooperation of the other communities and inter-communal goodwill. The memorandum noted:

> The Malays need help by obtaining it with the willing cooperation of the other more advanced communities but not help through legislation. While

> such legislation tends to make them a privileged class it also reduces them to a dependent and undignified community. They must not expect to be spoon-fed and be made to lose all sense of incentive but must be trained in the hard way to rely on their own efforts and initiative for success.[98]

The association concluded that willing inter-racial co-operation and goodwill will then ensue and bring with it a new era of hope for the Malays.[99] At the hearing on 24 August 1956, Lau Pak Khuan expressed some fears on the "special position" of the Malays, which had been proposed by the Alliance Party.[100] While they accepted that the Malays had certain rights with regard to land, they feared what was being planned by the Alliance was something more. Lim Lian Geok submitted that multilingualism was important because few Chinese could speak English or Malay. He said Kuo-Yu should be adopted as an official language in the various councils. Lau pointed out that the Chinese had demonstrated their loyalty when they formed the Kinta Valley Home Guard at the request of General Sir Gerald Templer during the Emergency.

A memorandum dated 24 September 1956 was submitted to the commission by a Tamil group representing a wide cross section of the community which had convened an All Malaya Tamils Conference (*Agila Malaya Thamilar Sangam*) on 25 and 26 August 1956.[101] The convenor of the conference held in Ipoh was T.V.M. Mahalingam, and the conference was declared open by federal legislative councillor S.O.K. Ubaidulla, who was also a Malayan Indian Congress leader. The conference was attended by 118 delegates and 157 observers from 109 Tamil organisations in the country.[102] The main focus of the memorandum was the issue of federal citizenship and safeguards for the Tamil schools and Tamil language. The memorandum noted in the opening statement the contributions of the Indian community to Malaya:

> The Tamils true to their tradition of doing silent and selfless sacrifices have converted this land of once impenetrable jungles into the present smiling land of plenty. Engaged in the noble task of building and developing Malaya the Tamils had little thought for their own welfare and advancement, and others who benefited by their services and sacrifices paid lesser attention to the welfare and uplift of the Tamils. So much so the Tamils who had striven hard for the welfare of others have been left far behind, educationally, economically and socially.[103]

The memorandum noted that the Tamil community was only asking "what is justly and reasonably due to them as 'pioneer nationals' of this country of Malaya."[104] The conference urged the commission to provide that the Tamil language be made one of the four official languages in Malaya in order "to preserve and develop the Tamil culture which is very ancient, vast, varied, and virile."[105] The group urged that Tamil and Kuo-Yu be made compulsory subjects in all schools and examinations in order to "preserve and sustain the growth of the languages and cultures" of the Tamil and Chinese communities.[106] They wanted early education for children to be in their mother tongue "in consonance with all accepted education principles."[107] The conference resolution proposed that English be taught in the third year in the vernacular primary schools and Malay in the fourth year to facilitate early education in mother tongue.

The conference wanted Tamil school teachers to be placed on the same scale as national schools and urged the government to establish Tamil-medium secondary schools in each state with hostel facilities.[108] The memorandum sought "equal and automatic citizenship rights, equal justice and equal opportunities as the sons of the soil for Tamils, Chinese and others who as British subjects and who have been pioneers in the work of developing Malaya in all spheres."[109] The memorandum noted that the Tamils were in a more backward state economically and socially than the Malays.[110] The memorandum stated: "What the Tamils want is a just and fair deal, not at the cost of the interests of other communities but on the merits of their standing, services, sacrifices and contribution to the Malays and Malaya."[111] They urged the government to implement the Land Development Scheme for the South Indian labourers as recommended by High Commissioner Sir Gerald Templer.

An interesting and significant memorandum was submitted to the commission on 14 July 1956 on behalf of the aboriginal peoples of Malaya by Datoh Panglima Kinta Haji M. Eusoff as the Aborigines Representative in the Federal Legislative Council who was based in Ipoh.[112] Although barely covering two pages, the memorandum provided an invaluable insight into the plight of the aborigines. According to the representatives of the aborigines, Datoh Eusoff, there were two main tribes – the Temiar and the Semai. The Temiar numbered about 8,000 and were found mostly in Perak and Kelantan. The Semai, totalling between 50,000 and 60,000, were mostly found in the central highlands of Perak.[113] The aborigines were divided into three ethnic groups and between 18 and 20 tribes. Datoh Eusoff said the tribes were divided into three groups – nomadic, static and on the fringe.[114] The Temiar on the whole were more settled than the Semai. The memorandum began by noting that until recently aborigines were only of academic interests to a few anthropologists and this was reflected in the name given to the department in charge of the aborigines, which was called "Museums, Archives and Aboriginal Research." While acknowledging that things had improved a little for the aborigines, the memorandum noted that there were still a lot of weaknesses in the measures taken to look after their welfare.[115]

Under the Aborigines Peoples Ordinance (No. 3 of 1954), an Adviser on aborigines was charged with the responsibility to conduct research on the aborigines and to advise the State and Settlement governments on matters related to aboriginal administration. However, the memorandum noted that the States and Settlements were not playing an active part in the administration and welfare of the aborigines (no state department had been created for aboriginal welfare) and this made it difficult for the Adviser with his limited resources.[116] Restrictions placed by Forest and Games department made it difficult for the aborigines to continue their way of life: "The aborigines are unable to continue their normal mode of life – hunting and fishing, exploitation of jungle produce (their source of cash income), kill games for their food, clear forest area for cultivation (food) – because of restrictions placed by the Forest and Games Departments," it noted, pointing out that the aborigines were in these forests long before the areas were gazetted as forest reserves.[117]

The aborigines wanted several issues safeguarded in the constitution. The memorandum urged that the aborigines be given equal status in matter of rights and privileges as the other communities and that they should suffer no discrimination.[118] They wanted a Department of Aboriginal Affairs to be set up with specific terms of reference to advance their social, economic and political interests.[119] They urged that aboriginal reserves be created to preserve their tribal lands with the tenure of these reserves secured.[120] The memorandum urged that the aborigines should be given surface and mineral rights in the reserves. "Also they should be allowed to hunt and fish, kill games for food and exploit jungle produce in the Forest Reserves, especially those inhabited by them. This is their normal way of life," the memorandum noted.[121] The memorandum urged that legal provisions should be enacted to prevent religious missionaries from proselytising the aborigines. The aborigines urged the commission to provide for aboriginal representation in the state and settlement levels as it would not be possible for them to elect a representative through popular election because of their small numbers.[122]

On the question of reservations, Datoh Eusoff told the commission during the hearing that he felt that the present system of reserves should be made more permanent.[123] He said,

> There were certain gazetted reserves and these were administered in theory by the States, but they appeared to have no interest in the condition of the tribes, and would provide no men to help him (the Adviser) in his work. Selangor was, however, more advanced in this matter than Perak.

He felt that the aborigines should be a federal subject, but Lord Reid pointed out that it would be difficult to make the aborigines an exclusively federal subject as the States would want to have a say in the reservation of their land.[124] On the question of missionaries, Reid felt that all religions should be prevented from proselytising.[125] To a question on boundaries posed by McKell, Eusoff said the boundaries on the map (provided by Eusoff) were strictly adhered to by the tribes but that these boundaries had no regard for State boundaries.[126]

A 20-page memorandum was submitted by the Eurasian Union of Malaya to the constitutional commission on 1 September 1956.[127] The Eurasian community, estimated at 12,000, was concerned about their future in terms of job opportunities, education and welfare and sought safeguards for fundamental liberties. The union's membership totalling eight regional associations comprised the North Johore Eurasian Association, Malacca Eurasian Association, Negri Sembilan Eurasian Association, Selangor Eurasian Association, South Perak Eurasian Association, North Perak Eurasian Association, Penang Eurasian Association and Kedah Eurasian Association.[128] The well-articulated memorandum signed by G. Shelley, the president of the union and a federal legislative councillor, was bound in fine binding paper of quality print. The first five pages of the memorandum gave the historical background of the community, beginning from the intervention of the Portuguese admiral Alfonso D'Albuquerque in 1511 in Malacca.[129] The memorandum noted the contribution of the community to education, quoting H.R. Cheeseman, Deputy Director of Education, who noted that girls' education in Malaya owed a lot to the Eurasian teachers who formed the backbone of the staff in the girls' schools.[130] The memorandum pointed out the contribution of the Eurasians to the army during the First World War, noting that there was a company of soldiers in Penang made up completely of Eurasians.[131] The memorandum quoted Malcolm MacDonald, then governor general of Malaya in a speech of 4 January 1948 describing the "native" character of the Eurasians:

> The Eurasians, like the Malays themselves, have no other homeland. They cannot look elsewhere for shelter or help in times of distress or danger. Their place in the country of their birth is as rightful as anyone's and they are playing an active part in the Government and the professions, in trade and labour here.[132]

The Union urged the commission to provide for a nominated member in the upper house to represent the Eurasians.[133] The memorandum noted:

> The identity of the Community must be preserved in an Independent Federation; there is a very real need to safeguard it against submergence by major communities. The Eurasian Community feels that the only way of offering such an assurance would be to provide for representation of the community at legislature levels.[134]

The Union fully supported the introduction of a common nationality, noting that: "It is only by a bond of national unity could we aspire to be a great nation. The binding force must be a common loyalty."[135] They wanted the continuation of their status as British subjects while embracing the Malayan nationality.[136] The Union urged safeguards for freedom of worship and for the separation of the church and the state.[137] They wanted the doctrine of religious liberty to be written into the constitution:

> Religion, truth and justice must be ever maintained in an Independent Federation. Violation of any of these tenets of human society would be a perversion of democracy and its ideologies. Nature and reason command individuals to particular forms of worship and the rights of citizenship should accord him full liberty in the exercise of such worship. The State must not interfere with religious convictions and their expressions except when these result in acts that are injurious to others.[138]

The Union wanted safeguards written into the constitution to protect the "legitimate interests" of the community and suggested the constitution should contain a clause which read: "In the exercise of his executive authority the *Yang di-Pertuan Besar* shall have the following responsibility, that is to say, the safeguarding of the legitimate interests of the Aborigines; Eurasian and other minority communities."[139] In the hearing given by the commission to the Eurasian Union on 31 August 1956, Lord Reid congratulated the association on the content of their memorandum and noted that the commission appreciated that the Eurasians had long roots in the country and were continuing to play an important part in its development.[140] Shelley told the commission the union was concerned with two main issues. First was that of religion. He said that the only thing that separated them from the Malays was religion. The Union was anxious about freedom of worship in the Federation in the future and urged the commission to safeguard religious freedom in the constitution.[141] Second was the issue of British nationality. Shelley said that members of his community would be prepared to accept British nationality after independence but hoped that conditions for such people would not be made intolerable.[142] Shelley said that the Union was also concerned with the question of "racialism." He said the government at present was constituted on a community basis and that the Eurasian community had tried to create a non-racial atmosphere and had not associated with any communal group. He said the community was anxious to ensure that in future the community could take its proper place as a member of the Malayan community. Shelley said very few Eurasians entered business and most of them were government servants or in the professions and hence felt some protection should be given to the community in the civil service.

The Malayan Christian Council (MCC) submitted a seven-page memorandum to the commission on 18 July 1956, and it was signed by the organisation's chairman, vice chairman and members of its standing committee.[143] The MCC comprised the Anglican Church, the Methodist Church, the Presbyterian Church of England, the Chinese Presbyterian Church of Malaya, the Mar Thoma Syrian Church, the Bethesda Church of Katong, the Orthodox Syrian Church, the Bible Societies in Malaya, the Salvation Army, the Young Men's Christian Association (YMCA), the Young Women's Christian Association (YWCA) and the Lutheran Church.[144] The memorandum expressed the need to safeguard the fundamental liberties[145] and emphasised the need to ensure "full religious freedom" was provided in the constitution.[146] The MCC urged the commission to take steps to safeguard the liberties and rights of all citizens as set out in Article 18 of the Universal Declaration of Human Rights (UDHR).[147] The council wanted the constitution to protect the right of religious groups to set up their own educational institutions. The memorandum noted,

> Every religious denomination or community shall have the right to establish and maintain its own educational institutions. No religious denomination or community shall be prevented from providing religious instruction for its pupils in any educational institution maintained by that denomination or community.[148]

The council stressed that no person should be compelled to pay any special tax, the proceeds of which are to be spent on the propagation or maintenance of any religion other than his own.[149] It wanted equal opportunities to be given to all communities for jobs in the civil service and emphasised that there should not be any discrimination on the grounds of race, religion, sex and place of birth.[150]

In the hearing before the commission on 23 August 1956, the MCC stressed that its main concern was that they should retain in the future "all rights and privileges they now held."[151] Dr Ho Seng Ong, the chairman of the MCC and director of the Methodist Education Board, told the commission that the constitution should ensure that there were no limitations regarding religious freedom and to enable the present field of religious freedom to be enlarged. Reid said that all that could be written into the constitution was some safeguard to prevent discriminatory action being taken. Rev. J. Sutton, associate general secretary of the MCC, emphasised that they were very concerned over the question of freedom for all people to choose their religion.[152] It was a fundamental and important right.[153] Reid said the commission could certainly consider the legal aspects of this question.[154] Ho raised the point of some groups proposing Islam as the new State religion. He said it would be more proper in a community of different races if the new independent state were to be a secular one giving no particular favours or privileges to any religion, as in the case of India.[155] Justice Abdul Hamid said that such a provision by itself would not prevent the legislative body enacting any law on the subject it saw fit to introduce.[156] Reid said that, as he understood it, what the Council wanted was a written guarantee of religious freedom for all and a declaration that the new Federation was a secular state.[157] The representatives of the council agreed that this was so.

The Malayan Sikhs' Union (MSU) presented a seven-page memorandum to the commission on 14 July 1956 signed by its President T. Mahima Singh.[158] The memorandum was the result of a meeting of representatives of Sikh Gurudwaras held on 19 May 1956 in Kuala Lumpur and drawn up by a special committee, the Malayan Sikhs' Representative Committee. The main focus of the memorandum were the issues of citizenship and fundamental liberties. The memorandum stressed the contributions of the Indians to Malaya which had brought prosperity to the country and urged the commission to embody the principle of equality of citizenship.

> Suffice it to say that the Indians have put in much hard labour and capital to develop rubber lands, in building roads and railways, in providing transport and maintaining law and order in this land of our adoption . . . The Sikhs have served the Federation of Malaya and Singapore faithfully and loyally and they intend to continue doing the same in the future. The Sikhs residing in Malaya have a definite stake in this country and would like to share the benefits and bear the responsibilities that the citizens of a country normally enjoy.[159]

The Sikhs Union wanted those born in Malaya and of age 21 years and above and willing to take an oath of allegiance to be given citizenship.[160] The organisation urged that people born of federal citizens should be given citizenship. Those who had resided in Malaya for ten years should be accorded citizenship.[161]

The MSU memorandum contained a long list of fundamental rights which was based on the Indian constitution.[162] The organisation stressed that the constitution of the federation should be secular.[163] A particular concern of the Sikhs was constitutional safeguards for the Punjabi schools and language and facilities for pilgrimage to Sikh holy shrines in India and Pakistan.[164] The memorandum also wanted the constitution to provide for the free flow of foreign capital:

> The Sikhs are aware that the history of prosperous nations shows that foreign capital has been an important and deciding factor in the prosperity and improvement of such countries. Malaya's need is no less now than it has been in the past. To attract foreign capital attractive terms ought to be offered and the security of taking out the capital from the Federation of Malaya to be assured to investors. As such we submit that there should be free flow of capital in and out of the Federation of Malaya.[165]

The memorandum was signed by eight prominent leaders of the Sikh community in the federation led by Mahima Singh who made up the drafting committee.[166]

The Persatuan Melayu Semenanjong (Peninsular Malay Union) based in Johore Bahru submitted a brief and general one-page memorandum dated 15 July 1956 to the commission.[167] The memorandum was signed by its President Ahmad bin Haji Abdul Rahim and focused mainly on the rights of the Malays and the issue of citizenship. The association wanted the federation, which was to include Singapore, to be called *Tanah Melayu*. It felt that citizens of Malaya should be the Malays living in Malaya and those of Malay descent living in the Malay Archipelago. The association proposed that Muslims of non-Malay descent could become citizens provided that they understood and spoke Malay, could perform Malay customs, declared themselves as *Bangsa Melayu* and owed undivided loyalty to Malaya. The association also submitted that non-Muslims could become citizens if they were born in Malaya or one of their parents were born in Malaya and were of 18 years and could speak Malay and understand and perform Malay customs and owed undivided loyalty to Malaya. All non-Malay citizens would be accorded the same rights as the Malays in terms of politics, economics and education. The memorandum stated that all citizens would be equal before the "national law" and all citizens would be guaranteed freedom of religious worship. The association wanted a strong central government. The central government was to comprise the Conference of Rulers, Council of Ministers and an Executive council, a legislative council and people's representation. It proposed that Malay should be the official language and Islam the official religion.

The Federation of Kwan-Tung Association of Malaya submitted a three-page memorandum to the commission on 16 July 1956.[168] The association, which represented Malayan Chinese who traced the origins of their ancestors to the Kwangtung province in China, had 17 branches in the federation and claimed to be writing on behalf of 1.3 million Chinese in Malaya.[169] The main focus of the association was the issues of citizenship, equality, language and education. The association wanted the constitutional commission to provide for the recognition of the principle of *jus soli* in the constitution. It proposed that a five-year residence should suffice for those intending to apply for federal citizenship. The association also wanted the constitution to provide recognition for the validity of existing citizenship rights obtained under the federal citizenship and state nationalities.[170] The association wanted the four main languages to be recognised as official languages, and for education in the mother tongue to be protected. The association pointed out that these rights were universal rights accepted by most democratic countries, and the association was not claiming any special privileges. Political equality, the memorandum stated, was the only solution for an independent Malaya, if peace and security was to be assured.[171] The leader of the Kwan-Tung Association, Leung Cheung Ling, told the commission at the hearing given on 21 August that the views expressed in the memorandum represented the views of the majority of the Chinese and non-Malays in Malaya.[172] The association pointed out the sacrifices made by the Chinese community in the last two wars and also during the eight years of the Emergency. The association wanted the four major languages to be allowed in the legislatures as the association found that some of the most suitable candidates could not speak in English or Malay. Lord Reid enquired who would bring unrest in the country as noted in the association's memorandum. A representative replied that there were noted communist terrorists who had been able to obtain recruits throughout the period of the Emergency and that this showed "there were people in Malaya who were prepared to cause trouble."[173]

An organisation called the Malaya Tamil Pannai based in Kuala Lumpur submitted a memorandum to the constitutional commission on 28 September 1956 following resolutions passed at a meeting on 18 August 1956.[174] The memorandum was signed by the organisation's Secretary K. Chidambaram. The memorandum in the main sought the preservation of the languages and cultures of the Tamil community and other minority races: "The New Constitution of the Federation of Malaya should guarantee the preservation of the respective racial languages and cultures which is a cardinal right."[175] The association wanted the constitution to make provisions in the constitution for "freedom of worship, freedom to learn the mother-tongue, and inalienable right to preserve their culture, customs and traditions." The association described the Tamils as the torch bearers and vanguard of Malaya's early culture and customs. The memorandum noted,

> The Tamils had historical connections with Malaya and they may justly be described as the torch-bearers and vanguard of Malaya's early culture and customs. That was indeed a reflection of the rich heritage, the religious, philosophical and cultural contributions of South India. Their culture had a profound effect on Malaya.[176]

The association argued that the preservation of the various cultures would lead to a united Malayan nation:

> We wish to assert here the existence and preservation of the various cultures and languages will be significant contributory factor towards the foundation of a united Malayan nation. The provision that we seek to be written into the Constitution will forever constitute a milestone in the march of Malaya.[177]

The association wanted stringent requirements to amend the constitution to safeguard the fundamental rights of the minorities and that any constitutional amendment should require a two-thirds majority of each House.[178]

Chambers of commerce and business organisations

The Associated Chinese Chamber of Commerce of Malaya submitted a three-page finely printed memorandum dated 25 June 1956 signed by its Chairman Chong Koon Lin.[179] The organisation represented all the Chinese chambers of commerce in the country. The first recommendation made by this organisation in its memorandum was the recognition of the principle of *jus soli* for the determination of federal citizenship.[180] The memorandum noted that prior to 1948 all persons born in the Settlements of Penang and Malacca were British subjects while those born in the other states were subjects of the rulers of the respective states and British Protected Persons. The principle of *jus soli*, the memorandum added, was recognised by the courts in the country.[181] The organisation noted that *jus soli* was an internationally recognised principle, adding that the Alliance Party also supported this principle, and urged the commission to provide for the recognition of the principle in the constitution.[182] The chamber said the requirements for those applying for federal citizenship were too strict at present and urged that the period of residence required for citizenship be reduced to five years and that the language test be abolished.[183] The chamber urged the commission to provide for multilingualism in the constitution: "It will constitute a great hardship not in keeping with democratic principles if any one language is adopted as official to the exclusion of others."[184] The organisation also urged the commission to ensure that the constitution provided for equality of citizenship:

> It is the considered opinion of our Chambers that when the Federation becomes a self-governing independent and democratic nation, provisions should be made in her Constitution to enable all of her nationals or citizens to enjoy equal rights and opportunities and to bear equal duties and obligations without distinction as to race, colour or creed.[185]

The chamber concluded its memorandum by reiterating the contributions of the Chinese community to the nation:

> The Chinese people in general and the merchants in particular have in no small measure contributed to the prosperity and well-being of this country. It is only fair and equitable that their share of labour in making the country what it is today should be recognised in the new Constitution.[186]

The Perak Malay Chamber of Commerce sent a memorandum to the commission dated 30 July 1956 signed by its Secretary Zapidin bin Ali.[187] The chamber urged that the Malays be given "first preference in everything be it politically, economically or culturally." It wanted the constitution to provide for a special minister for

Malay Economic Affairs to "promote and protect the economic interests of the Malays." They wanted a Malay bank to be set up for the Malays to serve as the nucleus of "Malays economic expansion." The chamber wanted land policy to be changed to ensure that only citizens of the country could "own land of perpetuity."[188] They wanted the constitution to outline stringent immigration policy. The chamber urged the government to set up facilities to train Malays in commerce, agriculture and other vocational fields to enable them to fully participate in the economy. The chamber recommended a policy of economic protection be provided in the constitution: "Towards this end a policy of economic protection should be introduced. No material available or producible in Malaya should be imported from overseas and in case of their indispensability a high taxation should be imposed on them."[189]

The Associated Indian Chamber of Commerce in Malaya sent a five-page memorandum to the constitutional commission dated 20 October 1956.[190] The chamber, which was represented by a member in the Federal Legislative Council, sought parity with the Chinese Chamber of Commerce in the legislative council in terms of one member for every two members for the latter. They hoped this could be implemented in the upper house of the bicameral legislature.[191] The chamber felt it was time to remove the obstacles for non-Malays to qualify for citizenship by birth in the second generation. The memorandum pointed out that since 1904 under the Naturalisation Enactment all that was required was a period of residence of five years and a statement from the applicant that he intended to reside permanently in the four Federated Malay States. There was no language qualification. Thus, the chamber felt that five years residence should suffice for citizenship by registration or naturalisation.[192] It suggested that the language qualification be suspended for two years from the implementation of the new constitution. The chamber pointed that a large majority of the Indians were agricultural labourers and were recruited on terms providing for repatriation "and thereby they were never given a chance to develop in themselves the idea of regarding Malaya as their home."[193] Only after assisted emigration had been stopped by the Indian government, it pointed out, was it possible for "an identity of interest to permeate and inform the Indians who decided to remain in this country forever."[194] This point, it noted, should be borne by those who criticised the Indians for being transients. Therefore, the Indians should be facilitated in their right to acquire citizenship.[195] The chamber hoped that the various languages and cultures would be preserved by suitable legislation without detriment to the building of a Malayan nation.[196] The chamber also urged that English which they felt had served as a cementing factor between the races and its prestige should be maintained.[197] The chamber supported efforts to protect the special position of the Malays so that they could take their proper place in education, administration, politics and the economy. But the chamber, at the same time, was against any attempt to take away or minimise the rights and privileges of the non-Malays.[198]

Trade unions and others

The Bar Council of the Federation of Malaya sent a brief three-page memorandum to the constitutional commission on 15 September 1956, which was signed by its

Chairman T. Rejeindra.[199] The Bar Council raised two main points: the first relating to retention of appeal to the Privy Council and the second on the appointment of judges.[200] The Bar Council noted that individuals appointed to the judiciary "should not only be completely impartial but should also be professionally as competent as possible."[201] The council noted that prior to 1935 appointments to the Bench of the High Courts of the Straits Settlements and the Federated Malay States were made largely from the civil servants with the necessary legal qualifications and partly from the local Bars. But subsequently appointments from local Bars were discontinued. The Council pointed out this was not because of shortcomings of the local Bar "but for reasons of recruitment to the Colonial Legal Service."[202] The Council urged the commission to ensure that the constitution provided for appointment of members of the local bar to judicial office including appointment as Supreme Court judges. It said potential candidates should be such "as to ensure the impartiality and freedom from political influence of persons appointed to be judges of the Supreme Court."[203] The Bar Council also urged the commission to provide for the continuation of appeals to the Privy Council so as not to endanger present standards.[204] It pointed out that the judicial committee of the House of Lords had a long tradition and "commanded universal respect and admiration."[205]

A joint declaration was sent by two teachers' association from the Indian and Chinese vernacular schools. This "declaration" dated 24 September 1956 was submitted to the constitutional commission by the Selangor Indian School Teachers' Union and the United Chinese School Teachers' Association.[206] The declaration, which resulted from resolutions made by the two associations, was signed by D. Rajeeloo, president of the Selangor Indian Teachers' Association, and Lim Lian Geok, chairman of the United Chinese School Teachers' Association. The declaration begins with the words: "We are the educational workers of the two major races residing in Malaya. The responsibility of educating the future generations of more than half of Malaya's population sought rests in our hands."[207] The first declaration sought that the medium of instruction in education of the various races should be their mother tongue. The second declared that the education of the various races "should enjoy equal treatment and equal opportunity of development." A third declaration wanted the languages of the three main races in Malaya – Chinese, Malay and Indians – to be included as official languages. The associations noted that their third point raised, the issue of official languages, may seem outside the question of education, but argued that they had learnt a lesson from the 1952 Education Ordinance: We have learnt a lesson from the Education Ordinance, 1952, and we know that if the language of any race is not recognised as an official language, it will be subjected to restrictions and liable to eliminated in due course. We therefore strongly demand that the language of the three major races – Chinese, Malay and Tamil – should all be included as official languages and that this should clearly be stipulated in the Constitution.[208] The associations at the same time agreed that Malay should become the national language.

The Federation of Malay Teachers' Association (*Kesatuan Persakutuan Guru2 Melayu Semenanjong*) with an address in Taiping, Perak, sent a memorandum to the constitutional commission dated 1 August 1956, and this was signed by its Secretary General Basir bin Udoh.[209] The association said it had 9,000 members and at a special meeting on 7 July 1956 the association adopted several solutions. The association wanted Malay and non-Malay students to study in one type of national school, whether they were government schools or government-aided schools. The association said that individual non-Malay schools should be allowed to be opened on condition that the Malay language was taught and the education was Malayan in character. The association felt that communal universities should be banned: "There should be one university only namely the University of Malaya with Malay as the medium of instruction and the other languages as a subject."[210] The association submitted that the constitution should only provide for one national language – the Malay language.[211] Malay should be the only medium in government business and government departments, it said.

Prominent Indian lawyer and federal legislative councillor, R. Ramani, raised several points on the issue of citizenship. He told the commission during a hearing that ever since the creation of the Federated Malay States there had been in each of the four Malay States a Naturalisation Enactment.[212] All that was required in the Enactment was that a person should be in this country for five years and if he declared that it was his intention to make this country his home, he would have all the rights and privileges of a natural born citizen. He noted that while previously there was no language test, this was required following the 1948 federation agreement. Chairman Reid pointed out that language tests were held in other countries for naturalisation and said that he did not see why the difference between five/ten years residence qualification was so critical. Ramani said that his plea was to revert to pre-war conditions. Indians, he noted, were brought here for specific periods until 1910 under the indenture labour system which required that they should go back every three years. This was modified in 1912 with the coming into force of the Labour Code on Indian Immigration. Up to 1941 the Indian labourer was never given any incentive to stay in this country. He referred to the British Nationality Act 1948 and said that there was no language test. He felt that this question of language test should be completely removed. He suggested that Indian British subjects should receive preferential treatment over Chinese alien immigrants. Ramani felt that Commonwealth citizenship should be enjoyed along federal citizenship. He noted that Indians although a minority were regarded as a majority. He said that Indians should be represented in the Upper House only if they were inadequately represented in the Lower House. Reid enquired whether there should be communal constituencies, and Ramani replied that there was no need for them. He added that a two- or three-member constituency as a temporary measure in those cases would be appropriate. Ramani felt that single-member constituencies would suit the present make-up as they did not take into account the racial rivalries. He did not see how the parliamentary system could work in the country for a generation. Ramani stressed that there should be a completely independent judiciary and that the Bench should also be the guardian of the constitution. He suggested the appeal to the Privy Council should be retained if possible.

Notes

1 See letter from R.T.M. Henry, Deputy assistant secretary, constitutional commission, to secretary, constitutional commission, 4 October 1956, CO 889/8/1 (2).
2 Summary record of the main points submitted by individuals and organisations in memoranda and at the hearings, 5 September 1956, CO 889/8/1 (1), C.C. 1003/5.
3 Ibid.
4 Ibid.
5 Ibid.
6 Ibid.
7 Ibid.
8 Memorandum by People's Progressive Party, 20 July 1956, CO 889/5 (1). The memorandum was dated 18 July 1956. The party's address was 7 Hale Street, Ipoh.
9 Ibid., p. 1.
10 Ibid., p. 3.
11 Ibid., p. 4.
12 Ibid., p. 4.
13 Ibid., p. 5.
14 Ibid., pp. 6–7.
15 Ibid., pp. 6–7.
16 Ibid., p. 7.
17 Ibid., p. 8.
18 Memorandum by the Labour Party of Malaya, 25 September 1956, CO 889/3 (5). The party's secretariat was at 59 Beach Street, Penang.
19 Ibid., p. 1.
20 Ibid., p. 2.
21 Ibid., p. 2.
22 Ibid., p. 2.
23 Ibid., pp. 2–3.
24 Ibid., p. 3.
25 Ibid., p. 4.
26 Ibid., p. 4.
27 Ibid., p. 4.
28 Ibid., p. 4.
29 Ibid., p. 5.
30 Ibid., p. 5.
31 Ibid., p. 5.
32 Ibid., p. 6.
33 Ibid., p. 6.
34 Ibid., p. 7.
35 Ibid., p. 7.
36 Ibid., p. 7.
37 Ibid., p. 9.
38 Ibid., p. 9.
39 Memorandum by Islamic Association of Malaya, 14 July 1956, CO 889/5 (1).
40 Ibid., p. 1.
41 Ibid., p. 3.
42 Ibid., p. 6.
43 Ibid., p. 7.
44 Ibid., p. 7.
45 Ibid., p. 6.
46 Ibid., p. 6.
47 Ibid., p. 7.
48 Ibid., p. 7.

49 Ibid., p. 9.
50 Memorandum by Party Negara Perlis Branch, 28 July 1956, CO 889/5 (5).
51 Summary record of third meeting of constitutional commission, 25 June 1956, CO 889/1 (4), p. 1.
52 Memorandum by Party Negara Perlis Branch, p. 1.
53 Ibid., p. 1. See also record of party's hearing before the commission on 28 July 1956, CO 889/1 (1), C.C. 2046.
54 Ibid., p. 2. See also record of party's hearing before the commission on 28 July 1956, CO 889/1 (1), C.C. 2046.
55 Ibid., p. 2.
56 Ibid., p. 2.
57 Memorandum by Straits Chinese British Association, Penang, 4 July 1956, CO 889/5 (1).
58 Ibid., p. 1.
59 Ibid., pp. 3–4.
60 Ibid., pp. 4–5.
61 Memorandum by Straits Chinese British Association, Penang, 14 July 1956, CO 889/5 (1), pp. 6–7. See also record of hearing given to the Straits Chinese British Association, 10 August 1956, CO 889/1 (2), C.C. 2048.
62 Memorandum by Straits Chinese British Association, Penang, p. 7.
63 Ibid., p. 7.
64 Ibid., p. 8.
65 Ibid., p. 10.
66 Ibid., p. 10.
67 Ibid., p. 10.
68 See record of hearing given to the Straits Chinese British Association by the constitutional commission, 10 August 1956, CO 889/1 (2), C.C. 2048.
69 Memorandum by Malay Society of Great Britain, 10 July 1956, CO 889/5 (1).
70 Ibid., p. 1.
71 Ibid., p. 1.
72 Ibid., p. 2.
73 Ibid., pp. 2–3.
74 Ibid., p. 3.
75 Ibid., p. 3.
76 Ibid., pp. 3–4.
77 Ibid., p. 4.
78 Ibid., p. 5.
79 Ibid., p. 6.
80 Ibid, p. 6.
81 Ibid., p. 6.
82 Ibid., p. 7. The memorandum was signed by Ibrahim Manan, chairman of sub-committee; Sulaiman Alias, secretary of sub-committee; and the members, Abdul Aziz bin Yeop, Ismail bin Alang, S. Agil Barakbah, Wan Daud, Hussein Onn, Ismi Ismail, S. Othman Ali, Wan A. Hamid and Zain Ahmad. The memorandum was dated 1 July 1956.
83 Memorandum by Pan-Malayan Federation of Chinese Associations, 20 July 1956, CO 889//8/6. See also CO 889/1 (21), C.C. 2060. Summary record of hearing given by the constitutional commission to the Pan-Malayan Federation of Chinese Associations, 24 August 1956. The memorandum was signed by associations from Penang, Kedah, Perlis, Perak, Selangor, Negri Sembilan, Malacca, Johore, Pahang, Trengganu and Kelantan.
84 Ibid., pp. 1–2.
85 Ibid., p. 2.
86 Ibid., p. 2.
87 Ibid., p. 1.

88 Ibid., p. 2.
89 Ibid., p. 3.
90 Ibid., p. 5.
91 Ibid., p. 3.
92 Ibid., p. 3.
93 Ibid., p. 4.
94 Ibid., p. 3.
95 Ibid., p. 4.
96 Ibid., p. 5.
97 Ibid., p. 4.
98 Ibid., p. 4.
99 Ibid., p. 5.
100 See summary record of hearing given by the constitutional commission to the Pan-Malayan Federation of Chinese Associations, 24 August 1956, CO 889/1 (21), C.C. 2060.
101 Memorandum submitted to the constitutional commission by the All Malaya Tamils Conference, 26 August 1956, CO 889/6 (1), p. 1.
102 Ibid., p. 1.
103 Ibid., p. 1.
104 Ibid., p. 1.
105 Ibid., p. 4.
106 Ibid., pp. 1–2.
107 Ibid., p. 2.
108 Ibid., p. 2.
109 Ibid., p. 2.
110 Ibid., p. 3.
111 Ibid., pp. 2–3.
112 Memorandum submitted by Datoh Panglima Kinta Haji M. Eusoff as aborigines representative, 14 July 1956, CO 889/5 (1), p. 1. See also record of hearing given to Datoh Haji M. Eusoff by the constitutional commission, 14 August 1956, CO 889/1 (7), C.C. 2055.
113 Record of hearing given to Datoh Haji M. Eusoff by the constitutional commission, p. 1.
114 Ibid., p. 1.
115 Memorandum submitted by Datoh Panglima Kinta Haji M. Eusoff as aborigines representative, p. 1.
116 Ibid., p. 1.
117 Ibid., p. 1.
118 Ibid., p. 1.
119 Ibid., p. 1.
120 Ibid., p. 1.
121 Ibid., p. 1.
122 Ibid., p. 2.
123 Record of hearing given to Datoh Haji M. Eusoff by the constitutional commission, 14 August 1956, CO 889/1 (7), C.C. 2055, p. 1.
124 Ibid., p. 1.
125 Ibid., p. 2.
126 Ibid., p. 2.
127 Memorandum by the Eurasian Union of Malaya, 1 September 1956, CO 889/8/7.
128 Ibid., p. 5.
129 Ibid., pp. 5–6.
130 Ibid., p. 8.
131 Ibid., p. 8.
132 Ibid., p. 9.

133 Ibid., p. 12.
134 Ibid., p. 12.
135 Ibid., p. 13.
136 Ibid., p. 14.
137 Ibid., p. 15.
138 Ibid., p. 15.
139 Ibid., p. 21.
140 Summary record of hearing given to the Eurasian Union of Malaya, 31 August 1956, CO 889/1 (1), C.C. 2000. The Eurasian Union was represented by its President G. Shelley, L.E. Labrooy, B.A. Skelchy and R.H. Beins.
141 Summary record of hearing given to the Eurasian Union of Malaya, 31 August 1956, CO 889/1 (1), C.C. 2000.
142 Ibid.
143 Memorandum by Malayan Christian Council, 18 July 1956, CO 889/5 (1). Rev. J. Sutton was the association's general secretary. See also summary record of hearing given to Malayan Christian Council, 23 August 1956, CO 889/1 (18), C.C. 2067.
144 Memorandum by Malayan Christian Council, p. 1.
145 Memorandum by Malayan Christian Council, 18 July 1956, CO 889/5 (1), p. 5. It wanted provisions for freedom of speech expression, assembly, to form associations and freedom of movement, among others, written into the constitution.
146 Memorandum by Malayan Christian Council, p. 1.
147 Ibid., p. 2.
148 Ibid., p. 3.
149 Ibid., pp. 3–4.
150 Ibid., p. 6.
151 Summary record of hearing given to the Malayan Christian Council, 23 August 1956, CO 889/1 (18), C.C. 2067, p. 1. The council was represented by Dr Ho Seng Ong, chairman of the Malayan Christian Council and director of the Methodist Education Bureau; Archdeacon R.W. Woods, acting for Bishop H.W. Baines as head of the Anglican Church in Malaya; Rev. R.L. Archer, bishop emeritus of the Methodist Church of Malaya; Rev. Roland Koh, acting vicar, St. Mary's Church, Kuala Lumpur; Rev. P.C. John, minister of Mar-Thoma Church, North and Central Malaya; and Rev. J. Sutton, associate general secretary, Malayan Christian Council.
152 Summary record of hearing given to the Malayan Christian Council, p. 1.
153 Ibid., p. 1.
154 Ibid., pp. 1–2.
155 Ibid., p. 2.
156 Ibid., p. 2.
157 Ibid., p. 2.
158 Memorandum by Malayan Sikhs' Representative Committee, 14 July 1956, CO 889/5 (1).
159 Ibid., pp. 1–2.
160 Ibid., p. 2.
161 Ibid., p. 2.
162 Ibid., pp. 2–5.
163 Ibid., p. 5.
164 Ibid., pp. 5–6.
165 Ibid., p. 6.
166 Ibid., p. 7. The memorandum was signed by T. Mahima Singh (president, Malayan Sikhs' Union), U.S. Gill (president, Khalsa Education Board, Malaya), Lall Singh (advocate and solicitor, Kuala Lumpur), S. Natha Singh (advocate and solicitor, Penang), Harbans Singh (president, Perak Sikh Association), Ganga Singh (teacher, Kuala Lumpur), Pritam Singh (superintendent of Police, Kuala Kubu Bharu) and Inder Singh (president, Sikh Temple, Sentul, Kuala Lumpur).

167 Memorandum by the *Persatuan Melayu Semenanjong* (Peninsular Malay Union) based, 15 July 1956, CO 889/5 (1)(b).
168 Memorandum by Federation of Kwan-Tung Association of Malaya, 16 July 1956, CO 889/5 (1).
169 Ibid., p. 2.
The memorandum was signed by representatives of four state branches.
170 Ibid., p. 2.
171 Ibid., p. 2.
172 Summary record of hearing given to Federation of Kwan-Tung Association of Malaya by constitutional commission, 21 August 1956, CO 889/5 (1), C.C. 2057. The other members who attended the hearing were Yap Mau Tatt, Chin Chee Meow, Cheong Fong and Yoe Fee Tan.
173 Ibid., p. 2.
174 Memorandum by Malaya Tamil Pannai, 18 August 1956, CO 889/6 (1).
175 Ibid., p. 1.
176 Ibid., p. 2.
177 Ibid., p. 3.
178 Ibid., p. 4.
179 Memorandum by the Associated Chinese Chamber of Commerce of Malaya, 25 June 1956, CO 889/3 (59).
180 Ibid., p. 1.
181 Ibid., p. 1.
182 Ibid., pp. 1–2.
183 Ibid., p. 2.
184 Ibid., p. 2.
185 Ibid., p. 2.
186 Ibid., p. 3.
187 Memorandum by Perak Malay Chamber of Commerce, 30 July 1956, CO 889/5 (1).
188 Ibid.
189 Ibid.
190 Memorandum by Associated Indian Chambers of Commerce, Malaya, 20 October 1956, CO 889/7 (1). The memorandum was signed by its General Secretary K.S. Gill.
191 Memorandum by Associated Indian Chambers of Commerce, Malaya, p. 1.
192 Ibid., p. 2.
193 Ibid., p. 3.
194 Ibid., p. 3.
195 Ibid., p. 4.
196 Ibid., p. 4.
197 Ibid., p. 4.
198 Ibid., p. 4.
199 Memorandum by the Bar Council of the Federation of Malaya to the constitutional commission, CO 889/6 (1), 15 September 1956, p. 1.
200 Ibid., p. 1.
201 Ibid., p. 1.
202 Ibid., p. 2.
203 Ibid., p. 2.
204 Ibid., p. 3.
205 Ibid., p. 3.
206 Joint memorandum by the Selangor Indian School Teachers' Union and the United Chinese School Teachers' Association, 24 September 1956, CO 889/6 (1) (C.C. 2160 and C.C. 2026).
207 Ibid.
208 Ibid.

209 The Federation of Malay Teachers' Association (*Kesatuan Persakutuan Guru2 Melayu Semenanjong*), 1 August 1956, CO 889/6 (1b).
210 Ibid., p. 1.
211 Ibid., p. 2.
212 Summary record of hearing given by constitutional commission to R. Ramani, 28 September 1956, CO 889/1 (31), C.C. 3003/1.

7 The judiciary

The judiciary is a central pillar in the workings of a parliamentary democracy and acts as the moderator between the government and its citizens in the enforcement of the laws and regulations. Under the doctrine of separation of powers based on the Westminster model, the independence of the judiciary is central to the effective functioning of the parliamentary democracy. Most British colonial territories embraced this doctrine at independence to ensure that there was a check and balance on the executive and the legislature, the two other components of the governing body. In fact, even before the achievement of independence, most colonial territories had a long tradition of the judiciary functioning independently, as a neutral arbitrator of the implementation of the laws of a state, devoid of any political intervention. They drew considerably from the workings of the judiciary in Britain and from established precedents and conventions in the older Commonwealth countries such as Canada and Australia. Underpinning the judicial system was the shared Common Law norms and precedents. Thus, considerable attention was given by the Reid constitutional commission and the main political parties in Malaya in their submissions urging the commission to entrench firmly the independence of the judiciary in the new constitution. The Alliance Party, the Malay rulers and a number of other organisations and individuals emphasised the independence of the judiciary in their submissions to the constitutional commission.

The judiciary in the federation was well-respected by the legal fraternity in the country and in the Commonwealth and had developed a long historical legal tradition. English law was first introduced in the country after the arrival of Francis Light in Penang in 1786. The precise date of the beginning of the application of English law in Penang remains contentious, however. Light had "acquired" the island from the Sultan of Kedah on behalf of the East India Company. The first professional judge arrived in Penang from England in 1801. The English Crown granted the First Charter of Justice in 1807 resulting in the establishment of a Court of Judicature in Penang.[1] Thereafter, the Common Law tradition was gradually introduced into the legal system in the nineteenth century in the Straits Settlements and later the Federated Malay States with the introduction of the residential system and state legislative councils. The jurisdiction of the courts in Settlements of Penang, Singapore and Malacca and the Malay states was governed by several

DOI: 10.4324/9781003542537-7

important legislation. First, the British Crown had legislative powers in the Settlements of Penang and Malacca, which were Crown colonies by the virtue of the British Settlements Act 1887 and 1945 and the Straits Settlements (Repeal) Act 1946.[2] This meant that the British parliament could pass legislation with respect to the two Settlements "without any constitutional limitation."[3] The British constitutional position under the 1948 federation agreement was governed by the Federation of Malaya Order in Council 1948 and as amended in 1955. This legislation was enacted both under the British Settlements Acts 1887 and the Foreign Jurisdiction Act, 1890. Second, the British Crown had full jurisdiction in the nine Malay states through various treaties with the Malay rulers. The Crown acquired legislative power in these states via the Foreign Jurisdiction Act, 1890.[4] It was under the Foreign Jurisdiction Act, 1890, that the 1948 federation agreement and state agreements had the force of law.[5] The Common Law system co-existed with the practice of Muslim law or *syariah* law, which was placed under the jurisdiction of the Malay rulers in the states. Various state enactments from 1948 brought matters relating to the Muslim religion within the legislative competence of the state legislative councils.[6] These courts were previously known as the *kadhi* courts and had limited civil and criminal jurisdiction and largely dealt with personal and property laws for Muslims.[7] During the period of British rule, the Common Law legal tradition soon became the dominant legal tradition in Malaya. Under the 1948 federation agreement, civil and criminal laws were subjects placed under the jurisdiction of the federal government.[8] Muslim law and Malay customs, on the other hand, were placed under the jurisdiction of the states, religion being a state subject. In the Settlements of Penang and Malacca, the federal government had legislative power over Muslim law (Clause 48 and Clause 110 and the Second Schedule). In the other states, the Council of State was authorised to legislate on Muslim law and federal law was limited to "ascertainment" (Clause 48 and Second Schedule).[9]

In 1946, a Supreme Court was established for the whole of the Malayan Union in Kuala Lumpur with a single chief justice and a number of judges under the Malayan Union Courts Ordinance No. 3 of 1946.[10] This law also provided for subordinate courts to be constituted.[11] Prior to this, there were a number of superior courts which exercised civil and criminal jurisdiction in the Straits Settlements, the Federated Malay States and the Unfederated Malay States which essentially operated independently.[12] Some efforts were made in the pre-war period to consolidate the judicial system in Malaya. In 1938, for example, a Court of Appeal for the Straits Settlements and the Federated Malay States was created.[13] Prior to that, there was a chief justice each for the Straits Settlements and the Federated Malay States. The Unfederated Malay States, on the other hand, had a number of superior courts. Thus in 1946, the judiciary in Malaya was reorganised into one national body under the Judicial and Legal Departments.

In the post-Second World War period, there were efforts to increase the number of locals in the judicial and legal service in Malaya. At the end of the war, there were only four qualified Malayans serving the judicial and legal service.[14] This situation improved a little thereafter, but the number of Malayans serving in the judicial and legal service still remained small. In 1955, the Malayans in judicial and legal service comprised one judge; 14 serving as court presidents, magistrates or senior assistant registrars; one legal adviser; and two deputy public prosecutors.[15] Thus, up till 1957 most of the senior judges were British. In the mid-fifties, the Federation of Malaya Bar Council had urged the high commissioner to appoint more local barristers to the Bench.[16] The judges that were elected to the bench were mainly from the Colonial Legal Service in Malaya, Malayan Civil Service and some British barristers. The Malayan Bar felt this method of selection was ignoring local talent. The chief justice summed up the situation aptly when he proposed a reorganisation of the judicial and legal service in late 1955 with Malaya moving closer to independence to achieve complete Malayanisation:

> There will be no lack of qualified personnel to serve in the two departments, but there is the shortage of experienced and seasoned lawyers within the Government Service, ready to take over the more senior appointments. There are available practising lawyers who might be induced to sacrifice their large earnings in private practice to accept positions on the Bench, but regard must be had to the young Malayans who have accepted law as their career and who are entitled, when they have gained the experience, to look forward to promotion to senior posts in both departments.[17]

The chief justice proposed the creation of a Federation Legal Service, comprising both judicial and legal posts in the government service to replace the Colonial Legal Service.[18] In 1956, the Conference of Rulers approved the setting up of a Federation Legal Service to staff all legal and judicial posts.[19]

When the constitution was being drafted in 1956–1957, there was a Supreme Court and a Court of Appeal at the federal level, with high courts and lower courts in the states. The administration of the courts was under the jurisdiction of the federal government which had unified the previous divided judicial system. There was a chief justice, and most senior judges were British. Nevertheless, the judiciary in Malaya was held in high regard by Malayans and the Commonwealth nations. Many elites in Malaya, including members of the royal households, in the past century were trained as barristers in England and had been admitted to the English Bar before returning home and were comfortable with the legal system based on Common Law traditions. Thus, the elites overwhelmingly wanted the continuation of Common Law practices and the judicial system based on the practices in England.

The two main actors in Malaya, the Alliance Party and the Malay rulers, felt strongly about the need for a sound judicial system in the country, and in their memoranda emphasised the need for an independent judiciary in Malaya, based on the doctrine of separation of powers found in most parliamentary systems. The Alliance Party in their memorandum stated unequivocally the need for an independent judiciary in keeping with the doctrine of separation of powers enshrined in most modern democracies: "The judiciary should be completely independent both of the Executive and the Legislature."[20] The memorandum noted further: "The Supreme Court should be vested with powers to decide whether or not the actions of both the Federal Executives and the Legislatures are in accordance with the Constitution."[21]

They wanted subordinate courts, high courts and a Supreme Court which would hear appeals from the high courts. They proposed that the judges should be appointed by the *Yang di-Pertuan Agong* and hold office till the age of 65 years. The Alliance suggested that the judges could be removed from office by the *Yang di-Pertuan Agong* on grounds of "misbehaviour or infirmity of mind or body" after an address by the *Dewan Raayat* (Lower House), which was supported by a majority of the members of the house and by votes of not less than two-thirds of the members present and voting.[22] Any motion brought into the house for the removal of a judge should have the support of not less than one-third of the total members of the *Dewan Raayat*. The Supreme Court would be vested with the powers to decide if the action of the Federal Executives and Legislature were in accordance with the constitution.[23] Interestingly, the Alliance suggested that the constitution should provide for a right of ultimate appeal to the *Yang di-Pertuan Agong*, who for the purposes of deciding these appeals should be assisted by a body of law councillors, appointed by him.[24] The Alliance's memorandum was silent on appeals to the Privy Council in the House of Lords in the United Kingdom.

The rulers shared similar views on the need for an independent judiciary vested with powers to decide constitutional disputes. In their memorandum to the constitutional commission, the rulers stated clearly that they wanted the existing federal judicial system to be retained.[25] Unlike the Alliance, however, the rulers wanted a Judicial Services Commission to make recommendations for the appointment of judges to the Supreme Court of the Federation.[26] The appointment itself would be made by the *Yang di-Pertuan Agong* on the advice of the judicial commission. The appointment of minor judicial positions such as registrars, presidents of Sessions courts and first-class magistrates and appointments to the Federal Legal Service would be the responsibility of the Judicial Services Commission. Their Highnesses, at the same time, wanted to retain the right to veto the appointment of any federal judicial officers who would perform in their respective states. The Supreme Court, in the view of the rulers, should be the determining authority in the adjudication of constitutional disputes, interpretation of the constitution and enforcement of fundamental rights of the citizens in the federation.[27] The rulers were in favour of retaining the right of appeal from decisions of the Court of Appeal in Malaya to the Privy Council in the House of Lords and suggested that a qualified Malayan should be appointed to the Judicial Committee of the Privy Council.[28]

The Malay rulers submitted that the status of the *syariah* religious courts which adjudicated on Muslim law should be reserved to the rulers. Their memorandum stated: "Their Highnesses consider that the status of the religious (Muslim) Courts is a matter for Their Highnesses within their own States. Further that the existing law relating to the ascertainment and enforcement of Muslim Law (*Hukum Shara*) and Malay Custom should be maintained."[29] The rulers noted that the appointment to the position of attorney general of the federation should be a political appointment.[30]

In addition, they suggested that Legal Service of the federation should be constituted under a permanent civil service head such as the solicitor general. Appointments to the legal service would be made by the Judicial Services Commission.

The rulers wanted the post of Legal Adviser to the States to be separate from the positions of Public Prosecutor and Federal Counsel:

> In principle the post of Legal Adviser to the State should not be filled from the Federal Legal Service, but should be filled from amongst suitable lawyers practising in the State concerned who may carry out the functions of State Adviser upon part-time basis.[31]

The Bar Council in their memorandum touched on two main issues relating to the judiciary while emphasising the need for meritorious selection for appointments to the Bench and the legal service. The first related to the appointment of judges, and the second concerned the retention of appeals to the Privy Council in the United Kingdom.[32] Individuals appointed to the judiciary, said the Bar Council, should not only be "completely impartial" but also be "professionally as competent as possible."[33] The council noted that prior to 1935, appointments to the Bench of the High Courts of the Straits Settlements and the Federated Malay States were made largely from the civil servants with the necessary legal qualifications and partly from the local Bars. Subsequently appointments from local Bars were discontinued. The council pointed out this was not because of shortcomings of the local Bar "but for reasons of recruitment to the Colonial Legal Service."[34] The council urged the commission to ensure that the constitution provided for appointment of members of the local bar to judicial office including appointment as Supreme Court judges. It said potential candidates should be such "as to ensure the impartiality and freedom from political influence of persons appointed to be judges of the Supreme court."[35] The Bar Council also urged the commission to provide for the continuation of appeals to the Privy Council so as not to endanger present standards.[36] Dato' Sir Roland Braddell, a respected senior lawyer who was involved in the drafting of the 1948 federation agreement, expressed concern over the calibre of the Bench in his meeting with the commission.[37] He told the commission that the "special position" of the Bench should be recognised and only the best qualified barristers, "irrespective of race, citizenship status or age" should be appointed to the Bench after they had sufficient practice in the country.[38] Another renowned local lawyer R. Ramani told the constitutional commission that there should be a "completely independent judiciary" and that the Bench should be the "guardian of the constitution."[39] He suggested the appeal to the Privy Council should be retained if possible.

The Reid Commission provided for the continuation of the Supreme Court with its existing powers and procedure but with enlarged powers in independent Malaya. The commission recommended (Article 114) a Supreme Court for the federation to be headed by a chief justice and with a maximum of 15 judges. While the commission noted that they did not want to make any considerable changes to the existing judicial system, they felt it was necessary to provide for a clearer distinction between federal and state powers.[40] The commission gave considerably more powers to the Supreme Court in the draft constitution, particularly in respect of interpreting the constitution.[41] Under the federation agreement, constitutional disputes and interpretations were adjudicated by an ad hoc Interpretation Tribunal. In the new constitution, the Supreme Court would handle such disputes. The commission said that states could not maintain their measure of autonomy unless they "are enabled to challenge the courts as *ultra vires* both Federal legislation and Federal executive acts."[42] The commission also pointed out that the insertion of provisions relating to fundamental liberties required the establishment of a legal procedure in which breaches of these provisions could be challenged. In addition, a method of securing a rapid decision on a constitutional question was provided in Article 121 along the lines adopted in other Commonwealth countries such as Canada, India and Pakistan.[43]

The commission did not support the proposal of the rulers for the setting up of a Judicial Services Commission for the appointment of judges. Instead, they adopted the suggestion of the Alliance and provided for the appointment of judges to the Supreme Court by the *Yang di-Pertuan Agong* in consultation with the chief justice (Article 114(2)).[44] The commission noted:

> We do not approve of the suggestion that Supreme Court judges be appointed by the Judicial and Legal Service Commission, since a body suitably composed for appointing subordinate judges (containing for instance, the Attorney-General) would not be suitably composed for appointing Supreme Court judges.[45]

In the appointment of a judge to the Supreme Court, the commission recommended (Article 115) that the person should have been an advocate of the Supreme Court for at least ten years or had served ten years in the judicial or legal service in the federation.[46]

The commission felt strongly on the need to maintain the independence of the judiciary and provided for strong safeguards in respect of the removal of judges. The commission provided (Article 116) that a judge could not be removed from his position except by an order from the *Yang di-Pertuan Agong* after an address in parliament passed by a two-thirds majority of members of each House of Parliament present and voting on the grounds of misconduct or infirmity of mind or body.[47] The commission recommended the age of retirement of judges should be fixed at 65 years, as they felt given tropical conditions in Malaya, the United Kingdom practice of life appointments would not be suitable.[48] The commission felt that the remuneration of a Supreme Court judge should not be "varied to his disadvantage" (Article 117) during his term of office and recommended that the salary should be charged to the Consolidated Fund (Article 90). While the commission felt that judges should not be beyond criticism, they maintained that the judges should be able to sit "fairly and freely, without favour and without fear."[49] They noted that judges should not exercise their functions with "an eye upon the activities of party politics."[50]

The commission gently rebuffed the request of the rulers that Their Highnesses should have a "veto" against the placing of a judge in a state (as provided under

Clause 79(2) of the federation agreement) unless Their Highnesses were first consulted. They felt the appointment of judges was a federal matter and noted in the report:

> We understand that no judge has been appointed to reside in any state without the consent of the Ruler having first been obtained but in our view this is not a matter which comes within the jurisdiction of a State authority.[51]

The commission agreed with the Alliance, the rulers and the Bar Council that appeals to the Privy Council should continue although some difficulties arose over the legal procedure as "Her Majesty will not in the future be the Fountain of Justice in the Federation."[52] The commission felt great advantages would be gained from the retention of the appeals to the Privy Council as this tribunal had much experience of adjudicating on other federal constitutions. The commission opined that the quality of the Bench in Malaya was not of high quality to determine complex legal issues such as fundamental rights or prerogative writs and did not anticipate that this quality could be raised through recruitment from the Malayan Bar within a generation.[53] They therefore felt that the appeals to the Privy Council should continue. Jennings had earlier suggested the possibility of the setting up of a Malayan Judicial Committee, to be possibly called the "Court of Appeal," comprising mainly of law Lords from the United Kingdom but also senior judges from the Commonwealth countries sitting in Malaya to adjudicate complex cases.[54] He felt taking the appeals to London may be too costly. In time, he thought the number of Malayans on this Malayan Judicial Committee could be increased and, eventually, Malayanised. The commission recommended that appeals to the Judicial Committee of the Privy Council could originate from the Supreme Court in the federation and the decision of the Privy Council could then be sent directly to the Supreme Court which would be bound to apply it.[55] The commission drew considerably from the judicial practices of Canada, India, Ceylon and Pakistan, and invariably the United Kingdom, in providing for a strong and independent judiciary in the tradition of the modern parliamentary system of government in the Commonwealth.

On the position of the attorney general, the commission rejected the rulers' recommendation that it should be a political position and preferred the practice in the United Kingdom where the attorney general was not part of the Cabinet. The commission noted:

> In some Commonwealth countries the Attorney-General holds political office. In others the political functions normally exercised by a political Attorney-General are exercised by a Minister of Justice or Minister of Law, while the Attorney-General (or Advocate-General) exercises the more professional functions of giving independent legal advice to the government, representing the government in the courts, and perhaps assuming responsibility for public prosecution. On the whole, we prefer the latter. In the United Kingdom

> the political and professional functions of the Law Officers are conventionally kept distinct and the latter are not regarded as within the jurisdiction of the Cabinet.[56]

In the Working Party, several points were raised in relation to the judiciary and some changes were made. The rulers, for example, submitted that if the judges of the Supreme Court were appointed by the *Yang di-Pertuan Agong*, then the rulers' concurrence should also be sought for these appointments.[57] Following discussions, the Working Party agreed that the chief justice would be appointed by the *Yang di-Pertuan Agong* after consultation with the prime minister and the Conference of Rulers (Article 114).[58] Other judges of the Supreme Court would be appointed by the *Yang di-Pertuan Agong* on the recommendation of the Judicial and Legal Service Commission and after consultation with the Conference of Rulers.[59]

The Alliance proposed that judges should be citizens as suggested by Justice Abdul Hamid in his minority report.[60] The Alliance, however, was of the view that judges who were not citizens before Merdeka Day should be allowed to continue holding office after independence. The Working Party accepted the Alliance's recommendation but added a proviso that for ten years after independence non-citizens could continue to be appointed as judges (Article 115).[61] On the removal of the judges, the Reid Commission had recommended that this could only be done on the order of the *Yang di-Pertuan Agong*, after an address by the parliament supported by two-thirds of the members present and voting. The Working Party modified this provision to provide for the removal of the chief justice and judges of the Supreme Court by the *Yang di-Pertuan Agong* on the advice of a tribunal specially constituted after consultation of the Judicial and Legal Service Commission (Article 116).[62] The Working Party accepted Article 121 enabling the *Yang di-Pertuan Agong* to refer issues of questions of law of public importance arising, but recommended that this provision should be limited to "questions of interpretation of the constitution" to avoid any difficulties.[63]

The Alliance and the rulers agreed that appeals to the Privy Council should be retained as recommended by the Reid Commission[64] and that an appropriate machinery should be devised to facilitate this process in view of the change in the position of the Queen in relation to such appeals after independence.[65] It was agreed that appeals to the Judicial Committee of the Privy Council should lie from the Supreme Court as recommended by the Reid Commission. The Working Party thought the advice of the Judicial Committee (of the Privy Council) should be conveyed to the *Yang di-Pertuan Agong* for transmission to the Supreme Court which would then make such an order to give effect to the decision of the Privy Council.[66] It was also agreed that the existing practice should be continued in regard to criminal case appeals to the Privy Council.[67] Clearly, the constitutional commission and the main parties placed much emphasis on the independence of the judiciary as an important underlying principle in the constitution and also ensured strong safeguards in the appointment of the judges of the Supreme Court.

Notes

1 R.J. Braddell, *The law of the straits settlements: A commentary* (Kuala Lumpur: Oxford University Press, 1982), pp. 1–21. See also Salleh Buang, *Malaysian legal history* (Kuala Lumpur: Dewan Bahasa dan Pustaka, 2015), pp. 3–6.
2 See note on the jurisdiction of the courts by Sir Ivor Jennings, 24 June 1956, CO 889/2 (1).
3 See note by Attorney-General T.V.A. Brodie to secretary, constitutional commission, 25 September 1956, CO 889/2 (11). Clause 154 of the Federation Agreement provides that nothing in the agreement shall affect His Majesty's sovereignty and jurisdiction over the Settlements.
4 See note on the jurisdiction of the courts by Sir Ivor Jennings, 24 June 1956, CO 889/2 (1).
5 Ibid.
6 See Note on Muslim law in the states by Justice Abdul Hamid, 20 June 1956, CO 889/2 (1).
7 Ibid. The *syariah* court's civil jurisdiction included betrothal, marriage, divorce, maintenance of dependents, custody of children, property inheritance, wills, *wakaf* (trust), *nazar* (donations), *zakat* (tithe of certain property payable annually by a person) and *fitrah* (a payment made by Muslims at the end of the fasting month of Ramadhan to be used for religious and charitable purposes). Criminal jurisdiction includes various punishments for offences under state Muslim law enactments, which include absence from Friday prayers, sale and consumption of liquor, desertion of wife, male found in suspicious proximity of a woman, unlawful solemnization of marriage and misuse of Quran and contempt of religion and religious authorities.
8 See note on the jurisdiction of the courts by Sir Ivor Jennings, 24 June 1956, CO 889/2 (1).
9 Ibid.
10 See Legal Report by Attorney-General, 15 April 1946, CO 717/149/9 (28). The Attorney-General K.K. O'Connor noted in his report: "The objects of this Ordinance as regards the Supreme Court, are to constitute one Supreme Court to have jurisdiction throughout the Union, and to confer upon that Court the powers and jurisdiction of all the Superior Courts which it replaces."
11 See Legal report by attorney-general, 15 April 1946, CO 717/149/9 (28).
12 Ibid.
13 Malcolm MacDonald to Sir Shenton Thomas, 10 August 1938, CO 272/624/1 (2).
14 See Memorandum by chief justice of Malaya, 20 December 1955, CO 1030/404 (1).
15 Ibid.
16 Memorandum of the Bar Council of the Federation of Malaya to the Reid Commission, 15 September 1956, CO 889/6 (1), p. 46.
17 See Memorandum by chief justice of Malaya, 20 December 1955, CO 1030/404 (1).
18 Ibid.
19 MacGillivray to secretary of state, 2 May 1956, CO 1030/404 (3).
20 Alliance memorandum, 27 September 1956, UMNO/SUA 154/56, p. 6.
21 Ibid., p. 6.
22 Ibid., p. 6.
23 Ibid., p. 6.
24 Ibid., p. 6.
25 Memorandum submitted by the rulers to the commission, September 1956, CO 889/8 (22a), p. 46.
26 Ibid., p. 46.
27 Ibid., p. 47.
28 Ibid., p. 47.

29 Ibid., p. 47.
30 Ibid., p. 48.
31 Ibid., p. 48.
32 Memorandum submitted to the commission by the Bar Council of the Federation of Malaya, 15 September 1956, CO 889/6 (1), p. 46. The memorandum was signed by the Bar Council Chairman T. Rejeindra.
33 Memorandum submitted to the commission by the Bar Council of the Federation of Malaya, p. 1.
34 Ibid., p. 1.
35 Ibid., p. 1.
36 Ibid., p. 47a.
37 Summary record of hearing given to Dato' Sir Roland Braddell, 11 September 1956, CO 889/1 (26), C.C. 2103, p. 2.
38 Ibid., p. 2.
39 Record of hearing by commission to be given to R. Ramani, CO 889/1 (31), 28 September 1956, C.C. 3000/1.
40 Report of the federation of Malaya constitutional commission, 1957, pp. 53–54.
41 Ibid., p. 54.
42 Ibid., p. 54.
43 Ibid., p. 54.
44 Ibid., p. 54.
45 Ibid., p. 54.
46 Ibid., p. 54.
47 Ibid., p. 54.
48 Ibid., p. 54.
49 Ibid., pp. 54–55.
50 Ibid., p. 55.
51 Ibid., p. 55.
52 Report of the federation of Malaya constitutional commission, 1957, p. 55. See also Summary record of 35th meeting of constitutional commission, 28 September 1956, CO 889/1 (38), C.C. 1000, p. 1.
53 See paper by Jennings, A Malayan court of appeal, 30 August 1956, CO 889/2 (1), C.C. 2000/30. See also summary record of meeting of constitutional commission, 27 August 1956, CO 889/1 (27), p. 6.
54 See paper by Jennings, A Malayan court of appeal, 30 August 1956, CO 889/2 (1), C.C. 2000/30.
55 Report of the federation of Malaya constitutional commission, 1957, pp. 55–56.
56 Ibid., p. 56.
57 Fifth meeting of Working Party, 28 February 1957, CO 941/85, p. 3.
58 Report of the Working Party, 29 March 1956, CO 941/86, p. 23.
59 Ibid., p. 23.
60 Fifth meeting of Working Party, 28 February 1957, CO 941/85, p. 3.
61 Report of the Working Party, p. 23.
62 Ibid., p. 24.
63 Ibid., p. 24.
64 Report of the federation of Malaya constitutional commission, 1957, p. 55.
65 Fifth meeting of Working Party, pp. 4–5. See also Report of the federation of Malaya constitutional commission, 1957, pp. 55–56.
66 Fifth meeting of Working Party, p. 5.
67 Ibid., p. 4.

8 The election commission

The federal constitution provided for the setting up of an independent election commission to conduct the general elections and to determine the constituency delimitation after independence. Article 106 of the Reid draft constitution provided for the setting up of an election commission to be headed by three members who would be appointed by the *Yang di-Pertuan Agong*. One of the three members would serve as chairman of the commission.[1] The commission had enormous powers under the constitution as an independent body to conduct elections and to determine any increase in the number of constituencies at every 10-year interval. They were answerable only to parliament. Elections had been conducted in the federation since December 1951 when the first local council elections were held in George Town in Penang, followed by the Kuala Lumpur municipal election in February 1952.[2] This was followed by local council elections annually from 1952 in the major towns in the country. State elections were held from 1954 and the first federal elections were held in July 1955 for the partially elected Federal Legislative Council.

The elections were traditionally conducted by civil servants led by the Supervisor of Federal Elections, and there was no separate body to conduct elections. Electors were registered during a fixed period, usually throughout the month of March each year. Two voter registrations had been held prior to 1956, according to J.A. Cradock, the then serving Supervisor of Federal Elections, in his testimony to the Reid constitutional commission in August 1956. Enthusiasm from the Malayan voters, however, was evidently lacking. Cradock noted that while the government had made efforts to register, there "was no great public enthusiasm to enrol."[3] Lord Reid noted he was informed that while 2.7 million people were entitled to register as voters, only 1.3 million had registered.[4] However, Cradock felt that it was more likely that 1.6 million were eligible to vote rather than the 2.7 million estimated. Malayan attitudes towards elections in these early years, the idea of democratic elections being a novel political activity to the people, were generally quite poor according to the election officers who gave their testimony to the constitutional commission.[5]

The constitutional commission in fact asked the Supervisor of Elections for the federation, T.E. Smith, who was responsible for conducting the 1955 federal

DOI: 10.4324/9781003542537-8

elections, during a hearing whether there should be an Election Commission in the federation. Smith did not respond directly to the question posed by the commission but said that whoever was responsible for elections, much of the work would fall upon the district officers.[6] Smith felt that revision of electoral rolls was easier as it involved shorter periods than the registration of voters as the later had to be constantly updated. Smith told the commission that the Constituency Delineation Committee was instructed to "weight the rural areas," in the preparation of electoral boundaries for the 1955 federal elections.[7] According to him, a rural constituency would have anything from 50,000 voters upwards, whereas the towns were divided into constituencies of approximately 90,000.[8] For the 1955 federal elections, 52 seats in the Federal Legislative Council were directly elected while the balance of 46 members were nominated to represent various interest groups such as business, commerce, plantations, trade unions and minorities. Smith felt that there was a certain apathy among the population in the towns which were mainly Chinese.

The commission agreed after discussion that all members of the lower house should be directly elected in single-member constituencies. Initially, the commission thought a minimum of 90 members or a maximum of 95 would suffice, and the average size of the constituency would be determined by dividing the total population by the total number of members.[9] They eventually suggested 104 constituencies, increasing by two-fold the total number of elected representatives in the then existing Federal Legislative Council. The commission recommended that total difference in population between any constituencies should not be more than 15%.[10] A guiding principle recommended by the commission was that no state should have a smaller number of members than its population demands, subject to certain minimum seats being allocated to the smaller states.[11]

The provisions for the setting up of an election commission and its functions were largely based on a working paper prepared by Sir Ivor Jennings.[12] He had suggested in the commission's discussions that a single election commission similar to India[13] would be desirable in the Malayan context to compile the electoral registers, delineate constituencies and organise elections for the states and federation.[14] Article 324 of the Indian constitution provides for the setting up of an election commission headed by a chief election commissioner and a number of other election commissioners for the preparation of electoral rolls and the conduct of all elections to parliament, state legislatures and the offices of president and vice president.[15] Jennings' paper essentially defined the mode of appointment of the election commission's members, the functions of the commission, delimitation of the federal and state constituencies, qualification of electors and election laws in general. Jennings drew on his previous experience in drafting the constitutions of Ceylon[16] and Pakistan, both of which had autonomous election commissions, and the provisions of the Indian constitution, to define the role and functions of the Malayan election commission.[17]

The constitutional commission had considered the question of whether the position of the members of the election commission should be a full-time or part-time job and eventually decided that it should be a full-time job as provided in Article

106 of the draft constitution.[18] The draft constitution prepared by the Reid Commission provided for the formation of an election commission which would have the responsibility of conducting elections and the appointment of returning officers.[19] The constitutional commission was keen to ensure that the election commission was completely independent and impartial and provided for the setting up of a permanent body.[20] This is similar to the provision for the appointment of the election commissioners by the president of India to maintain the independence of the commission.[21] Pakistan and Ceylon also provided for the appointment of the election commission by the head of state. To ensure there was no conflict of interest, the constitution required that the members of the commission should not hold any office of profit.[22] This was a standard requirement for office bearers of election commissions in India, Pakistan and Ceylon in order to ensure that there was no conflict of interest.

The independence of the election commission is further emphasised by the fact that the commission's members cannot be removed except on the grounds and in a manner of removal of that of a judge of the Supreme Court (Article 106).[23] A Supreme Court judge could only be removed on the order of the *Yang di-Pertuan Agong* following a vote in parliament which is supported by not less than two-thirds of the members present and voting. This is similar to the conditions found in India, Pakistan and Ceylon.[24] The terms and conditions of the commission members were protected and would be determined by the *Yang di-Pertuan Agong* and later by an Act of Parliament. The draft constitution provided that the remuneration of the election commission members shall not be diminished during their term of office.[25] To strengthen the independence of the commission, the constitution provided that the remuneration of the commission would be charged to the Federal Consolidated Fund, as was the case with the judiciary.[26] This was intended to place the commission beyond the dialectics of party politics.

The importance of the election commission is reflected in the guidelines provided in the draft constitution by the commission to the *Yang di-Pertuan Agong* in regard to the appointment of the election commission's members. Clause 3 of Article 106 in the draft constitution stated that in the appointment of members of the election commission, the *Yang di-Pertuan Agong* "shall have regard to the importance of securing an Election Commission which enjoys the confidence of all democratic political parties and of persons of all communities."[27] Such a guideline is also found in the constitution of Pakistan and places a special burden on the governor, or the king in the Malayan case, to ensure that the appointees to this office were members of the community who were held in high regard by the society. The draft constitution provided for the Election Commission to have several main functions. These (Article 108) included the duty to delimit federal and state constituencies, to prepare electoral rolls and to revise them annually or at intervals that the parliament may provide and to organise federal and state elections and senate and local council elections if requested by a state. Under Clause 4 of Article 108, the election commission was empowered to make rules for the purpose of its functions.[28] In essence, the election commission was to be an autonomous body responsible only to the parliament and the king.

The draft constitution provided some guidelines to the election commission in the delimitation of federal and state constituencies. The constitutional commission had deliberated considerably on the delimitation of constituencies and expressed some concern over the potential for gerrymandering. The election commission was advised to give due consideration to four elements: the distribution of population in the state (Article 109), the sparsity or density of the population in several parts of the state, the means of communication and the distribution of the different communities.[29] The election commission was expected to maintain the equality of the number of electors as the principle of representation but could depart from this principle to the extent of 15% of the electors in a constituency. The Reid Commission had considered an alternative idea of a three-member constituency "a primitive form of proportional representation," as Jennings put it, (each voter having three ballot papers each to fill) in the hope that the "majority community would dissipate its vote and the minority would concentrate them."[30] This model was based on the system of electoral representation in Ceylon which had introduced multiple-member constituencies. Jennings thought that this more sophisticated form of proportional representation would be difficult to introduce to an "illiterate electorate."[31] This model was intended to ensure adequate representation of the various ethnic interests. In the end, however, the constitutional commission decided to recommend single-member constituencies and leave such questions of proportional representation to the discretion of the election commission that would be formed.

The Reid Commission recommended a total of 104[32] parliamentary seats for the first post-independence election expected in 1959. The election commission was formed on 4 September 1957 to prepare the rolls for the first post-independence elections. The Reid Commission, by a majority, did not provide for direct elections to the Senate and suggested a majority be elected by indirect elections and the rest be nominated for a number of years by the *Yang Di-Pertuan Agong*.[33] McKell and Hamid disagreed with the majority and felt that the terms of reference required the commission to provide for the setting up of a fully elected Senate.[34] In his draft provisions on the election commission, Jennings had recommended a novel form: for the elections to the Senate the whole state should form a single constituency, and each voter would have as many votes as there were seats to be filled.[35] The electoral rolls for elections to the lower house would also be used for the election of senators.

The provisions on the election commission also outlined the qualifications for voters (Article 112). The voter or elector should be a citizen, 21 years of age, not found to be of unsound mind, was a resident in the constituency for six months preceding an election and not subject to any disqualification as a result of corrupt or illegal practices at elections.[36] These provisions were drawn mainly from the constitutions of India and Pakistan with some minor changes. The provisions in the constitution of India in particular had been tried and tested (the constitution of Pakistan only came into force in 1956) and thus provided the constitutional commission with a useful template to construct the provisions in the Malayan federal constitution. In a sense, the provisions in the Malayan constitution were more clearly framed and organised than the provisions of the constitutions of India and Pakistan, the Reid Commission benefiting from the drafting of these earlier constitutions.

The main functions of the election commission were to delimit federal and state constituencies and to prepare electoral rolls for elections to the parliament, state assemblies and municipalities and any local authority in the state. The duty of the commission to assist in the conduct of local elections if requested by a state legislature is clear from Jennings' draft:

> Where the Legislature of a State so authorises, the Election Commission may undertake, on such terms as to payment as may be agreed, to organise and conduct elections to the Municipal Council of any Municipality within the State or to any other local authority or class of local authority within the State.[37]

In Jennings' draft, he recommended that the number of federal constituencies should be equal to the state quota (as provided during the 1955 general election). But no state should have less than two federal constituencies. Jennings recommended that each state shall be divided into constituencies in a manner that each constituency should have nearly an equal population.[38] The election commission was asked to give due consideration to three features; first, the sparsity or density of the population; second, the means of communication; and third, the distribution of the different communities.[39] This was to be done in such a manner that "while maintaining equality of population as the principle of representation, it may depart therefrom to the extent of fifteen per centum of the population more or less."[40] The margin of difference between the constituencies hence, the commission felt, should not be too wide.

Jennings' draft was intended clearly to provide for greater rural weightage so that a Malay majority would emerge in parliament.[41] The constituency delineation committee in 1954 had been instructed to ensure that there was greater rural weightage when drawing up the electoral boundaries for the first federal elections in 1955. There was some concern in the commission and outside that if the urban and rural parliamentary seats were divided in equal proportions based on the district as the unit of representation and on population, there was potential for a Chinese majority to emerge in the federal legislature.[42] Jennings observed that based on the 1947 census and on the unequal size of the districts, there were 45 districts with a Malay majority, 8 with a Malay plurality, 25 districts with a Chinese majority and 6 with a Chinese plurality.[43]

Jennings in his working paper on a potential model of distribution of voters based on the "unequal" district as the unit of representation argued it would ensure a Malay majority. Jennings estimated that if the unit of representation, for example, was 40,000 persons per seat (if the district was regarded as the unit of representation), there would be 81 Malay seats and 51 Chinese seats.[44] But he felt that this total number of seats (132) was too big for a House in a bicameral legislature. On the other hand, if the unit of representation was 50,000 persons per seat, this would produce a federal legislature with 59 Malay seats and 36 Chinese seats. This he felt would be more appropriate, and there would be no danger of the Chinese "swamping the Malays."[45] He noted in his paper that the Chinese and Indians were concentrated in the towns and other densely populated areas and added: "It follows that, if the district is regarded as the unit of representation the Malays must have a sufficient majority. What that majority is depends on 'the unit of population' for purposes of representation."[46] In regard to the delimitation of state constituencies, Jennings recommended that the number of state constituencies should be such multiple of federal constituencies as provided in the constitution.[47] Invariably, the Reid Commission drew from the provisions for an election commission in the constitutions of India, Ceylon and Pakistan with some adaptations to suit the multiethnic Malayan political environment in the formation of an election commission and in determining its duties and ensuring its independence.

Notes

1 See Article 106 in Reid draft constitution, pp. 36–37, and Report of the federation of Malaya constitutional commission, 1957, p. 30.
2 See Fernando, *The making of the Malayan constitution*, p. 20.
3 Summary record of 17th meeting of constitutional commission, 4 August 1956, CO 889/1 (21), p. 1. The meeting was also attended by G. Hawkins (State Election Officer, Selangor) and E. MacDonald (Chief Registration Officer, Controller of Manpower).
4 Summary record of 17th meeting of constitutional commission, p. 3. MacDonald told the commission that according to his calculations, the granting of *jus soli* would give citizenship rights to 716,000 people, of whom 392,000 would be under the age of 18.
5 Summary record of 17th meeting of constitutional commission. The commission interviewed J.A. Cradock (supervisor of federal elections) and several election officers. See also Summary record of 36th meeting of constitutional commission, 1 October 1956, CO 889/1 (39), p. 2.
6 Summary record of 39th meeting of constitutional commission, 4 October 1956, CO 889/1 (42), p. 3.
7 Ibid., p. 3.
8 Ibid., p. 3.
9 Summary record of 50th meeting of constitutional commission, 11 October 1956, CO 889/1 (53), p. 1.
10 Ibid., p. 1.
11 Ibid., p. 2.
12 Paper on election commission by Sir Ivor Jennings, 15 October 1956, CO 889/2 (4), C.C. 2000/43. See also Summary record of 50th meeting of constitutional commission, p. 2.
13 The election commission in India was formed in 1950 as an independent body as provided in the Indian constitution.
14 Paper on the state constitutions by Ivor Jennings, 31 August 1956, CO 889/2, C.C. 2000/19, p. 4.
15 See Constitution of India, Part XV.
16 Jennings appears to have drawn much from the provisions of the 1946 Ceylon constitution. The Soulbury Commission had recommended in its draft constitution for Ceylon the setting up of a Delimitation Commission to be appointed by the Governor-General, consisting of three persons, one of whom shall be the chairman. The commission was tasked to divide the provinces of the island into electoral districts. See Report of the Commission on Constitutional Reform, Ceylon (London: Her Majesty's Stationery Office, Cmd. 6677, 1945), p. 113. See also Martin Wright, *British colonial constitutions*

1947 (Oxford: Clarendon Press, 1952), pp. 526–527. The Ceylon constitution (Article 41) provided for each electoral constituency to be based on a population estimate of 75,000. The Ceylon constitution also provided for multiple member (two or more) constituencies to provide for a better representation of the diverse communities.

17 Paper on election commission by Sir Ivor Jennings, 15 October 1956, CO 889/2 (4), C.C. 2000/43. See also Summary record of 61st meeting of constitutional commission, 19 October 1956, CO 889/1 (64), pp. 2–3. The election commission in Pakistan was formed in March 1956 and a Department of Election formed in October 1955 conducted the elections in Ceylon (now Sri Lanka). Both election bodies were autonomous and only answerable to their respective parliaments.

18 See Summary record of 61st meeting of constitutional commission, pp. 2–3. See also Summary record of 62nd meeting of constitutional commission, 19 October 1956, CO 889/1 (65), pp. 2–3 and Reid draft constitution Article 106, p. 37.

19 Summary record of the 50th meeting of the constitutional commission, 11 October 1956, CO 889/1 (53), p. 2. See also Article 106 of the Reid draft constitution.

20 See Report of the federation of Malaya constitutional commission, 1957, p. 30.

21 See Clause 2 of Article 324 of the Indian constitution.

22 Paper on election commission by Sir Ivor Jennings, 15 October 1956, CO 889/2 (4), C.C. 2000/43.

23 See Reid draft constitution, p. 37. See also Report of the federation of Malaya constitutional commission, 1957, p. 30.

24 See, for example, Clause 5 of Article 324 of the Indian constitution which states that the Chief Election Commissioner shall not be removed from office "except in like manner and on the grounds as a Judge of the Supreme Court."

25 Paper on election commission by Sir Ivor Jennings, p. 1. See Reid draft constitution, p. 37, and Report of the federation of Malaya constitutional commission, p, 30.

26 Report of the federation of Malaya constitutional commission, p. 30.

27 See Reid draft constitution, Article 106 (3), p. 37.

28 Ibid., pp. 37–38.

29 Ibid., p. 38.

30 See Jennings' paper on state constitutions, 31 August 1956, CO 889/2, C.C. 2000/19, p. 5.

31 Ibid., p. 5.

32 See Early draft of Part IV (The Federation) of constitution, prepared by Justice Hamid, 22 October 1956, CO 889/2 (1), C.C. 2000/44, p. 4. See also Article 40 (1) of Reid draft constitution.

33 See Reid draft constitution, Article 111, p. 39, and see also CO 889/2 (65), paper by Jennings, Distribution of population, 29 June 1956.

34 See Report of the federation of Malaya constitutional commission, 1957, pp. 25–26 and note by McKell and Hamid, p. 34. McKell and Hamid noted, "Under our terms of reference we are asked to make provisions for a federal form of constitution for the whole country as a self-governing unit based on parliamentary democracy with a bicameral legislature. This involves in our opinion the setting up of a Federal Parliament consisting of two Houses, each House being fully elected on an adult franchise."

35 See Jennings' draft provisions on the election commission and elections, 15 October 1956, CO 889/2 (4), C.C. 2000/43, p. 3.

36 Reid draft constitution, p. 40. See also Summary record of the 50th meeting of the constitutional commission, 11 October 1956, CO 889/1 (53), p. 2.

37 Paper on election commission by Sir Ivor Jennings, 15 October 1956, CO 889/2 (4), C.C. 2000/43, p. 2.

38 Ibid., p. 2.

39 Ibid., p. 3.

40 Ibid., p. 3.

41 Paper on distribution of population by Ivor Jennings, 29 June 1956, CO 889/2 (1), C.C. 2000/5, pp. 1–2.

42 Paper on distribution of population by Ivor Jennings, 29 June 1956, CO 889/2 (1), C.C. 2000/5, p. 1. The population of the federation in 1956 was 6,250,000 persons, comprising 49% Malays, 38% Chinese, 11% Indians, and 2% others.
43 Paper on distribution of population by Ivor Jennings, p. 1.
44 Paper on distribution of population by Ivor Jennings, p. 2. According to Jennings formula, if the population was under 20,000, the district would be merged with another district. If the population was between 20,000 and 60,000, the district would form one electoral seat.
45 Paper on distribution of population by Ivor Jennings, p. 2.
46 Ibid., p. 1.
47 Paper on election commission by Sir Ivor Jennings, 15 October 1956, CO 889/2 (4), C.C. 2000/43, p. 3.

Sources and bibliography

Primary sources

Documents consulted at the national archives in Kew, Britain

CAB128	Cabinet Minutes
CAB129	Cabinet Memoranda
CO 537	Colonies General, Supplementary and Original Correspondence
CO 717	Colonial Office: Federated Malay States, Original Correspondence
CO 889	Reid Commission Constitutional Documents
CO 941	Government Committee Reports
CO 1022	Southeast Asia Department: Original Correspondence
CO 1030	Far Eastern Department: Original Correspondence
DO 35	Dominion Office and Commonwealth Relations Office: Original Correspondence
FCO 141	Foreign and Commonwealth Office
FO 371	Foreign Office: General Correspondence

Other primary sources

Sir Ivor Jennings Papers at the Institute of Commonwealth Studies, University of London, London

Documents consulted at the Arkib Negara, Kuala Lumpur

United Malays National Organisation (UMNO) Files
Malayan Chinese Association (MCA) Files
Tan Cheng Lock Papers

Documents consulted at the Institute of Southeast Asian Studies, Singapore

Tan Cheng Lock Papers
H.S. Lee Papers

Other government publications

Federation of Malaya Agreement, 1948 (Kuala Lumpur: Government Printers, 1948).

Federation of Malaya Constitutional Proposals 1957 (White Paper).

Report of the Federation of Malaya Constitutional Commission 1957, (London: Her Majesty's Stationery Office, 1957, Colonial No. 330).

The Constitution of India, 1949.

The Constitution of Pakistan, 1956.

The Constitution of Burma, 1947.

Report of the Commission on Constitutional Reform, Ceylon 1945, (London: Her Majesty's Stationery Office, Cmd. 6677, 1945).

Secondary sources

Books and chapters

Allot, Antony, *Essays in African Law*, London: Butterworth, 1960.

Amery, L.S., *Thoughts on the Constitution*, London: Oxford University Press, 1956.

Ampalavanar, R., *The Indian Minority and Political Change* in Malaya, *1945–1957*, Kuala Lumpur: Oxford University Press, 1981.

Andaya, Barbara Watson and Andaya, Leonard Y., *A History of Malaysia*, London: Palgrave, 2001.

Arasaratnam, S., *Indians in Malaysia and Singapore*, London: Institute of Race Relations, 1967.

Bagehot, W., *The English Constitution*, Oxford: Oxford University Press, 2001.

Bari, Abdul Aziz, *Malaysian Constitution: A Critical Introduction*, Kuala Lumpur: The Other Press, 2003.

Basu, Durga Das, *Constitutional Law of India*, New Delhi: Prentice-Hall, 1991.

Braddell, R.J., *The Law of the Straits Settlements: A Commentary*, Kuala Lumpur: Oxford University Press, 1982.

Buang, Salleh, *Malaysian Legal History*, Kuala Lumpur: Dewan Bahasa dan Pustaka, 2015.

Ching-hwang, Yen, "Historical background," in Lee Kam Hing and Tan Chee-Beng (eds), *The Chinese in Malaysia*, Shah Alam: Oxford University Press, 2000.

Cowan, C.D., *Nineteenth-Century Malaya: The Origins of British Political Control*, London: Oxford University Press, 1961.

Fernando, Joseph M., *The Making of the Malayan Constitution*, Kuala Lumpur: Malaysian Branch of Royal Asiatic Society, 2002.

Fernando, Joseph M., *Federal Constitutions: A Comparative Study of Malaysia and the United States*, Kuala Lumpur: University of Malaya Press, 2007.

Fernando, Joseph M., *The Alliance Road to Independence*, Kuala Lumpur: University of Malaya Press, 2009.

Gorman, Daniel, *Imperial Citizenship*, Manchester: Manchester University Press, 2006.

Harding, Andrew, *Law, Government and the Constitution in Malaysia*, Kuala Lumpur: Malayan Law Journal, 1996.

Harding, Andrew, *The Constitution of Malaysia: A Contextual Analysis*, London: Bloomsbury Publishing, 2012.

Hashim, Mohamed Suffian, *An Introduction to the Constitution of Malaysia*, Kuala Lumpur: Government Printer, 1972.

Hickling, R.H., *An Introduction to the Constitution of Malaysia*, Singapore: Malayan Law Journal, 1960.

Ibrahim, Sheikh, *The Constitution of the Islamic Republic of Pakistan*, Lahore: P.L.D. Publishers, 1992.

Jennings, Ivor, *The Constitution of Ceylon*, London: Oxford University Press, 1949.
Jennings, Ivor, *The Law and the Constitution*, London: University of London Press, 1961.
Jennings, Ivor, *The British Constitution*, Cambridge: Cambridge University Press, 1971.
Joshi, G.N., *The Constitution of India*, London: Macmillan, 1950.
Kratoska, Paul H.., *The Japanese Occupation of Malaya, 1941–1945*, London: Allen and Unwin, 1998.
Lau, Albert, *The Malayan Union Controversy, 1942–1948*, Singapore: Oxford University Press, 1991.
Means, G.P., *Malaysian Politics*, London: Hodder and Stoughton, 1976.
Parkinson, C.N., *British Intervention in Malaya, 1876–77*, Kuala Lumpur: University of Malaya Press, 1964.
Purcell, Victor, *The Chinese in Malaya*, London: Oxford University Press, 1967.
Santhanam, K., *The Constitution of India*, New Delhi: Hindustan Press, 1951.
Sheridan, L.A., *The Federation of Malaya Constitution*, Singapore: University of Malaya Law Review, 1961.
Stockwell, A.J., *British Policy and Malay Politics during the Malayan Union Experiment, 1942–1948*, Kuala Lumpur: Malayan Branch of Royal Asiatic Society, Monograph 8, 1979.
Thio, Eunice, *British Policy in the Malay Peninsula, 1880–1910*, Kuala Lumpur: University of Malaya Press, 1969.
Tregonning, K.G., *A History of Modern Malaya*, Singapore: Eastern Universities Press, 1964.
Trindade, F.A.. and Lee, H.P.. (eds), *The Constitution of Malaysia: Further Perspectives and Development*, Singapore: Oxford University Press, 1986.
Wah, Yeo Kim, *The Politics of Decentralization*, Kuala Lumpur: Oxford University Press, 1982.
Wheatley, Paul, *Impressions of the Malay Peninsula in Ancient Times*, Singapore: Eastern Universities Press, 1964.
Winstedt, R.O., *A History of Malaya*, Kuala Lumpur: Malayan Branch of Royal Asiatic Society, 1935.
Wright, Martin, *British Colonial Constitutions 1947*, Oxford: Clarendon Press, 1952.

Articles

Andaya, Leonard Y., "Orang Asli and the Melayu in the history of the Malay Peninsula," *Journal of the Malaysian Branch of the Royal Asiatic Society*, Vol. 75, No. 1, 2002, pp. 23–48.
Fernando, Joseph M., "Elite inter-communal bargaining and conflict resolution: The role of the Communities Liaison Committee in Malaya, 1949–1951," *Journal of Southeast Asian Studies*, Vol. 43, No. 2, June 2012, pp. 280–301.
Fernando, Joseph M. and Ho Hui Ling, "British and Commonwealth legacies in the framing of the Malayan constitution, 1956–1957," *Britain and the World*, Vol. 8, No. 2, 2015, pp. 181–203.
Fernando, Joseph M. and Shanthiah Rajagopal, "Fundamental liberties in the Malayan constitution and the search for a balance, 1956–1957," *International Journal of Asia-Pacific Studies*, Vol. 13, No. 1, 2017, pp. 1–18.

Newspapers

The Malay Mail
The Straits Times
The Times

Index